ACCLAIM FOI
THE DARK ~~FACE OF HEAVEN~~

You won't want to miss *The Dark Face of Heaven*. Dr. Colli is a renowned counselor whose skill dramatically touched the lives of many who were battling grievous trauma. This informative and easy to read book presents multiple inspiring case reports of those who triumphed over the tragedy in their lives. For everyone who has faced seemingly insurmountable challenges in their lives, this highly recommended book offers a profound message of hope and reassurance.

—Jeffrey Long, M.D.
Author of the New York Times bestseller *Evidence of the Afterlife: The Science of Near-Death Experiences*

Rilke taught us that buried in our deepest fears may lie our greatest treasures. Likewise, in this book, Janet Colli shows us that terrible childhood and other traumas may contain the seeds of personal transformation and profound healing. A master and innovative therapist, Colli demonstrates through recounting a series of inspiring case histories that she has become adept at helping her clients harvest these seeds of renewal and regeneration. The result is a book that offers hope to all those who, like Colli's clients, may be searching for the door that will lead to their own rebirth into wholeness.

—Kenneth Ring, Ph.D.
Author of *Lessons from the Light*

The subtle roles of mind, belief and intentionality, as well as our overt behaviors, shape the unfolding of destiny in each human, and hence, our destiny as a species. Each of us must learn to manage these very difficult issues that this book addresses so well.

—Edgar Mitchell, Sc.D., Ph.D.
Apollo 14 Astronaut and Founder of *Institute of Noetic Sciences*

This masterwork absolutely validates and honors the struggles of humanity for all time. To read it is to embark upon the epic journey of healing the author chronicles. I have never experienced a book that so personally, beautifully, painfully, hopefully, and at the same time rigorously explores the journey toward wholeness, as well as the power of transformation through trauma. I am not the same person I was who first picked up the book. Thank you, Janet, for your extraordinary gift.

—Tav Sparks
Director of Grof Transpersonal Training, Author of *Movie Yoga: How Every Film Can Change Your Life,* and *The Wide Open Door: The Twelve Steps, Spiritual Tradition and the New Psychology*

The Dark Face of Heaven is amazing and amazingly powerful. It is a handbook for dark times, and a lifeline. Beautifully conceived, informative and transformative. It will be a part of my life from now on. When storms rage, I have *The Dark Face of Heaven* to inspire and support me.

—Whitley Strieber
Author of *Communion* and Host of *Dreamland*

Anyone who reads newspapers, watches television, listens to the radio, or receives blogs on the Internet is aware of the epidemic of trauma in today's world. Military combat, sexual abuse, bullying, physical and mental illness, and natural disasters can all lead to traumatic experiences. But the story need not end there. *The Dark Face of Heaven* is filled with remarkable accounts of people who emerged from their trauma transformed; what didn't kill them had made them stronger. In this book, Dr Colli tells her readers how to use spiritual awakening, psychic opening, and shamanic imagery to come through their dark night of the soul into a luminescent daybreak, one that is not only life-changing but life-affirming.

　　—Stanley Krippner, Ph.D.
　　Co-author, *Haunted by Combat: Understanding PTSD in War Veterans*

The Dark Face of Heaven shows how traumatic experience often catalyzes ways of knowing beyond the physical. It's a great read, a book that prompts one to search for similar emotional drivers of transformation.

　　—Dennis Briefer
　　Engineer and Board Member of John E. Mack Institute

I feel totally at peace with this book because I agree with the author.

Janet and I have lived the experience of conscious participation in life and health, free of guilt. Our surrender and acceptance of our mortality *becomes a therapist* and leads to saving our authentic life. We thereby derive physical benefits from the transformation. Self-induced healing is not a spontaneous event. It is created by achieving our true potential through the harmony we create in our new life—free of the wounds of the past. Years ago my articles were refused by medical journals as "interesting but inappropriate," and by psychotherapy journals as "appropriate but not interesting." We need to realize that mind, body & spirit are not separate entities but are one, as Janet demonstrates. Medicine and psychiatry need to open their approach to treating the whole person and their experience, and not just the disease. For years, I called myself *a Jungian surgeon*. Understanding healing as she does, I could say the same thing about Janet.

—Bernie Siegel, M.D.,
Author of *Faith, Hope & Healing* and *A Book of Miracles*

THE DARK FACE OF HEAVEN

JANET ELIZABETH COLLI, PH.D

TRUE STORIES OF TRANSCENDENCE THROUGH TRAUMA

Grateful acknowledgment is made to the following for permission to reprint previously published material:

Reprinted by permission from Changes of Mind: A Holonomic Theory of the Evolution of Consciousness, by Jenny Wade, the State University of New York Press © 1996, State University of New York. All rights reserved.

Excerpts from I'm The One That I Want, by Margaret Cho, copyright © 2001 by Margaret Cho. Used by permission of Ballantine Books, an imprint of Random House, a division of Random House LLC. All rights reserved.

Any third party use of this material, outside of this publication, is prohibited. Interested parties must apply directly to Random House LLC for permission.

Printed in the United States of America.

ISBN-13: 978-1499626650

ISBN-10: 1499626657

Cover Design: Will Bueche
Interior Design: Brian C. Short
Cover Photo: Scott A. Gaul

www.sacredencounters.com

THE DARK FACE OF HEAVEN

To Thomas,
without whose loving support and encouragement
I likely would not be alive,
much less a clinician and author.

And to all those, known and unknown,
who, in the face of trauma,
surrendered to an evolutionary dynamic.

Table of Contents

Mutant Mystics Among Us

W riting a foreword can be a deeply personal matter. This one is, anyway. You deserve to know why I am writing it. I have corresponded with Dr. Colli for a few years now. We have never met, but I immediately recognized in her writings a clear resonance with the vast things that my own writing and life have been orbiting around for decades, like nervous objects getting closer and closer to some super-massive black hole at the center of everything.

That hole, I have come to see over the years, is trauma. But not just trauma. Trauma is god awful. Trauma is, in turns, horrific, devastating, gory, cruel, sickening, and dehumanizing. But sometimes, sometimes, for reasons that we do not really understand, trauma can and does also function as a trigger of transformation and transcendence.

I do not use such words lightly. I am a historian of religions by training and profession. Most people would recognize my field as "comparative religion." I specialize in comparative mystical literature, that is, texts from around the world that express and transmit some of the most extraordinary and extreme human experiences on record. By no means accidentally, the two most common languages for expressing mystical states are the languages of "death" and "sexuality," and probably in that order. In short, trauma and energetic transformation.

I began my professional career with a dissertation on a famous Hindu saint, Ramakrishna Paramahamsa (1836-1886), who appears briefly in these pages as well, by the way. Among other things, I suggested in that dissertation, which became my first book, *Kali's Child* (1995), that the saint had been sexually traumatized in his youth, and that these sufferings "opened him up" for later adult states of blissful ecstasy, elaborate vision, altered states of energy, and a divinization that his disciples could palpably feel in his presence. I did not reduce the saint's mystical experiences to his sexual trauma, that is, I did not explain away his altered states of consciousness and electric transmissions (*shakti-pat*) as displacements of his sexuality, as a classical Freudian reading might. Rather, I suggested that we read his sexual trauma as a trigger, as a breaking open into other dimensions of our shared humanity (and divinity). It was in this way that I affirmed both the saint's stunning religious states and his equally obvious psychosexual

3

sufferings.

I was hated and harassed for many years for this suggestion. Indeed, in some sense, I still am. At the time of this writing, I am "dead" on the Internet—"killed off," I assume, for the same crime. If you Google my name, you will see that I died the same year that I finished my dissertation (1993).

There were other, more thoughtful responses, of course. While I was being tracked by my haters and aspiring censors, I was also being sought out by a number of quiet, profound human beings who had been sexually traumatized in their youth and then later experienced deep spiritual states and visions in their adulthood. They had always sensed that there was some mysterious connection between the early sexual trauma and the later spirit life, but they could not understand what or why this might be. They felt mostly confusion and shame over this intuited connection. They could not understand how something so terrible could be connected to something so beautiful. Then they read *Kali's Child*. For the first time, they understood that they could read their early sexual trauma as a trigger, and not a cause, of their later mystical states. They understood that their adult states of transcendence need not be reducible to the horrible shame of their youth. In essence—I do not know how else to put this—the book helped to heal them.

Since that first book, I have written many others. I have looked again and again at what I have come to call "the traumatic secret" in the lives of scholars of mysticism, including my own anorexic sufferings stemming from the sexual repressions and denials of Roman Catholicism (*Roads of Excess, Palaces of Wisdom*). I have analyzed the same secret in the life, loves, and healing ministry of Jesus in early Christian memory (*The Serpent's Gift*), in the American counterculture and the human potential movement (*Esalen*), in the history of psychical and paranormal phenomena (*Authors of the Impossible*), in the alien abduction literature, and in the lives of the authors and artists who create science fiction and superhero comics (*Mutants and Mystics*). With each new turn of the spiral, that original intuition about trauma as a potential trigger of transcendence has become more and more precise and more and more acute.

The black hole.

Or the dark face of heaven.

As a therapist, Dr. Colli does not work with texts. She works with people—like you, like me. Through them, she has come to under-

4

stand that, yes, trauma is horrible, but that, in some remarkable cases (including those recounted in the pages that follow), it can trigger transcendent states of knowledge and vision that fundamentally—physiologically, energetically, neurologically—alter, re-wire, and gift the person who undergoes them. An individual is struck on the head and begins to manifest psychical capacities. A young woman is raped by a family member and finds herself floating on the ceiling during the rape, or drawn deeply to spiritual things later in life. In Dr. Colli's own language, in these instances, "extraordinary experience appears to be the portal to a biologically-based transformation of the human personality." Or again: "What happens is *evolution*—the future of the brain."

The future of the brain. Evolution. These are very strong words. They are outrageous words, really. But for anyone who has known such states of suffering and consequent altered states of mind and energy, they are eerily familiar and immediately persuasive. The truth, for those who know it, really is fantastic.

And outrageously hopeful. *The Dark Face of Heaven* is many things, but, above all, it is a book of hope, compassion, and personal courage. In its pages, Dr. Colli tells the story of her own suffering, trauma, and transcendence. She walks her talk. We are then privileged to listen in, as it were, on the results of her therapy sessions with a number of profound, quiet human beings, who share with Dr. Colli, and now us, their own stories of trauma and transformation. These are individuals "gifted through damage," who possess a "fire in the brain," who vibrate "like a battery," who know the outer as the inner and the inner as the outer. These are the individuals who truly understand, who have ears to hear, who know the traumatic secret. These are the mutant mystics walking among us.

Jeffrey J. Kripal
J. Newton Rayzor Professor of Religious Studies at Rice University
Houston, Texas
4 May 2013

THE DARK FACE OF HEAVEN

Definition. Transpersonal: Existing *above and beyond* the personal or cultural paradigm; involving non-ordinary or altered states of consciousness. Transpersonal psychology includes mystical, numinous, supernatural, and sacred experience.

My psychotherapy practice covers panic attacks, anxiety and depression, posttraumatic stress from childhood sexual abuse, eating disorders and cancer. There is no shortage of suffering on our planet. No doubt there is a disturbance in the energy field surrounding my office.

Yet I also see Kundalini awakenings and spiritual emergency, "experiencers" of close encounters, "seers" of visionary and near-death experience. In short, what I call subtle realm experience. Between my practice of Clinical and Transpersonal psychology there is no major schism. This is most uncommon as therapy practices go. Atypical. Yet I have no shortage of clients. They flock to me muttering, "You don't think I'm weird? *Cra-zy?*"

"No," I say.

Many times they answer, "I've never told anyone this—my entire life."

Yet this range, this variety and assortment, in short, this plethora of experience should be nothing new to any therapist. This embarrassment of riches is the birthright of any human.

History supports my claim. *Every known civilization has had truck with the transcendent.* The history of humanity *is* unavoidably a history about The Other Side—that repository of mystic beings whose deeds and doings create myth. Their heavenly and hellish abodes spring from the font of the zero-point field (ZPF), yet are colored by the imprint of humanity's collective unconscious. Residents (denizens from beyond) include any guardian angel and bug-eyed alien, as well as ghostly apparition. Not to mention, Buddha and Jesus Christ, Satan and dead grandparents, Zeus, Spiderman and Men-In-Black.

Luckily, there are always those among us who participate in, and who *translate* the other side, whether shaman, medium, priest or saint. Or almost every person I work with in transpersonal therapy. Major movements of consciousness have been expressed by the change in nomenclature from *shaman* to *priest* to *patient.* Let us begin with an historical view of the evolution of consciousness on planet Earth.

Summing up our historical past for fifty to one-hundred thousand years is straightforward: Shamans and tribal societies. The symbolic revolution that cave art expresses—by which animals *emerge* from rock imbued with mystic power—bespeaks a different consciousness than ours. What to the modern mind are deemed hallucinatory states and visionary trance were once the norm, allowing converse with what we now interpret as the *supernatural*.

As that era ended and we skip forward some fifty thousand years, the modern era began, along with our resident state of subject-object consciousness. In other words, the separation of reality into *it, me, us and them*. Subject-object consciousness ("I," the subject, perceiving a world of separate "objects") views the world as such: me *versus* you (and everything else). We break up the unified field with each act of perception; hence, a world of discrete, separate objects appears to us. A vast dissociation underlies the separation of church and science; and a chasm between the *supernatural* and the material, physical realm has reigned supreme ever since.

Now consider that part of the modern era that heralds the birth of psychology. *Therapy*. Psychotherapists are modern day shamans who mediate our connection with the transcendent realm of healing. Therapy, good and proper, is about facilitating that connection. Therapy is not about diagnosing and medicating pathology, that is, balancing levels of serotonin and whatnot in unbalanced brains. Therapy is about healing our traumas and growing our neurophysiology to enable us to reach beyond ourselves, to shrink the difference between *it, me, us and them*.

And ultimately, to reach the stars.

That may not be such a long reach, after all. For the heavenly bodies are also reaching out to us. "The stars have moved closer. Perhaps they move closer every night."[1] Accordingly, after many thousands of years of evolution, the subtle realm is encroaching on our territory. The barrier between the supernatural and the natural is melting before our eyes. This unprecedented growth of consciousness calls for a "new" psychology. Better yet, we need to merge Clinical and Transpersonal Psychology to deal effectively with our life experience, its range, variety and assortment—that embarrassment of riches that is the birthright of any human.

Now, back to history.

During the eighteenth and nineteenth centuries, the effects of what were once considered witchcraft and satanic possession were determined by modern society to be mental illness. Responsibility was shifted from evil forces deemed *outside* the brain—to dysfunctional workings *inside* a sick mind. *Psychopathology*. But the collective pendulum had overzealously swung over to reductionism. Scientism: the religion of science. Religious and mystical experiences were regarded as mere artifacts of brain dysfunction. As political movements fostered secular, republican governments instead of monarchies—and science held sway over clericalism and the church—the scientific investigation of trauma flourished.

By the late nineteenth century in France, some of the best scientific minds of the day endeavored to explain that quintessential psychological disorder of women: *hysteria*. Jean-Martin Charcot, the father of neurology, had hospitalized, female patients demonstrate bizarre physical sensations and trance states—not based on physical pathology. In those days, conversion reactions such as paralysis were as popular and widespread as today's anorexia or the "cutting" of teenagers. It was Pierre Janet who truly recognized the psychogenic basis of these disorders: *trauma*. Sigmund Freud, studying at the Salpêtrière hospital in Paris, at first "exported" key elements of this work to Vienna, but later disavowed the real live trauma of his female patients. *So much for the scientific approach.* The childhood sexual trauma that resulted in these complex disorders and strange behaviors was far too disturbing to the bourgeoisie Viennese. The supernatural seemingly did not have a snowball's chance in hell.

But it is hard to keep a biological impulse down. Spiritism overtook Europe in the early 1850's. *Always, we have traffic with the transpersonal realm.* C. G. Jung had gone beyond his teacher and mentor Sigmund Freud's rigid analysis of the psyche into id, ego and super-ego—to pioneer an understanding of the psyche's individuation process, as well as archetypes from the "collective unconscious." Amazingly, a little known influence in the C. G. Jung's development was a stint with mediums. Indeed, table-turning on the continent at the turn of the century played an integral part in what has been termed "the discovery of the unconscious."

"Ivenes," Jung's medium, incarnated the spirit of her grandfather, changed dialects while somnambulistic, was instructed by "clear spirits" and journeyed to Mars. All too soon Jung grew disenchanted. "After about two years of experimentation we all became rather weary of it."[2] Carl Jung's autobiography does not mention the fact that six months after his departure from the group, Ivenes was caught red-handed, faking "apports," physical objects allegedly produced by spirits. Jung was no doubt disconcerted by the scam. But he himself had already caught on to the medium's "trickery."

Incredibly, the great Swiss perceived some true measure in the "independence and maturity of her personality." In fact, the germ of Jung's theory of individuation grew from this insight: "I learned from this example how a No. 2 personality is formed, how it enters a child's consciousness and finally integrates it into itself."[3] Jung deemed medium-ism a growth mechanism of the unconscious that overcomes obstacles in the psyche's development.

All in all, this was the one great experience which wiped out all my earlier philosophy and made it possible for me to achieve a psychological point of view. I had discovered some objective facts about the human personality. Yet the nature of the experience was such that once again I was unable to speak of it.[4]

That speaks to the difficulties we still face when trying to explain such transcendent growth of consciousness, much less to separate out the authentic from the overblown, imaginary or inflated. Jung's colleagues—like so many of mine who are unable to countenance the growth potential of medium-ism—were left behind in the collective dust of disbelief and skepticism.

And so mesmerism survived as *hypnotism*, with sole authority and credibility sought by universities and nascent psychiatrists. Even Freud worked altered state, hypnotic cures upon his so-called hysterical patients, whom history deemed victims of sexual trauma and abuse, even if Freud did not. Over one-hundred years of trauma research have revealed the dissociative processes and out-of-body states that the psyche resorts to under the threat of chronic abuse ... and death. *Without a doubt, trauma plays a role in the evolution of consciousness.*

Early science fostered the awareness of the dangers implicated with hypnotism, ranging from crude sexual seduction by the "magnetizer," to crimes committed under hypnosis. Freud himself could not reconcile his female patients' seeming ability to "dream up" sexual transgressions—with his conventional view of patriarchal Viennese society. So-called "fantasies" of sexual abuse were relegated to the division of the psyche that served instinctual drives, heralding from the mythic land of the Oedipal complex. Freud was much more *comfortable* initiating the rigid ritual of psychoanalysis. Highly emotional and reactive, Freud's patients seemed to inhabit a realm somewhere between conventional reality and fantasy-land.

What Freud could not fathom was the relationship between trauma and the subtle realm—to which this book is dedicated. No, I do not refer to so-called "false memories" or fantasy prone personalities. The sexual abuse Freud's patients claimed was materially, physically real. Real life trauma. It was not artificial, imagined or invented. Certainly not an Oedipal or Electra complex—sprung full-blown from the Id.

Yet I can relate to Freud. Holding a Ph.D. in Clinical Psychology, I specialize in *extraordinary* human experience and healing. Extraordinary, so-called. Modern day witches, clairvoyants and shamans, sashay into my office everyday. Saints, psychics, healers, animal communicators "people" my practice. I am half-jokingly referred to as the shaman's shaman.

With a solid footing in mainstream trauma work, I help people process the life-shattering events that ushered in the transpersonal. Victims of incest, physical or emotional abuse and neglect, they have learned through dissociation to "tune into" the *subtle realm*—the realm beyond consensus reality. So much so that one of my earliest mentors said, "Show me a psychic, and I'll show you someone who has been traumatized."

Indeed, research in social psychology has shown that a somewhat higher incidence of childhood trauma is linked to certain transpersonal experience, for example, close encounters and near-death experiences.[5] The theory is that trauma fosters the development of a quality called *psychological absorption*. And psychological absorption lends itself to the perception of altered states and realities that generally escape the attention of others. After all, nothing stimulates other-worldly perception better than the dissociative, out-of-body states resorted to under life-threat.

One of the foremost trauma researchers of our time, Dr. Judith Herman, pays homage to this preternatural development: "The pathological environment of childhood abuse forces the development of extraordinary capacities, both creative and destructive. It fosters the development of abnormal states of consciousness in which the ordinary relations of body and mind, reality and imagination, knowledge and memory, no longer hold."[6] That being said, these "extraordinary capacities" clearly relate to the psyche's capacity to foster healing.

When privy to a near-death experience, no doubt about it, you are altered. Near-death research has uncovered effects as far-reaching as reduced fear of death, reports of psychic ability and healing gifts, a predilection for eating more fruits and vegetables, as well as a tendency to disable wristwatches and electrical appliances—presumably due to

11

changes in the physcial body's electromagnetic field.[7]

Transpersonal psychologists such as myself have much to teach. Transpersonal states of consciousness are precisely where reality is constructed and *de*constructed. Alternate or otherworldly realities *vie* with material reality. The subtle realm and the material world are both *real*—in their own respective ways. After all, the imaginal realm is imagin-*al*, not imagin-*ary*. "Not only is the imaginal realm ontologically real, it is also a world that has form, dimension, and most important for us, *persons or entities*."[8] So the spirit world and the material world are both eminently real. But they are *not* equivalent. *Not* interchangeable. Their *crossover* should give us pause....

Their *meeting point* is where authentic miracles of healing happen.

No, I do not make a good skeptic. I have seen far too much sound evidence that the subtle realm can have *material* healing effect. The material, physical world can be most responsive to co-creation. Synchronicity, that Über-lord of coincidence, a *superior* kind of coincidence, is where mind and matter meet. Synchronicity is one form of *co*-creation. Which brings us back to C. G. Jung.

At a pivotal time in his development, Jung was driven to communicate with his anima figure through fantasies and images, dutifully recorded in his Red Book and his Black Book. Only his family life and work-a-day, professional life enabled him to stay grounded in a normal life, in the material world. "The unconscious contents could have driven me out of my wits."[9] That ready admission, as well as its solution, gives us grounds for hope.

With any luck, my clinical cases highlight the relationship between trauma and the transpersonal. Single case studies gained prestige with Freud. They can provide a solid framework upon which to portray a previously unknown process. A single case study can disclose the process by which a compulsively disordered psyche successfully negotiates healing. One case study can be worth its weight in gold.

Like Carl Jung, we modern-day shamans need fortitude to mediate the connection with the transcendent realm—for those who access altered states and face "other worldly" realms. Ultimately, we psychotherapists help translate those states and realms into healing. In so doing, we bridge the gap between Clinical psychology and Transpersonal—and foster *the psychology of the future*. The psychology of the future reflects the whole human personality and its potential to reach into other realms, to co-create reality. Not for nothing was Jung originator of the notion of synchronicity, where the human psyche touches the cosmos and shapes events. Try doing *that* on a regular basis. Have a go at mediating the healing of an individual psyche, as well as the collective. Transpersonal psychotherapy.

Like true marriage, it is a job made in heaven. Or rather, a job made bringing heaven down to Earth.

CHAPTER 1

IN THE MIDDLE OF SOMEONE'S DARK NIGHT OF THE SOUL SOMEWHERE IN THE UNIVERSE

The world is a den of thieves. And night is falling. Evil is breaking its chains and goes through the world like a mad hound. The poisoning affects us all.... No-one goes free.

Ingmar Bergman, *Fanny & Alexander*

T

herapy.

You are possessed. Naturally, you seek therapy. You are among the fortunate. Psychotherapy was not always an available form of support during the history of human suffering. The ancestry or lineage of psychotherapy is illustrious nonetheless. Aboriginal shamans—from our earliest known time—came first. Shamanism is not lost, I promise. The best therapy has a shamanic *twist*.

Therapy, simply put, gets to the bottom of what possesses you. What spirit or Ghost of Christmas Past possesses you to sit down and *spill your guts* over me, a near perfect stranger?

You may be young, early twenties, new to this game of life. Or in the prime of it. Nowadays we have mid-life crises in our thirties or forties. At the drop-of-a-hat. No matter. The Dark Night finally caught up with you. You have been outrun and overtaken by some form of suffering. Some *undigested* piece of your life experience, some virulent thought-form or memory trace has been energized, triggered to come forth. Like a zombie, it staggers towards you, gesturing and speaking what sounds like gibberish. Long dead and buried underground, it has been dissociated mainly so you could survive in this dog-eat-dog world.

Your suffering has finally surfaced—*encrypted*—in symptoms psychiatrists readily diagnose and medicate. But rarely, if ever, treat.

Therapists at their best are modern-day shamans—the divinely chosen *go-betweens*. We submerge ourselves in your inner realm, the Underworld (the unconscious); or we ascend to the higher regions of Heavenly awareness to intercede on your behalf. Or (if you choose) we accompany you—*in full egoic consciousness*—to fight your own handpicked demons. Yet we are not your only helpers.

What a profound teaching that your worst symptom is your greatest ally.

Be thankful for your symptoms and disorders. They are your best and truest friends. Not a popular view in the West. We live in the land of warfare: the war against cancer, the war against poverty, drug wars, the war against terrorism. We are decades past the World Wars, the wars-to-end-all-wars. Yet no warfare has succeeded. In warfare, we seek to suppress and conquer the enemy. Suppression is the name-of-the-game in Western, allopathic medicine. Psychiatry followed suit.

15

Little wonder. Wise women, midwives wielding herbal remedies, were hunted as witches between 1500 and 1650. The history of Western medicine *is* warfare. The medical lineage of the United States, England and Western Europe is writ in blood. *Witch hunt.* Anywhere from a few hundred thousand to nine million women were murdered. The 1486 treatise widely used in trials, The Malleus Maleficarum (The Witches Hammer): "all witchcraft comes from carnal lust which is in women insatiable." Little wonder symptom suppression is widely held as the paradigm underlying Western, allopathic medicine.

Witch hunters believed the "good witch" (the midwife) did more harm than anyone, healing without recourse to the Church. The College of Physicians, organized by physicians and surgeons in 1518, had ultimate say over the sanctioned practice of medicine. The Acts of Incorporation branded "smyths, wevers, and women" as interlopers and accused the latter of sorcery. Make no mistake about it, many women died for the suspected practice of medicine, whereupon all worldly possessions of the woman became property of the Church.

Yet the therapies sanctified by the early Church were born of the subtle realm: shrine cures, pilgrimages to holy places, relics of saints and martyrs. Christian churches in England used the technique of *incubatio* (incubation sleep), modeled after the divine sleep cures of the Ascelpian temples of Turkey and Greece. The patron saints of healing were invoked to diagnose and bestow cures—during some species of sleepstate. Surely these are shamanic methods using altered states to invoke visions of spirit guides. Only the names have changed.

"The ostracism of the shamanic aspect of women's medicine, at first economic and political in nature, later became necessary because science could not account for what appeared to be transpersonal phenomena."[1]

Transpersonal phenomena? Spiritual awakening and psychic openings, out-of-body and near-death experiences, lucid dreams, and other altered states *are revealed during trauma therapy.* Transpersonal experiences of otherworldly beings, survival after death, reincarnation, memories of birth and prenatal life *are* therapy, in and of themselves.

Transpersonal psychology is the psychology of the sacred. And trauma *initiates* the transpersonal. When the skin-encapsulated ego is "split open" through trauma, our capacity to heal is unfettered and unbound. Trauma can initiate one into altered states and otherworldly realms that support healing. Yet this revolutionary finding is largely unappreciated within traditional psychology. Call them what you will—witches, wise women or healers, I wager that shamans still walk the earth. Much of modern medicine, psychiatry and psychology have simply gotten off track.

Unwittingly we take psychotropic medication (along with Vicodin for pain) peddled by a pharmaceutical industry: *anti*-depressive, *anti*-anxiety or *anti*-psychotic medication is routinely prescribed. *Anti*. Neti neti. Neither this nor that. What are we running away from? Where are we running? This blind, panicked running does *no one* any good—and does not routinely masquerade as treatment in older cultures. Tibetan medicine, functional or integrative medicine, homeopathy, naturopathy, Aryvedic medicine (to name a few), all function differently.

Simply put, the disorder itself carries the *seed* of its cure. Somehow those treating the so-called mental disorders never caught the drift.

Your biggest symptom is your greatest dream trying to come true. That is taught by those of us who translate psychology into the healing of physical or mental symptoms.[2] *The psychology of the body*. Symptoms are simply trying to enlighten you. What better way to get your attention? Symptoms and disorders carry the configuration, the code of your awakening. The following are a few preliminary codes worth cracking.

Bipolar disorder I or II, Borderline personality disorder (BPD), every therapist's nightmare until treatments like Dialectical Behavior Therapy (DBT). Dissociative identity disorder (DID), a.k.a. Multiple personality disorder (MPD), Eating disorders (EDS), Obsessive compulsive disorder (OCD), Panic attacks, with or without agoraphobia, Posttraumatic stress disorder (PTSD), simple or complex. Oppositional defiant and Conduct disorders.

Yet at the 22nd Annual Trauma Conference, trauma expert Bessell van der Kolk shared his "disdain, disgust and concern about our diagnostic system." Many of the above disorders *boil down to*, or *begin with* Developmental Trauma Disorder (DTD): trauma and abuse during early childhood, along with a loss of attachment. That one diagnosis, for which field trials are now being conducted, ought to be included in the updated version of the current bible of psychiatric labels, the *Diagnostic and Statistical Manual of Mental Disorders* of the American Psychiatric Association, although it causes serious trouble for the diagnoses Oppositional Defiant and Conduct Disorder. "Our diagnostic system is a total fraud right now, just like *crazy. And when your diagnostic system is crazier than the people you treat, you really are in bad trouble*." When 87% of those diagnosed with Borderline Personality Disorder have a very serious history of trauma and neglect starting before the age of seven, the diagnosis itself and its diagnostic criteria are due for an overhaul.

Our kids are getting medicated into *oblivion*. No society can afford to have ten percent of your population raised on anti-psychotic drugs. So they will *never* be able to feel the pleasure of discovery, the *pleasure* of interpersonal relationships that gets killed by antipsychotic agents. It's a true national disaster. And an economic disaster.[3]

Some of those traumatized, abused kids grow up to be my clients. Yet those who have experienced trauma or *a dark night of the soul* often develop special awareness or enhanced perceptual abilities. Extraordinary experience appears to be the portal to a biologically-based transformation of the human personality. My cases chronicle the healing of cancer, panic attacks, eating disorders and traumatic brain injury. Consciousness transforms when our ego identity is threatened and our hearts are challenged to open. Moreover, such growth or transformation is a natural evolutionary process that anyone can access. Disturbances such as depression, anxiety or physical illness can be vehicles of growth.

What are these strange concoctions of psychological and behavioral symptoms but the unresolved grief, hurts and general misery of your life—in cipher or code? The *un*told, *un*cooked, *un*digested crumbs of your existence. Misery gets your attention. Attend to it. Ladle it up, *soup du jour*, and outpour. How better to absorb the savory, thick pea soup of your life? Together, analyst and analysand establish a bond that binds and siphons off (even if drop-by-drop) the deluge of consolidated, coagulated sorrow that symptoms represent.

Ever had a dream about a filthy dirty, overflowing toilet? A toilet that would not flush? This is *prima materia* held inside that just will not go down. You have not been able *to stomach* something or other. This is material long overdue for processing and releasing. Or a dream where you "take a dump" in public? Were you bare-assed, embarrassed and ashamed? (That is one woman's recurring nightmare, whose alcoholic *bad ass* father humiliated her as a child by taking down her underpants, and powdering with talcum her behind. Still shy, *embarrassed* if seen, trauma still haunts her nervous system.) Carl Jung's prospective patient, a straight arrow German officer, dreamt of an idiot child sitting on a chamber pot smearing himself with feces. Jung would not touch the case. C. G. *washed his hands* of that one.[4]

18

Carl Jung found that the first dreams the patient presents can prognosticate the course of therapy. A much better prognosis is a dream where the washing machine is draining onto the floor, but the patient knows how to fix it! Stop the washer; get buckets for the overflow; re-set the dial for another cycle. Translate: Safely contain overwhelming emotion within the confines of supportive therapy, wherein the clothes (persona) can get free of personality problems or difficulties. *Clean up your act.*

Now we're *cookin'*. This stuff is hot. *Caliente.* Symptoms (materialized dreams of the central nervous system) serve to *turn up the heat* in order to work their transformation. Psychotherapy facilitates a phase shift. Symptoms (as do dreams) have their own intelligence, their own language. Therapy is a translation from one level of reality (or language) to another. *My heart melts.* Just can't stomach it. That burns me. *Like a dagger in my back.*

When brain scans map the wholesale firings of a neuronal nexus, what lights up more brain matter than any other matter? Metaphor.[5] Expect lots of metaphor in these pages. I mean to inflame your senses, ignite your mind, to *light up* your neurons like fireworks—like a lightening flash—with imagery that will "... burn, burn, burn like fabulous yellow roman candles exploding like spiders across the stars and in the middle you see the blue centerlight pop and everybody goes "Awww!"[6]

Jack Kerouac, alcoholic, shining light to generations of All Americans, who "cracked the corporate, conformist facade of the 1950s wide open," and ushered in the Beat Generation ("young people in the 1950s who rejected the traditional values, customs and dress of Western society and experimented with Eastern philosophies, communal living and illegal drugs"). Altered states—from using the likes of "tea" (marijuana), alcohol, goofballs, "benny" (Benzedrine "uppers"), even shots of morphine, "M"—became entrenched in America as the *means of transcendence*. Yet Kerouac died hemorrhaging blood like any skid row drunk.[7]

The wolf howls outside the gates of the temple of conformity. Deeply spiritual (if not religious), Kerouac's prose illuminates our way as we contemplate altered or *non-ordinary* states of reality (and their risks) on our path to Wholeness. I evoke Kerouac's spirit (if not his addiction) to guide us. Even as addiction and Death loom large in our collective, we herein invoke Spirit to turn the lower spirits *(dipsomania)* to Religiomania. *Spiritum contra spiritus* (Higher Power opposes alcoholism).[8]

Therapy is nothing if not following Nature. Creation. The Higher Intelligence that permeates within us and without us. C. G. Jung,

Swiss giant among nascent psychoanalysts, and later "discoverer" of archetypes and the collective unconscious, was asked in his eighties if he believed in God. He replied, "I don't need to believe; I know."[9] That is exactly what I say, what seems to unfold during transpersonal therapy.

The extraordinary beauty of the truth (to cop a phrase from crippled, Mexican artist Frida Kahlo). It has been called names as various as Higher Power, or Inner Healer. Creation. "It is the *nirvana* of Buddhism, the *samadhi* of yoga, the *satori* of Zen, the *fana* of Sufism, the *shema* of the Kabbalah, and the Kingdom of Heaven of Christianity."[10] However named, whatever called, an indisputable Higher Intelligence holds us. Carries, contains, enfolds us. Whether or not we allow it, or go kicking and screaming over the cliff—of the hardened rock of our self-identity. In short, whenever we truly surrender. Whenever Thy Will is done.

Finally, that day has come.

For some, the cure is as simple as crying. Catharsis is an energetic release—an experience of spiritual release and purification brought about by raw, uncooked emotion. Or healing might "slip in" under the guise of a new perspective, tantamount to a New World order. "My father didn't love me." "I was just a child." "My mother never touched me." "I never told anyone about the abuse."

"Let go and let God," is said in Alcoholics Anonymous (AA). Surrender, as Bill Wilson (AA's founder) did, and by so doing (or *not* doing) sparked a collective Miracle of Healing—from crippling addiction to Wholeness. Not mere symptom relief. Not merely *coping* but going for the cure. The following are highlights from Bill's letter to Carl Jung (January 23, 1961). "I doubt if you are aware that a certain conversation you once had with one of your patients, a Mr. Rowland H., back in the early 1930's, did play a critical role in the founding of our Fellowship."

Clear once more of alcohol, I found myself terribly depressed.... In utter despair I cried out, "If there be a God, will He show Himself." There immediately came to me an illumination of enormous impact and dimension.... My release from the alcohol obsession was immediate. At once I knew I was a free man. Shortly following my experience, my friend Edwin came to the hospital, bringing me a copy of William James' "Varieties of Religious Experience." This book gave me the realization that most conversion experiences, whatever their variety, do have a common denominator of ego collapse at depth....

In the wake of my spiritual experience there came a vision of a society of alcoholics, each identifying with and transmitting his experience to the next—chain style.... This concept proved to be the foundation of such success as Alcoholics Anonymous has since achieved. This has made conversion experiences—nearly every variety reported by James—available on an almost wholesale basis. Our sustained recoveries over the last quarter century number about 300,000.[11]

"....lay every newcomer wide open to a transforming spiritual experience." However healing happens, it is larger than and *encompasses* human ego—operating, as it does, outside our paltry plans. When you have seen enough cases of healing, you are convinced beyond belief. It is a force to be reckoned with. *When healing happens it is healing to behold it.* Let us behold some of my most remarkable people. Monica, Judith, Abbey. Nick. What happens *to* them happens *through* them. *Healing.* A higher-order Intelligence takes over and provides order. Session by session, as individual consciousness is changed. Case by case, transformation is ordained. Neuron by neuron, until neural pathways are born. Brain by brain, until our collective is transformed.

What happens is *evolution*—the future of the brain.

Miracles of healing happen as a matter of course. It is Nature's way, pure and simple. A seemingly spontaneous, gone-into-remission healing is simply Nature having her way with us—in fast motion. Healing is an efficiency of energy, *efficiency being the essence of spirituality*, according to Shree Maa, one of India's most beloved and respected Saints.[12] When our hearts open (and the background music of our lives is heard), we heal. Our energy runs free and clear. All things can heal. *Cancer.* A broken heart. Every day I step into my office, I witness jealousy, fear and anxiety, allergy or lethargy transform. Through *grace*, all things heal. Some spaciousness, a modicum of freedom between you and your misery is created. Better still, that misery is *transmuted* in the telling, reconfigured in the reliving.

You will never be the same. *And so it flows, and it flows, and the river goes.* So too, flow the so-called "mental diseases" and "personality disorders," those deformations of the psyche, and their symptoms. Until they *go.* Give us *leave.* Wholesale transformation is happening on our planet. Mental structures are melting away.

Get thee behind me, Satan, said the Lord. (The theory advanced by the Church was that the causation of disease was Satan.) Jesus

21

Christ brought the healing of disease to the realm of possibility—by the *laying on of hands*. Healing: to rid of a wrong, evil, or painful affliction. Better yet, to make Whole. It may not be popular to say this but it needs saying nonetheless. *Healing* is the common ground between medical science and religion. The meeting place of science & spirituality. The secular & the sacred. *Where the rubber meets the road*. And healing happens when we therapists—modern-day shamans—shake our rattles and walk our talk.

Is the evil of Satan (as well as our symptoms) a mere reflection or a facet of our own (un-owned, unrecognized) false face?

If *only* Hitler had been psychoanalyzed, good and proper. Hitler, illegitimate, oft-beaten "brat" of a raging, alcoholic father and battered mother, who died of breast cancer *before his eyes* (Mein Kampf is cancer "germs" writ large and projected wholesale onto Jews). Adolf Hitler was, after all, diagnosable as personality disordered. Multiple-substance dependent, Hitler was also a sexual deviant. A Coprophile (for arousal, his women "shat" upon him, the ultimate act of self-loathing, projected onto Jews).[13] If only Hitler had been dually-diagnosed and duly treated, World War II might never have devastated the Modern World, so-called. *If only, what if.* Therapy in bygone days was hit-and-miss.

But my point is made. World leaders, from the Narcissistic personality disordered Fidel Castro (and Sarah Palin) to the sexually-addicted Bill Clinton, to the fatherless Barack Obama, are notably not exempt from needing the succor of an analyst's couch. From George Bush to George W's father complex, we flounder and invade. Indeed, the modern world's gone mad. Mass murderers like Pol Pot abound. Sadistic Saddam Hussein and his brutal torturing sons, the delusional, off-the-charts, North Korean Kim Jong-il, Egypt's Mubarak and Libya's Gaddafi. Dick Cheney (a Reptilean, for sure) and Donald Rumsfeld playing soldier boy—these are not far behind. The bygone Pharaohs, Kings and Queens, the Ayatollahs, Shahs and present day Presidents surely serve as projections, writ large upon our flat screen, 3-D TVs and smartphones.

Projective identification, according to some therapists. According to others, *archetypal bleed through* of universal symbols.

Rumplestiltskin and Voldemort.

Politicians and world leaders alike share the stage with Project Runway contestants and American Idols. We all stand to gain (and lose) from their melodramas, theatrics and histrionics. And unfulfilled promises.

Yet everyday in my office material arises that would shock and astound—the aforementioned overlords, world leaders and trendsetters. *Who are they to steal our healing thunder?*

Enough of them. Ensouled (cherishing deeply), I write to bear witness to you, unsung heroes and heroines—on the analyst's couch. I am taking you, reader, on the journey of those who cry for help in the middle of their dark-night-of-the-soul, somewhere-in-the-universe. Above all, I bear witness to transpersonal therapy, wherein the trauma of one connects to the healing of all. Countee Cullen, poet, said it best.[14]

Any Human to Another

The ills I sorrow at
Not me alone
Like an arrow,
Pierce to the marrow,
Through the fat
And past the bone.
Your grief and mine
Must intertwine
Like sea and river,
Be fused and mingle,
Diverse yet single,
Forever and forever....
Your every grief
Like a blade
Shining and unsheathed
Must strike me down.
Of bitter aloes wreathed,
My sorrow must be laid
On your head like a crown.

Transpersonal psychotherapy. Let it begin.

CHAPTER 2

OPENING MOVES

In many cases in psychiatry, the patient who comes to us has a story that is not told, and which as a rule no one knows of. To my mind, therapy only really begins after the investigation of that wholly personal story. It is the patient's secret, that rock against which he is shattered. If I know his secret story, I have a key to the treatment.

C. G. Jung, *Memories, Dreams, Reflections*

S ecret stories. Each secret story is precious. Every story is unique. Each case conveys a multiplicity of clinical considerations. Diagnoses of disorders are but summations of symptoms that carry a certain configuration, the code of awakening—to be cracked wide open. Yet even as individual psyches are fractured, splintered, and *transformed*, the result is the growth of human consciousness. *Therapy has evolved to aid this growth of consciousness.*

And through the yawning maw of Creation arrives the psychology of the future. Still, the psychology of the future is virtually as straightforward as the sharing of secret stories. And truly, the greatest story to be told is one where trauma results in shattering and dissociative states—yet the personality expands and develops. I am describing a specific dynamic through which personal healing happens and ultimately, the human personality unfolds. Species-wide.

Therapy has evolved in service to this dynamic.

I share secrets in these chapters, personal stories, with an emphasis on the creation of, amplification and integration of, *parts* within a fractured self—formed through trauma. Fractured selves make themselves known through these parts, and their enhanced perceptual abilities. Non-ordinary states of consciousness are *de rigueur* to secret selves. As our secret selves begin to be wholly integrated through therapy, the human personality transforms. In short, I invite you to witness wholesale healing.

This chapter introduces some "secret selves" you may already know. Our cultural icons marvelously *superbly* exemplify these mixed-up states and messed-up parts. So before introducing some unknown remarkable people, I shine the spotlight on film stars, artists, comedians and rock stars. For example, what do songwriter Joni Mitchell and artist Frida Kahlo have in common, that is, besides their obvious artistry?

Both artists suffered some crippling of limb from childhood polio.

After her bloody miscarriage, Frida Kahlo began to draw and paint her anguish in a unique style, forged from a *religious* Mexican genre, which defined her work until the end of her life. Art Historian, Victor Zamudio Taylor: "In Detroit, Frida Kahlo, for the first time, consciously decides that she will paint about herself, and that she will paint the most private and painful aspects of herself.... And to reveal herself and tell her story as the only choice and alternative she has to live a full life given her physical condition."[1] Muralist and marriage partner Diego Rivera: *"Frida began work on a series of masterpieces which had no precedent in the history of art—paintings which exalted the feminine qualities of endurance of truth, reality, cruelty, and suffering. Never before had a woman put such agonized poetry on canvas."*[2]

What was Frida's physical condition that caused her so much torment and suffering? Turn back the clock....

Frida's agonizing miscarriage was the indirect result of a bizarre accident during college that, upon closer inspection, seems fated. A trolley car had crashed into her flimsy wooden bus, leaving her impaled on a handrail—an iron rod—completely pierced through.

Her spinal column was broken in three places in the lumbar region. Her collarbone was broken, and her third and fourth ribs. *Her **right leg** had eleven fractures and her **right foot** was dislocated and crushed.* Her left shoulder was out of joint, her pelvis broken in three places. The steel handrail had literally skewered her body at the level of the abdomen; entering on the left side, it had come out through the vagina.[3]

At least thirty-two surgeries were required, most on her spine and her *right foot*. Frida's subsequent immobilization, and frustration at being immobilized by surgeries nevertheless had its compensations. She had never before thought of painting until she languished in bed from the accident. "Now you see that to suffer a little always serves a purpose."[4]

However, all her damage and suffering was an echo, a mere reverberation of the original trauma. What shattered Frida at the outset, I say, was childhood illness. Poliomyelitis was precursor to that seemingly freak accident.

Stricken with polio at six years, Frida spent nine months confined to her room, her freedom of movement curtailed by polio. Her right leg remained withered. Frida was later mercilessly taunted as *Frida la coja, pata de palo* (Frida the gimp, with the peg leg). The broken bird became introverted, "self-fascinated," as well as an outgoing "character," in order to overcome her withered *right* limb.

During that time Frida discovered what some would call an imaginary playmate. Breathing vapor onto one window pane of her bedroom, drawing with her finger *a door*, whereupon "full of great joy and urgency, I went out in my imagination, through this "door," … and I went down with great haste into the *interior of the earth*, where "my imaginary friend" was always waiting for me."

> She was agile and she danced as if she weighed nothing at all. I followed her in all her movements and while she danced I told her my secret problems…. But from my voice she knew everything about me…. When I returned to the window I entered through the same door drawn on the glass pane. When? For how long had I been with her? I do not know. It could have been a second or thousands of years…. I ran with my *secret* and my joy as far as the furthermost corner of the patio of my house, and always in the same place under a cedar tree, I cried out and laughed, surprised at being *alone* with my great happiness and with the so vivid memory of *the little girl*.[5]

The little girl was always waiting for me, Frida says. *Always*. Her great joy and urgency speaks to a specific emotional and mental state she had realized; clearly it required a sustained effort to achieve passage to this secret world. The consistency of her experience—the same window pane, the same "door," and the same place of return—speaks to a parallel reality. The subtle realm, I say.

It is this *going out in the imagination* that I highlight. In short, dissociation: the separation of normally connected mental processes. Dissociation is the basis for the fractured parts that *good enough* therapy regroups, rejoins and recreates into a whole person (whereas *great* therapy hones that whole into a fantastically functional self). After all, *going out in the imagination* is responsible for that widespread change of the personality that ultimately evolves our species.

Frida never forgot her "double." "Thirty-four years have passed since I experienced this magic friendship and every time that I remember it, it revives and becomes larger and larger inside of my world."[6]

So real and true is this dynamic of shattering, dissociation and *going out in the imagination* that, with respect to it, uncanny parallels exist in the development of other artists as well. Consider the life of enormously popular singer, songwriter Joni Mitchell. Like Frida, painting her anguish in a unique style, Joni hit her matchless stride with her album *Blue*. Steven Holden, Music Critic for The New York Times: "It was naked, pulsating, great poetry. *Blue* just went to a level of psychic pain and honesty that no-one else had *ever* written before. And no-one else has written since."[7]

This cathartic album has been called "precise notes on a nervous breakdown, death and rebirth."[8] It was written in the language of *spiritual emergency*, where one's ego defenses suffer a breakdown only to reach a re-ordering of reality and ultimately, a high-order functioning. Joni later spoke to the veils of perception being "pulled off," and the transparency of seeing and hearing "every artifice in a voice." This is a lady who speaks of mysticism ("I was a little 'God mad' at the time"), and ego malformation—in the same sentence.[9] Pure visionary experience through psychological descent, breakdown and dissociation.

I'll tell you what you have to go through to get an album like that. That album is probably the purest emotional record that I will ever make in my life. You wouldn't want to go around like that. To survive in the world you've got to have defenses. And defenses are in themselves a kind of pretension. And at that time in my life, mine just went. They went and you could call it all kind of technical things. Actually it was a great spiritual opportunity but nobody around me knew it was happening.[10]

Yet somehow Joni knew how to stoke the fires of transformation.

I moved up into the Canadian backbush to a small sanctuary where I could be alone. Live with kerosene, stayed away from electricity for about a year. I turned to nature. I was really *down*, and with that came a tremendous sense of *knowing nothing*. Western psychology might call it a nervous breakdown, but in certain cultures, they call it a shamanic conversion.

I read nearly every psychological book I could lay my hands on, and threw them all against the wall basically. But depression could be the sand that makes the pearl. Most of my best work came out of it. If you get rid of the demons that are disturbing things, if you get rid of them, then angels fly off, too. So there is the possibility in that mire—of an *epiphany*.[11]

Shamanic conversion? Naturally. Strengthened and stoked, through a "different, un-drug-induced consciousness."[12] Certainly. Joni has since shared what C. G. Jung would call her wholly personal, secret story. What shattered (and elevated) Joni Mitchell at the outset was prolonged childhood illness, *a shamanic illness*, eerily like Frida Kahlo's. The effects that unfolded in Joni Mitchell were likewise profound.

"I had a lot of childhood illnesses, and we moved a lot. You can see in early pictures of me that I started out as an extroverted, hammy kid. But a number of moves, then polio, scarlet fever, chicken pox bordering on smallpox, nearly dying with measles—all of that isolated me a lot."[13] *Joni was nine years old when she, like Frida, was struck with polio.* Nobody knows where Joni caught polio; diagnosing it took the doctors a few days to figure out what she had, whereupon she was shipped by ambulance plane to Saskatoon.

> The polio ward was annexed off of St. Paul's hospital with trailers, with ramps leading up to them. So we were isolated from the rest of hospital population and it was presided over by these *rustling* nuns. And as Christmas neared, there was a terrible longing to go home.... And [my mother] brought me a small Christmas tree. And decorations. Which I still have three of them that I put on my Christmas tree every year.
>
> The therapist had been in that day, and I'd said, "I want to go [home] for Christmas"—"Well, you can't," he said. *Why not?* "Well, you know, you can't walk." *What if I walked,"* I said. He said, "You can't, you can't even stand up. I said, "What if I stood up and walked?" And he just hung his head. He didn't answer me. So I thought, okay. I'm going home for Christmas....
>
> They used to bring these scalding rags, and pin them all over you, and bring you up to just before blistering, it was scalding. And the therapist would come in and try to *bend* you back into shape. And it was *terribly* painful. So one day I said, Okay, I want to try to walk. I don't know who I prayed to—I think I prayed to the tree—but I made a promise to whatever it was. I *addressed* it to the tree—I said, *I am not a cripple*. I am *not* a cripple. I am *not* a cripple. You know, I'm going home for Christmas. If I can pull this off, *I'll make it up to you,* you know.
>
> So I walked, I went home for Christmas. So polio, in a certain way, did me a solid, kind of germinated an inner life, I think, also, and a sense of the *mystic*. Definitely, it was *mystical* to come back from that disease."[14]

Ultimately, this intense act of prayer—powerfully distilled under threat of being forsaken as a *cripple*—opened Joni to an otherworldly perspective on life, and unearthly powers of concentration. She speaks to her mystical connection in discussing the process of songwriting. "A lot of it is being open, I think, to encounter. And in a way, in touch with the miraculous."[15] She speaks to the process of *going out in the imagination* in the following. "I do a lot of night-writing. I need solitude to write ... 'cause I have to go *inside myself so far*, to search through a theme."[16]

Graham Nash: "Watching her write is a most interesting process. It's almost like she *channels*. She was gone for hours. I mean, she was physically right there, but she wasn't there; she was gone. I'd say things to her, and she wasn't even listening. She was gone. And it was a great thing to see. A great thing to see someone taken away by—vision."[17]

David Crosby: "Throughout her work, there is an effort to make the music be skybound. To relieve the body of temporality. And once she gets there, *whoof*—it's almost a chant, this need for release and transcendence, to ride above the culture, to be in the sky, to reflect—to not be *in* it, but to look down upon it."[18]

Her ability to dissociate into powerful prayer is, in itself, an altered state. Though begun under duress of childhood illness, it obviously initiated Joni into her "shamanic conversion," and the self-absorption so necessary to her exalted artistry.

Speaking of her poor health that has lasted throughout her adulthood, Joni says, "Every decade I have a few rounds with death, you know."[19] Death becomes the lady.

*

Consider the work of Dr. Kenneth Ring, social psychologist and one of the founders and foremost researchers of the field of near-death studies. Knowledge of near-death experiences (NDEs) is widespread in our collective. Homer Simpson's cartoon dog, knocked unconscious, was ordered, "Stay away from the tunnel of light!" The NDE is highly relevant as an extreme form of dissociation. Dr. Ring's study, *The Omega Project*, linked NDE's with a higher incidence of childhood trauma.

The Omega Project found that near-death experiencers (NDErs) reported they experienced more abuse and trauma as children than control subjects. Experiencers were more likely to show dissociative tendencies—although not to a pathological extent. Dr. Ring argues that child abuse and trauma play a central role in promoting sensitivity to NDEs and even UFO experiences. For experiencers may develop a dissociative response style, which in turn, promotes "tuning into" other realities. Childhood illness, trauma and abusive childhoods certainly facilitate entry into the spiritual subtle realms.

At last we know the price of evolution.

Trauma, according to Dr. Ring, stimulates the development of "an extended range of human perception beyond normally recognized limits."[20] He even hypothesizes an encounter-prone personality, with the quality termed by psychologists as "psychological absorption" as its hallmark. Psychological absorption is the ability to focus attention on one's inner reality to the exclusion of the external environment. Frida Kahlo's and Joni Mitchell's great facility with altered states is likely a compensatory skill for those who have suffered significant trauma.

As for other changes, the Psychophysical Changes Inventory on Dr. Ring's questionnaire revealed the following:

Almost one half of [experiencers] (compared to about 15 percent of the control groups), for example, claim that their nervous system now functions differently than it did before, and not quite a third of them (compared to about 7-8 percent of the control groups) also assert that their brains are "structurally different" than before....

Finally, there is a clear tendency for experiential respondents to describe that they have undergone a kind of mind expansion.... well over half of them (compared to less than one quarter of the control groups) report that their psychic abilities increased after their encounters.[21]

Moreover, subjects were *twice to four times* as likely to report that they now experience the following: 1) sensitivity to light, 2) hearing acuity, 3) mood fluctuation, 4) psychic abilities, and 5) healing gifts. The Life Changes Inventory found significantly greater changes for the following values: appreciation for life, self-acceptance, concern for others, materialism (decrease), quest for meaning and spirituality. There was widespread agreement that such experiences are an integral part of an evolutionary growth spurt towards greater spiritual awareness and higher consciousness.

In summary, the data suggest a psychophysical transformation, that is, "certain changes that affect their physiological functioning, nervous system, brain, and mental processes so as to permit a higher level of human nature to manifest."[22] The general implication of these changes is voiced by Dr. Ring in the following: "Extraordinary encounters appear to be the gateway to a radical, biologically based transformation of the human personality."[23]

It is just such radically transformed humans of whom I write.

But before we get carried away, *singing praise of the evolutionary potential of the body electric*, we need to attend to trauma. Healing trauma is what therapy is all about. And a great deal of trauma comes at the hands of others. Frida and Joni, initiated in childhood through the trauma of physical illness, give way to other cases of people profoundly rent through human ignorance or cruelty. Case examples of cultural icons, nonetheless. The following exemplifies neuropsychiatric illness stemming from, or stimulated by a singular form of trauma.

Karen Armstrong painstakingly chronicled the unnatural life of a postulant and nun in the Catholic Church before the reforms of the Second Vatican Council. The emotional deprivation she suffered gave rise to depression and spiritual aridity. Without recourse to help from her religious superiors, she was traumatized by a raging and unreasonable Novice Mistress ("Mother Walter"), and victimized by the repeated sexual advances of a priest (her religious superior: an unnamed "Father"). Due to overly strict dietary restrictions ("mortification of the flesh") and the enforced intake of food such as dairy that her lactose intolerant body could not absorb, she routinely vomited and became severely anorexic.

"All this bleeding, fainting, vomiting—I suddenly wondered, was it because I was forcing myself to achieve the impossible?"[24]

Karen Armstrong, one of the western world's foremost commentators on religious affairs, and author of A History of God, describes her own out-of-body experience during what was later diagnosed as an epileptic seizure.

Suddenly in the special hush that heralded the deep isolation of the next eight days, a long disembodied sound broke into the waiting stillness, agonized, fighting for breath, on and on with a will of its own. What was that strange, keening scream that sounded like an animal caught in a trap? Where was it coming from? Then from a long way off I saw myself, my eyes clenched tightly shut, my mouth gaping and contorted and from it coming the unearthly cry. Nuns hurried round. They slapped me, shook me, but could not quell the sound. Finally I watched myself crumble through their arms in an awkward huddle.

Then something snapping. The sound stopped. Two selves pulled apart. Blackness.[25]

Karen would later recover from this foray into the life of a religious that amounted to a life *against* God. But her gut wrenching experience of dissociated selves describes an out-of-body experience (OBE). Karen's traumatic shock (or seizure) was such that she dissociated from her physical body. She saw herself "from a long way off." Karen observed the wailing, the nuns' response—everything—from outside her body.

Human consciousness has evolved a ready response to the unthinkable. Unbearable emotional trauma produces a profound altered state. While helpless and without the possibility of *physical* escape, a simple alteration of consciousness preserves our survival. If nothing else, OBEs are a very powerful adaptation. This alteration of consciousness is similar to hypnotic trance. Common features of both include calm, enhanced perception and altered sensation like numbing of pain; depersonalization and derealization (change of personal identity, and the reality of the world), and change in one's sense of time.

"People in captivity become adept practitioners of the arts of altered consciousness."[26] Two cultural icons demonstrate the arts of extreme states *par excellence*.

Comedian Margaret Cho and rock star Jim Morrison of The Doors have much in common. School served as the theatre where they both acted out their response to abuse on the home front. Victimized, Margaret was bullied for years during her childhood.

But I stayed at that same school for five more years, which is forever when you are a kid, and I must admit, *it wore me down*. I think I lost something there—an interior brightness. The luster and the silver lining and the Tootsie Roll center and the brave one in me went far underground, now surfacing, twisted, perverted, deformed, with a dowager's hump and a bad nervous tic, but tougher still.[27]

As males tend to externalize the abuse, Jim, according to his younger brother, sometimes *was* a bully. Schoolteachers noted his angry, seemingly irrational behavior.[28]

But in terms of substance abuse, Margaret and Jim were both on par. Both lived a life of near-suicidal substance abuse (one died from overdose) presumably *intended* to relieve unbearable emotional pain. It was self-medication gone awry. Traumatized people use psychoactive drugs to regulate their internal, intolerable emotional states. Feelings of anger and betrayal. *Depression.* Hurt people use drugs and alcohol to deal with helplessness and terror, to produce numbing effects like dissociation, and to control hyperarousal and intrusive symptoms such as nightmares. *And* to simulate well-being. But it is less than effective medication. Traumatized people are at great risk of developing dependence on alcohol or other drugs.

In the midst of a drug overdose, Margaret was fortunate to have, if not a classic near-death experience, at least an out-of-body experience.

> I am convinced I did die once. I did so many drugs one night, on top of an already-raging whiskey drunk, I floated off into a deep, drowsy place....
> I saw my body beneath me and I couldn't get back. I tried to move my body from where I was, but I couldn't. I stayed up there on the ceiling, trapped by the shadows, terrified, trying to get my mouth to say, "Call an ambulance." I couldn't get down for the longest time, and then after a while, the fear subsided. I knew I was going to die. It was okay. I didn't fight it.
> I died.[29]

Surrendering to Death proved productive. Not long afterwards, Margaret became convinced that she could not stop drinking and that she really *was* going to die. Margaret mobilized.

> I was sick of myself. I was sick of living this way. I was sick of dying.
> I realized I did not want to die.
> I wanted to quit drinking.[30]

Margaret's near-death propelled her towards becoming sober. "Since I had been getting high every day for all of my adult life, being sober was an altered state unto itself."[31] That stunning statement is indicative of traumatic shock. Altered states are *de rigueur* for one who experiences ongoing emotional trauma. Just why had Margaret been so intent on altering her resident state of mind?

Margaret "tended to despise sex, ever since that first awful time."[32]

He was twenty-two. She was fourteen. *Jailbait.* Hardly consensual sex.

> I was in shock because I didn't know him. He was on top of me and it happened so quickly. I didn't say yes, but I didn't say no either. It was like a flash and he was inside me and it felt cold and hurt in a way that I couldn't explain and I thought: He is raping me, yes, he is raping me—or is he? During it, I silently thanked my family for making me go to long church services, because that taught me to leave my body at a young age—those skills really do come in handy.[33]

One of my own clients, raped while still a virgin, confided during therapy that powers of concentration *honed by sports training* had given her the ability to partially dissociate from the pain—by focusing on the digital clock on the nightstand while she was being raped.

Altered state "skills" notwithstanding, Margaret Cho speaks to a seemingly permanent, dissociative split that results from such shock. "And still to this day I drive by that shitty apartment on Oak Street and I look up into the broken windows and there is part of me still up there in that place."

What do comedian Margaret Cho and Jim Morrison of The Doors have in common? Both Margaret and Jim broke through a self-imposed silence and cultural denial about childhood sexual abuse. In the following Margaret speaks to the ongoing trauma throughout her adolescence, and the toll it took.

> My body had started to develop earlier than other girls my age, and I had been the object of keen interest of many of my father's friends and a male relative, and I had already received countless touches that felt rude and invasive. I was wary of men, especially older ones, and did my best to stay away from their leering glances, grabby hands and personal questions.[34]

Finally, Margaret discloses what she refers to as "my childhood molestation by a family friend."[35] Yet Margaret was one sexual abuse survivor whose extreme altered state experience—her near-death—served to wake her up. It is legitimate to marvel at this extraordinary capacity of the mind. She ultimately learned to use her trance capability to enrich her present life rather than escape from it. "At times the survivor may even attain a feeling of participation in an order of creation that transcends ordinary reality."[36] Transcending mundane, material reality is precisely what Margaret's inner *felt* sense of comedy is all about.

> When the crowd is with you, the jokes are fresh, your timing is just right, and the moon is in the seventh house and Jupiter aligns with Mars. You feel like you are exactly where you should be, and there is nothing better. Comedy is a rare gift from the gods, an awesome invention. It propels you right into the heart of the universe.[37]

Thank you, Margaret. "Traumatic events serve as powerful activators of the capacity for trance."[38] Jim Morrison, whose own capacity for trance was initiated by trauma, would agree.

> Jim was the greatest American rock star of his era. Jim styled his band "erotic politicians," and relentlessly urged his huge audience—at the height of the dangerous sixties—to break on through the doors of perception, to free themselves from robotic familial conditioning, to seek a higher, more aware consciousness. Doors concerts—throbbing with war-dance rhythms and superheated intimacy—were as close to the experience of shamanic ritual as the rock audience ever got. The Doors captured the unrest and the menace that hung in the air of the late sixties like tear gas, and they did it with hypnotic cool.[39]

Yet it was anything but cool for Jim Morrison. *"For me, it was never an act, those so-called performances. It was a life-and-death thing—an attempt to communicate, to involve many people at once in a private world of thought."*[40] More likely, Jim's private world of unending pain. But "hypnotic" is dead right. Jim Morrison mused about the state of mind induced by a "hypnotic river of sound" that left him free "—to let my subconscious play it out, wherever it goes."[41] And he manipulated his own mind to achieve that self-hypnotic state.

> I used to have this magic formula, like, to break into the subconscious. I would lay there and say over and over, "Fuck the mother, kill the father, fuck the mother, kill the father.' You can really get into your head just repeating that slogan over and over. That mantra can never become meaningless. It's too basic and

can never become just words, 'cause as long as you're saying it, you can never be unconscious.[42]

Nobody around Jim realized that he was actually suffering from an untreated, posttraumatic stress condition, in essence, an unending nervous breakdown *("Ray, I want to quit. I just can't take it anymore. I think I'm having a nervous breakdown ... I don't feel so good")*.[43] Stemming undoubtedly from multiple traumas (some self-induced) from which he never recovered, Jim's *complex posttraumatic stress disorder* evolved into numbing self-medication (like drinking to blackout almost every night), and near-suicidal behavior. Besides screaming "maniacally" in clubs, and slapping the faces of fans who asked for an autograph, Jim was also known for "walking around West Hollywood, picking up skinny, boyish-looking girls, taking them back to his motel, and trying to sodomize them."[44]

Bill Siddons, The Doors' Manager: "I knew Jim had a lot of serious problems. I didn't know what they were. I just knew he would put more alcohol into his body than anybody ... I thought he was trying to commit suicide, because the quantities didn't make any sense to me."[45]

Of course, his behavior makes absolute sense in light of a diagnosis of posttraumatic stress disorder (PTSD). Not for nothing was the Doors epic song, *The End,* featured in the movie *Apocalypse Now.* Charlie Sheen's character virtually writhes in alcohol-soaked tremors of the disorder. *The End* is the quintessential song about PTSD.

According to drummer, John Densmore, The Doors' message was one of "endarkenment" (backlit by the sixties search for enlightenment).[46] Without a doubt, Jim's poetry was dark and ominous. Sex was conflated with rape and bleeding virgins. Hangmen and tombstones figured. Napalm. *Impending death.* Songs in which the Lizard King leaves his mother's body rotting in the ground. Jim's version of high school featured crashed school buses and raped cheerleaders. A screenplay featured a homicidal hitcher.

Joan Didion: "[The Doors'] *music insists that love is sex and sex is death and therein lives salvation.*[47]

The genesis of Jim's ascent to rock stardom included college-age, psychedelic binges of daily doses of still-legal LSD, "dangerous plant euphorics like belladonna and jimsonweed, plus mass quantities of alcohol." Jim stopped eating and within six weeks lost thirty-five pounds.

Yet LSD serves as a nonspecific *amplifier of the contents of the person's psyche*, both personal and collective. One of Jimmy's LSD trips

featured a spectacular flashback to the Indian car wreck he had witnessed as a child.[48] Young Jimmy had witnessed the aftermath of ve-
hicular accident—a truckload of migrant Indians hurled onto the road,
dying painful deaths. No small trauma for a boy of six years old. Could
one or more of the Indians, indeed, have launched and lodged his
airborne spirit inside the confines of Jimmy's psyche, a "child's fragile eggshell mind"? A Shamanic Overlord to his boyhood self? That
notion of Jimmy as possessed was disseminated by none-other-than
Morrison himself. There stood the Shaman, revealed a thousand-fold
by his own pounding, grinding *orgasmic* music (not to mention, by his
flagrant masturbation against microphone stands).

Yet that earliest childhood trauma most certainly prefigured something even more horrendous in Jim's epic life. Not for nothing did he
rage seemingly uncontrollably against injustice.

Anyone inquiring more than superficially into Jim Morrison's
life immediately realizes that the story of his childhood is crucial
to understanding what happened to him later. First, he remained
very childish his entire life. Second, when Jim began perform-
ing in public, he abruptly severed all contact with his family and
never saw his parents again. Third, his early act was a graphic re-
write of the ancient Oedipus legend, in which he sang of killing
his father and fucking his mother in front of tens of thousands
of his fans.

Why did Jim Morrison hate his parents so much? Why did he
hate himself? How was he able to create such pure American
music out of his own anguish?[49]

Whatever happened to Jim likely happened during his adolescence.
Classmates and teachers later remembered that Jim underwent a distinct personality change, noting his depression and angry, impulsive
behavior. Jim's notebook sketches at thirteen "specialized in obscene
drawings of people with surreally exaggerated sexual organs and enormous assholes, obsessively inking in bodily fluids, especially excre-
ment, menstrual blood, mucus and sperm."[50]

Jim Morrison *was* the original Back Door Man, whose same entitled song memorialized rear-entry (sodomy). Should we be surprised
by his claim—on more that one occasion—that he was the adolescent
victim of just such a depraved assault? Ripped from his throat, his
piercing scream echoed throughout his songs. How nakedly revealing,

his raging Oedipal epic, *The End*: "Father, I want to kill you. Mother, I want to fuck you." In May of 1970, Jim described being sexually abused as a teenager—to his lawyer, Max Fink. Apparently it was not the first time he made that claim.

In 1997, a California woman, Linda Ashcroft, published an account of her relationship with Jim that she claimed lasted from 1967 to 1970. Among the confidences she claims Jim shared with her was the story of being raped by his father during a disciplinary beating while he was in high school, presumably in Alexandria. Jim, she claimed, told her that he missed dinner one night and that his father took him upstairs for a man-to-man talk that ended in a depraved sexual assault. Ashcroft's book, Wild Child: Life with Jim Morrison, was published first in London with this allegation, but when the book was published in America in 1998, the allegation was deleted from the text, presumably for legal reasons.[51]

Some nature of early sexual transgression, followed by massive, daily doses of LSD and ultimately, derailed by chasers of beer and whiskey and ... voila!
Transfiguration.
Trauma experts agree that there is no greater trauma than sexual transgression. As far as *going out in the imagination*, its dissociating effects are considered by far the greatest of all traumas. Some sexual trauma, by virtue of its physical intrusion, can signal a life-threat. Such sexual trauma *is* a near-death experience—the greatest dissociative experience of all.

The history of psychology is shot through with psychiatry's inability to fathom just how great are the deformations and permutations of the psyche that result from such trauma as sexual abuse. Or to reconcile the giftedness of such a "No. 2 personality," to coin C. G. Jung's phrase about his medium Ivenes. Far from what The New York Times terms a "supernaturalism that seems bizarre to most Westerners," such a bent, whether mystic, magical, paranormal, or spiritual, is a natural inclination of our entire species. East or west, we have the same basic *human* neurophysiology. Perhaps Karen Armstrong's early brush with organized religion's lack of authenticity lead to her later doubt, "I knew better than to expect revelations, visions, or voices telling me what I must do. That happened only to a very few."[52]

Say not so. Secret stories reveal the giftedness of our cultural icons, of whom many come traumatized to the table, yet bearing revelations, visions and voices, speaking to us from the silver screen.

Marilyn Monroe suffered from addiction to barbiturates (sleeping pills), alcohol abuse and Borderline personality disorder—no doubt from an upbringing that included early abandonment and childhood sexual molestation she disclosed she had suffered while in foster care. (Margaret Cho could relate. "Taking tranquilizers with my booze, I felt like Marilyn Monroe."[53]) Marilyn drugged-out volatility yet woman-child vulnerability projected a *numinosity* across the silver screen that surely had its genesis in sexual trauma.

Def. *numinous*: having a mysterious power that suggests the presence of a spirit or god. Or charisma of a Hollywood Movie Star.

Many are the deformations of character diagnosed by clinical psychology, yet almost certainly initiated by trauma and neglect, though transformed by talent. Narcissistic Personality Peter Sellers ("The Life & Death of Peter Sellers"), Passive Aggressive Andy Kauffman ("Man on the Moon") Sociopath Stephen Glass ("Shattered Glass"), one of the mid-90s most sought-after journalists in Washington, D.C., whose stories for the policy magazine *The New Republic* turned out to be sheer make-em-ups. Any fan of Woody Allen's knew well before Dylan Farrow's claims that he was turned on by neurotic, suicidal women barely of age. Director Roman Polansky's taste runs towards the pubescent. James Dean was sexually molested by his church pastor, according to the late Liz Taylor.

Forget the analyst's couch. *Analysis in the West happens at the movies.* Never before in human history has psychological knowledge been so readily available to a sophisticated audience. The Arts and Sciences are ever represented. Sadistic Personality Disordered, Pablo Picasso, and Obsessive Compulsive Disordered (OCD) Howard Hughes. Not to mention, Nichola Tesla.

Gifted, no doubt. Joseph Conrad, plumbing the heart of darkness of incipient insanity, could relate. *The horror! The horror!* experienced by any one of these cultural icons.[54] Their dire straits and their channeled energies pave the way for my own clients.

One cardinal rule of therapy. *God sets my appointment book.* That is fortunate for both me and my clients. We are well met. The following people set an appointment with me and destiny—to share how they *woke up* to find themselves in-the-middle of their dark night of the soul, somewhere in the universe.

But first, my own story.

CHAPTER 3

JANET: MY STORY

The route to freedom from the despair and helplessness we feel is through surrender—the very thing our egos are fighting. The experience of total personal surrender is a necessary prerequisite for connecting with a transpersonal source.

Stanislav Grof, *The Holotropic Mind*

P sychospiritual rebirth.
   When I first read those words, I was electrified. Exhila-
rated. I recognized myself, how I had changed. I was like
someone who had struggled for years with baffling symptoms of an
unknown syndrome—someone newly receiving a diagnosis, and certain promise of a cure. This path was known to others. Charted. What
I had undergone was known—several long decades of suffering and its
swift change. Those words conferred acknowledgment. Confirmation.

Psychospiritual rebirth. Yes, I had truly been touched and transported home.

Telling one's story is something few therapists do, certainly not
within the context of somebody else's therapy. Self-disclosure is
frowned upon in traditional psychology, and for good reason. But I
want to tell my story for it provides a template for extraordinary experience and healing—initiated through childhood trauma. As such, it
is a story worth telling.

More than anything it provided my training as a transpersonal
therapist. Once you have experienced deep energetic healing—psycho-
spiritual transformation—you have been reborn. And along with that
comes some modicum of wisdom in facilitating the death and rebirth
of others.

But first, those words. I found them in Stanislav Grof's story about
his own mother's healing from a near-fatal bout after a toxic response
to poison oak. Little did he know during it that she was convinced her
healing resulted from a powerful vision of the Indian saint Sai Baba,
who "reached inside her body and performed miraculous healing."

Within an hour, my mother's condition improved as if by magic. She regained physical strength and her mind cleared. As the
day was breaking, she decided to step out of the house on our
large deck to watch the sunrise over the Ventana wilderness and
observe the Pacific Ocean. She was ecstatic, and her eyes were
radiant. "Stan, you live in an incredible place!" she said enthusi-
astically. "The air is so clear here, and all the colors are radiant!
Have you ever noticed the sparkles in the branches of these pine
trees? And look at the reflections of light on the waves!" There

43

was no doubt she was experiencing what I had witnessed many hundreds of times in my work with psychedelics and, more recently, with Holotropic Breathwork—a profound psychospiritual rebirth! [1]

My own healing came after several near-fatal bouts from a toxic response to my own poisonous life. The first thirty years of my life were hell on wheels.

*

I was deprived of food all throughout my childhood. That is a startling disclosure. Still, I have scarcely said those words before. I have said many other words, "My father was manic depressive. My mother had an eating disorder. I was neglected." But I never so starkly named it for what it really was. I was deprived of food such that my physical growth was stunted. This happens to nutritionally deprived children when nobody notices, when no outsider intervenes. That revelation is equally as devastating as the realization that no functional adult was on the scene.

But do those words accurately describe my memories? In third grade a kindly neighbor was so appalled at my appearance she asked if I'd been ill. I only knew I felt ashamed to be so noticed. Much to my humiliation my parochial school, eighth grade nun called me an example of "emaciation" in spelling class. I still cringe at that one. I struggle to capture the exact flavor of my sad childhood. Let me take you back.

My inner battle over food lasted until I was twenty-nine. In an age where three out of every hundred adolescent girls in the United States are affected by an eating disorder such as anorexia, bulimia or binge-eating, that is not remarkable. [2] But my problematic eating started long before my teen years. My conflict over food was passed down from my mother, and circumscribed my life. That conflict comprised my most basic sense of self. Food, after all, is one of the most primary of relationships that impinges upon the child from the outside world. I first knew that I was *unseen* by not being fed properly; I knew that I was rejected by my parents' frustrated response. So instead of rejecting my parents, so necessary to my survival, food became the enemy. I rejected food.

My memories outline the seeds of conflict that would play an integral part in my personal history. But thwarted instincts make for more than mere revenge. Above all, my story embodies the Jungian principle of regeneration. *Instincts that are thwarted—by redoubling back to the source of life—lead ultimately to renewal.* Even for the malnourished and undersized, such growth or transformation is a natural evolutionary process. Psychospiritual transformation. A thin, green shoot can break concrete.

I remember being fed. Feeling was everything. But the act of being fed in comfort, with the feeder in harmony with my needs, did not give rise to a conscious memory. It was only when my needs sharply differentiated from my mother's that "I" came into being.

And "I" felt miserable.

I sensed my mother by the food she spooned into my mouth *before I had swallowed.* My mouth was full but she did not stop. Strapped in a highchair, I was captive to her insensitivity. Then "I" could not swallow at all. Mute and unable to move that mountain of food in my mouth, I felt outraged. *Why doesn't she know what I am feeling?* A part of me came alive in that moment: a sense of self.

Little did I know that my mother would devastate my body with her own eating disorder throughout my childhood.

*

I remember a large room, filled with long tables and row upon row of people; it was to be a special occasion for eating. Surely a new experience. My older sister's memory of a banquet is tinged with pleasure. But some sense of my mother's fright was conveyed to me on a purely physical level. For I was fed and nervously overfed by my mother until I threw up without warning. *What a relief!*

I do not remember shame. Throwing up was a "natural" act to me, a reassertion of equilibrium. What I do remember is the waitress kindly suggesting that I might like a dish of Jell-O later. *No, no more food!* But her hovering attentiveness was not disturbing. She did not seem overly upset. Solicitous, she was offering food out of concern. That I remember these attitudes as noteworthy suggests that they differed from my parents. Indeed, they did. My older sister's memory completes the tale.

"Daddy was furious you threw up all over like that!"

*

Something *strange* had happened. Sometime between two and four years old, I was fed poisonous food. I remember being hospitalized. *Munchausen's syndrome* comes to mind—when a caretaker, often the mother, makes their child physically sick, in part to secure attention. But the truth is more complex. At the very least, my illness fit a disturbing pattern not unknown to my physician father. In third grade, I witnessed a fight between my mother and father, whose marriage was disintegrating. *My father accused my mother of trying to poison him.*

I remember lying in my bed at home, after my hospital stay. It was my bed with sides—a crib. I was contemplating a *problem.* Somehow I had gotten the impression that my food poisoning came from eating "bad" cottage cheese. Maybe that was gleaned from hearing the grownups talk. Maybe so. Somehow I jumped to the conclusion that cow dung (*ka-ka,* in babytalk) had gotten into my cup of cottage cheese. Salmonella food poisoning—to which children are most susceptible—is not fantasy. Salmonella bacteria does stem from fecal material. But to my child's mind, my eating tainted food was a mishap that could not help but amplify my growing sense of unease about eating.

I remember struggling and having to be held down in the hospital bed by two nurses to be given a shot. *Two* nurses, one on either side of tiny *me.* I told my sister about the nurses. We reenacted the scene with embellishments to portray its full dramatic impact. My sister was impressed I had been so plucky. A sense of my power to resist was just beginning to invigorate me. But there is something else that clings to my mind. Try as I might to shake it, the images remain.

I am lying in a white hospital bed with my legs up in slings and needles in my legs. I cry in vain for an uncompromising nurse to take the needles out.

As a young adult, I asked my physician father about my memory. Nonplused by medical events that were routine to him, he tried to assure me that the episode had been nothing serious. *Nothing to him,* I thought, *and everything to a child.* Almost as an aside, he said that I had been in the hospital to treat the dehydration that had resulted from food poisoning.

Dehydration would conceivably be remedied intravenously to restore fluids. No wonder I had a phobia of needles. Whatever the actual circumstances of my encounter with needles in that hospital, years later it set the stage for my refusal *for three years* to take the chemotherapy

routinely administered by an IV.
Routine to them, but everything to a child.

*

I remember squatting down on the floor of my bedroom. *Thinking.* The intensity of my thought virtually blotted out any visual perception of the outside world. I was focusing on a mental image of "a hot-dog." I was contemplating eating it. And I did not feel good.

Any other child's body might have responded with appetite: *Oh, joy!* But my body spoke up with discomfort, a distress associated with eating. A powerful connection born of fear was made, linking the two experiences: eating and discomfort. Out of the swirling darkness of undifferentiated consciousness, a decision was formed, a judgment made. "I," brave pioneer on the new frontier of Ego Development, forged my self-identity with the claim: *I don't like to eat!*

I was dismayed. Perhaps I was aware that this amounted to a declaration of war against my parents. But the "rightness" of my newfound knowledge was indisputable. My body did not lie. Moreover, "I" came into focus and all my sensory memories clicked perfectly into place with this pronouncement. I was aware of my father's presence in the next room. Something felt *wrong.* Some *thing* was wrong ... and the *thing* that was wrong was *me.* "I" was bad. I did not eat enough.

"If you don't eat more, I'll have to give you a shot."

It was a grim threat but one within the realm of possibility. My father carried needles in his black, funny-smelling bag. My father gave big people shots all the time. Maybe they were bad, too. Choking back my tears, a weight settled upon my shoulders. A blanket of depression muffled my anxiety. Except when I thought about food.

How many times I was traumatized by that threat, I do not know. But it happened enough times that I became uneasy about my own father. Needless to say, this had a disastrous effect on our relationship. This changed relationship made for a profound contrast to my early adoration.

Until my parents' separation when I was eight, I lived in a small, Midwestern town (pop. 1,950). Since the days of the horse and buggy, doctors have played an important role in rural farming communities. My father, as the town doctor, was revered for his medical savvy, and accorded a privileged status—while scorned for his Cuban heritage. Cuban, charismatic and highly emotional, my father stood out from the dull, monotone mentality of Midwestern farmers like a tropical bird living in a cornfield. The farmers were staunch Republican; my father was the lone Democrat. The white winters alone were enough to fuel the black depressions that ruled my father in predictable cycles, frozen cycles of icy, black depression.

It was the season of chaos and contradiction in my life. *White and black, love and hate*, I both loved and feared my father.

I loved being lifted off my feet and "danced" around the room to the strain of musicals such as *South Pacific* and *My Fair Lady*. My father's Latin sensibilities felt at home with the lyrics' extravagant sentiments. They went straight to the heart of something he felt deep inside. "One enchanted evening, you may see a stranger," the lover crooned. "Never let a woman in your life!" the bachelor exploded. Singing with his Cuban accent, my father heartily agreed, though he pronounced the "w" in "woman" as "g." Daddy was *home* to me—the center, or heart of me—and an exotic Latin lover, all rolled into one.

"Wouldn't it be love-erly?" And it was.

I loved being my father's sweetheart. Daddy's darling. I loved his heartfelt singing, our pretend dancing. Best of all, I loved sitting side by side. I felt supremely loved. *Safe,* up to that point. My story illustrates the power of trauma—for it generated a "split off" aspect of my personality such that, after my traumatic hospitalization and its aftermath, I always felt like a fearful, regressed child in the presence of my expansive father. Henceforth, I assumed a dissociated distance from my own father.

Yet I was not the only target of my father's irritability or upset. Sometimes daddy got mad at mommy—in episodes that ended with daddy taking to bed. Mommy nursed him with soup. Campbell's Tomato Soup out-of-a-can was opened with the electric can-opener that was accorded the significance of a status symbol. But that accorded privilege was balanced by a deficit in discernment. Little did the conservative citizens of our small town realize that daddy's sick days came as the result of substance abuse.

My physician father was prone to self-prescribing doses of Phenobarbital to manage his manic depression. Only as an adult did I learn that given the accessibility of drugs, the medical profession was all too prone to substance abuse. And all-too-prone in the 50's and 60's to covering up addiction. This was the last vestige of an era of denial. Alcoholism was just coming out of the closet as "physiological disease," instead of "moral affliction."

As a child, I could only just perceive that daddy's "sick days" came at shorter intervals as the fights increased. Too young to realize that my father's bipolar episodes were increasing, as far as I was concerned, a demonic possession was underway. Dr. Jekyl and Mr. Hyde-like transformations were *de rigueur* around my house. Either my father was loveable, excitable Ricky Ricardo, or sometimes I got my father mixed up with the next best thing to the devil himself—to those of Cuban heritage: Fidel Castro. Spying Castro's picture on a magazine cover, I confused the grownups' vitriolic remarks about my Cuban father. Vaguely I wondered, *Was daddy Fidel Castro?*

*

Food became a point of contention between my parents. Just how deep the conflict was between my mother and food, I could not begin to appreciate. Food, along with all its myriad associations like cooking and eating, had become the enemy.

To say that my mother was not at home in the kitchen would be a gross understatement. Never mind Cuban fare, she could not even cook American. I remember her trying to get us kids to eat potatoes au gratin—from a box. *Betty Crocker*, or some such stuff. My siblings declared it detestable and refused it, even ran away from the table when it was served. As the baby, I could not get away with such tricks. Not able to run fast enough, I was forced to eat a gluey portion. I vaguely wondered what was wrong with my mother that she could eat that moldy-tasting mess.

Something was missing from our privileged status as the doctor's family. That privilege did not make for peace. Well-being was compromised, as was my health. I stopped feeling well. Stopped feeling *good*. As a child I articulated this vague feeling as *something is wrong with me*. I was not eating enough to satisfy a bird. Anxious and scared about mealtimes, I stopped eating much at all. I grew increasingly sickly, which only infuriated my father.

I remember eating out with my parents and company. Too young to eat at the adults' table, I sat off to their side, unseen witness to the enacted drama. My father remarked with disgust that my mother could not even eat "a child's plate" of spaghetti. Had my mother, *a grownup*, ordered a child's portion? Apparently so. It would appear that she had done it to avoid the scene that would follow if she did not *clean her plate*. This was my first realization that my mother herself was a picky eater. A finicky, fussy eater. Someone who said, "No, I refuse to eat."

But she was not saying that now. *Why is she letting him bully her in public?* This playacting did not make much sense to me. I pondered its meaning many times in the years to come. I became aware that my mother did not want *me* to eat either. In fact, she seemed to be actively discouraging me. She never made my breakfast. And after my parents' separation, my mother stopped making dinners, too. She seemed to spend a lot of time in bed. She herself often ate only bananas, cottage cheese, and Milky Ways. I became adept at heating up frozen and canned food, eating alone at the kitchen counter.

School lunches tell the tale. My parochial school did not serve hot lunches; we *brown-bagged* it. As my mother never supervised meals, I was forced to fend for myself in the kitchen, packing anything edible I could find. So I packed a sandwich daily—a slice of white bread cut in half, covered with a mayonnaise spread, dotted with pickles. Day after day. With no adult to supervise, and with little food in the cupboard, my lunches were hardly nutritious. *Desert?* A slice of stale Christmas fruitcake, an unappetizing present from an aunt, wrapped in saran.

How such a lunch passed muster with the nuns is only understandable given their concerns. They were obsessively preoccupied with monitoring the noise level and ensuring that we did not swap food. But the kids that flanked me sure did notice. I remember Mary Ann, a child destined to become anorexic after an early pudginess marked her for childish taunts. No wonder she was hefty; her mother packed *fabulous* lunches, complete with overstuffed sandwiches, chunky soups in a thermos and homemade desserts. No Twinkies for her, but generous portions of wholesome food—testament to a mother's dependable love.

Mary Ann noticed my pitiable fare. *Fruitcake in February?* No retort could mask my shame. It remained lodged in my memory as a visceral reminder that mealtime harbored potential disgrace. The habitual nervous state of my innards around mealtime was scarcely conducive to good appetite.

I became obsessed with food. When confined to bed with the flu, I occupied myself by cutting out pictures of food from magazines. My starvation diet was even more noticeable during times of sickness. Famished, I was often served only a glass of milk. Grossly neglected in the material world, a hearty imagination came to my rescue. I contented myself with fantasy food—magazine cut-outs of food—assembled into imagined menus. I could handle food symbolically, could savor it in my mind, if not my body. Little wonder an obsession was born.

Ultimately, poor diet and appetite combined to produce the poorly nourished body and vaguely depressed personality that were mine throughout grade school. *Something was wrong with both me* and *my mother.* It was all too confusing for me to express, much less to figure out. As it turned out, my parents had motives that were well beyond my childhood years to comprehend. Only as an adult could I begin to understand and forgive.

*

From early childhood, I had been aware of my father's bouts of "sickness." He would stay in bed for days, wrapped in blankets, groggy and grizzled, his hair sticking out in tufts all over his head. I remembered mother bringing him soup and ice cream. It was routine with us, if worrisome. But I had never known *why* "daddy is sick." I had never questioned that part of our world. It was normal to me, even if "wrong" to my cousins, somehow smacking of disgrace. I had simply felt sorry for my daddy. A decade later, I was less approving when I discovered that my father binged on Phenobarbital in an effort to self-medicate his manic depressive disorder (Bipolar II).

Physician, heal thyself. Yet my father could not heal himself. Doctors themselves need doctors. As an adult I tried to get my father the care he needed; I even contacted the AMA, which was of surprisingly little help. Doctors misusing drugs were a well-kept secret within the staunch medical community. My father's colleagues looked after themselves by looking the other way. And living in the backwaters of a mid-western farming community, rife with secrets, did not help. In the end, I could not save my father.

But it was a slow initiation into the facts of my father's life. Each successive summer after high school, my father would sink deeper during my visit. And each summer, I felt more dread at the prospect of going, and more depressed during my visit. *Why did I go?* Ultimately I felt as helpless in the face of my father's demands as I felt in the face of our depression. For by now I shared in the depression that was the precursor of each binge.

Somehow the cyclic process of depression, when *amplified* by Phenobarbital, plunged my father down into the depths of his psyche where he would confront his own demons. Anger, guilt and shame. And only such a thorough breakdown of defenses would allow some release. *White or black. No half-tones would do.* Truly his states were primal. Little did I know that I was about to undergo the same breakdown of the psyche.

My depression culminated during a month-long stay in which my father was near-comatose from overdose. His co-dependent companion, determined not to intervene and jeopardize his medical license, stationed me by his bed *lest his breathing stop.* Eunice had years of experience "saving" my father's life. By now the initiation had gone beyond mere care-taking into the realm of life or death. This was more than I could bear. But the numbness that mercifully settled over me would not allow me to feel it.

Typical procedure, when my father would not stop taking pills, was to schedule a vacation. We were packed off to Disneyworld.

Eunice had long ago discovered that a vacation would provide the necessary intoxicant to counteract the sedatives and help my father pull out of it. However, a week in Disneyworld totally unnerved me. I remember the blaring trumpets and the merciless hot sun while gripping the seat of the monorail, lest I lose control. I remember my father trying to drive *onto* the "off ramp" of a freeway. I remember he insisted I carry today's equivalent of $5,500—in cash in an envelope in my purse. Meanwhile, I virtually stopped eating and sought refuge in every restroom we passed. I remember talking to myself constantly, desperately clinging to some semblance of sanity in that glaring, nightmarish world. But my muttering went unnoticed by my father, who was passing into the hypomanic phase and talking enough for the two of us. He was on his way into "the white light" of expansive and attractive energy; I embodied the dark, contracting and repulsive pole.

*

Home. Nearly incapacitated, I flew back to Ohio where my phobias about eating and vomiting resumed *en force.* I suffered from some strange malady in which I *wanted* to eat and gain weight, but my fear of nausea and vomiting prevented it. In retrospect, I see that these phobias also represented an unconscious act of rebellion. *I will not stomach being treated like this.* But as it was unconscious I could not heed the message. I was also afraid to fall asleep, lest something *I could not name* would overwhelm me. Something finally did overwhelm me. I bottomed out with a full-blown hallucination brought about by sleep-deprivation and near-starvation.

In the trees of my own back yard, I *saw* the dark and sinister mean-inglessness of the universe ... and I heard it. A black vacuum, stealthily sucking the light out of life, was hidden in the silence. *In the very foliage*. For the next five years, the stark terror of that vision never left me. Indeed, it would inform—and impede—my graduate career in philosophy. I had stumbled upon the stark embodiment of Jean Paul Sartre's Nausea.

Terrifying beyond words, only words could redeem me.

My arduous recovery consisted of a singular practice. I. Practiced. The. Control. Of. Concentrating. On. Every. Word. I. Read. Control was essential. Lest the Demons within the silence—that I so desperately kept at bay—escape into the phenomenal world. It took incredible integrity, not to mention enormous energy, to keep the lid on *that nameless something* that could annihilate the world.

Terrifying beyond words, was the world beyond words. Only years later, did I find that in the world of gurus, that *world beyond words* had another meaning:

> When you first enter into the world of no-mind it looks like madness—the "dark night of the soul," the mad night of the soul. All the religions have noted the fact; hence all the religions insist on finding a master before you start entering into the world of no-mind—because he will be there to help you, to support you. You will be falling apart but he will be there to encourage you, to give you hope. He will be there to interpret the new to you. That is the meaning of a master: to interpret that which cannot be interpreted, to indicate that which cannot be said, to show that which is inexpressible. He will be there, he will devise methods and ways for you to continue on the path—otherwise you might start escaping from it.[3]

No-mind or not, escape I did. Traumatized, I fearfully fought off that Nausea for years. Jean Paul would have been impressed. Not ready for the world of no-mind, with only a philosopher as master to guide me, I chose escape.

In surviving that experience, I gained a healthy respect for the psyche's natural timing. *Even madness has its season, its rhythm and its reason*. How could I, without support, open to the anguish of a broken heart? It would take years to build the support I needed to trust any expression of anger and grief, much less the void. During this virtual breakdown, hardly anyone even knew that I was sick! I barely alerted the counselor I was seeing at the university counseling center. And faced with a cold, analytical psychiatrist who averaged the heights of my parents to calculate my stunted growth, I pulled myself together. I gathered the shards of self-trust I had earned by learning the hard way *not to trust a doctor.*

It would take a few more years for my next healing crisis to erupt. But my experience of terror had convinced me that when language "stopped," other realms of consciousness began.

*

I had opted out of academia in order to pen a book about the origins of Western civilization and the foundation of rational thought. I believed I had cracked the code of Plato's dialectics—in actuality, an esoteric, secret practice. Plato's personal letters alluded to a mystical vision whereby "the first and highest principles" (the abstract forms, such as Truth and Beauty) were known. Yes, Plato's dialectics led to experience *inexpressible* by language. So an esoteric act of Mysticism gave birth to Rational thought. Surely that would rock the cradle of Western civilization.

However, writing such a book would prove to be no mean task. After all, Alfred North Whitehead had written that all of philosophy is nothing but "a series of footnotes to Plato." But I was not totally alone. This forbidden knowledge was also the heart of Robert Pirsig's "Zen and the Art of Motorcycle Maintenance." Alas! I heeded no warning from Pirsig's own breakdown and hospitalization. Beware to those who break with consensus reality and step outside the collective consciousness. Isolated from social reality, I broke down in my own way.

My descent into my own form of madness was timed with the arrival of an old friend and former lover, a mathematics professor from Ohio State University, for a summer visit. His overbearing masculine energy and my submissive response mirrored too closely my relationship with my father. Suddenly my rebellion against the Greek rationalism *founded in a patriarchal system* was playing out on an intensely personal level. The source of my "eating complex" was about to become conscious. Once again a nightmarish nausea made me afraid to eat even while I was terrified of being hospitalized. Unable to voice my fears, I withdrew from the outside world in order to face what seemed my demise. And indeed, the end of that life was near.

In a pattern that would be repeated in my future bout with cancer, my crisis sparked a dream. *A poor black woman lived in a hotel room with her young daughter. While the mother left her daughter at night to consort with men, the daughter suffered from neglect, not even having enough food in the refrigerator to eat.*

I turned to C. G. Jung for dream interpretation. Jung's concept of *the animus,* the masculine part of the feminine psyche, articulated the awareness that I needed. In a flash of intuitive understanding, I recognized that I had become ill *from paying too much attention to the masculine element, just like my mother.* Scared of my father as a child, the nightmare of Disneyworld had continued the trend. I needed to correct the imbalance between an animus-figure who was a glutton for attention, and a starved inner child.

With that illumination, the energy went out of a nervous complex that had lasted almost twenty years, whose energy dispersed into a more healthy form in my life. My obsession about eating and fear of nausea—that amounted to an eating disorder—healed virtually overnight. It was a first-hand experience of *spontaneous remission.* Moreover, it taught me that an energetic shift underlay the *transformation of consciousness* that is the basis for all healing. Thus began my training in developing the sensitivity to energy that remains fundamental to my therapeutic practice.

There followed a creative awakening in which I redefined myself, thereby loosening the boundaries of my tightly constricted ego. Heretofore an intellectual, I opened to my artistic side. A class in graphic design introduced me to my keen sense of color and shape. From construction paper and scissors, I developed an art form of painted cut & pasted paper designs, reminiscent of Matisse.

I continued to study dream interpretation. These diverse talents coalesced when a noted psychic, consulted for a life reading, summed me up unseen as an *interpreter of symbolic language.* Finally my visionary approach to life made sense—from analytical philosophy to art and dream interpretation. And that definition of myself marked a turning point in my life's direction. Validating myself was the first step towards seeking a profession in the healing arts.

*

The last time I saw my father alive was in Florida. I was almost twenty-eight. As my older sister prepared to give birth to her first child, my father was a nervous wreck. Life and death converged as the old generation made way for the new. My father broke under the strain. I was determined not to break down, too.

For virtually the first time, I defied my father. I resolutely resisted his efforts to draw me into the fracas between himself and my sister. Staunch supporter of my pregnant sister, I stayed at her house instead of his. My father turned to Phenobarbital. Sober for two years since retirement, the drug hit my father hard. However, I had finally *stopped* his world. Something in my refusal to be bullied brought his life-long descent to a standstill. Something in him snapped *open*. He gave in and moved in temporarily with us.

Suddenly transformation took hold. Long accustomed to his mood swings from black depressions into the white light of positivism, I was unprepared for this one. My father entered a state of heightened awareness. Long into the night, he told me the story of my mother's and his relationship, and his insecurities as a Cuban man with an American woman—that lead to his first misuse of drugs during his medical residency. He left a legacy of knowledge I would need in order to heal from the wounds of my childhood. My tape recording of our nightly sessions is simply entitled, "Dr. Colli."

My father was in a mental state at once manic, mystical and child-like. I myself was exhausted. Finally my father agreed to check himself into the psychiatric unit of a Veterans Administration hospital until he calmed down. So ebullient that he was actually looking forward to it, we traveled several hours by taxi. I returned to my sister's home in the Florida backwaters. However, under their care, my father quickly became delusional, "hearing" the loudspeaker announce my sister's death in a car accident. I reassured him as best I could by phone. But I just couldn't take care of my father anymore.

We got word the next day. Left unattended, my father hung himself by tying a rubber shower hose around his neck and dropping to his knees. That is what we were told. My father died the day after his first grandchild—*a boy*—was born.

*

I flew back home in shock.

Having lost my father was tragic enough. Eliseo M. Colli had barely entered into his Florida retirement. The Florida climate, reminiscent of his native Cuba, would surely have helped stem the black depressions that we suspected were made worse by harsh Illinois winters. Besides being filled with all the distractions that retirement offers, his life would have included the singular joy of helping raise his only grandson. Yes, my father's premature death was tragic indeed. But it was how I lost my father—the garish nightmare of a self-willed death by strangulation in a psychiatric ward—that haunted me.

In that state of mind, only six months after his death, I made the sorry trip to my father's home in Florida to sort out his belongings. There I came to hear about nearby Cassadaga, a town almost exclusively inhabited by old-world psychics. I was well-schooled in Edgar Cayce's prophecies. Known as the "sleeping prophet," Cayce perceived subtle energy realms that extended beyond ordinary sensory awareness. By the time Cayce died in 1945, he had given clairvoyant readings for more than 8,000 people. I was enthralled by the prospect of meeting someone of his ilk.

Artless signs outside Cassadaga houses advertised the services of those within. I chose a modest home—in that town of modest homes from a bygone era—where I was met directly by two psychics: an unassuming man and his female companion. Lucky me, I was next in line for a reading.

I had hoped to receive advice about my father's estate. But my memory only extends to their unexpected dire faces, giving me a grave warning. They prognosticated mainly about my physical health, asking if I felt any untoward digestive symptoms. And they warned me to get myself *immediately* to a doctor because I was in danger of becoming seriously ill. If I acted quickly, perhaps it was not too late to avert the terrible fate they saw in store for me. The male psychic, helpless in the face of what he clearly considered life-threatening, also recommended I eat radishes.

Eat radishes? A crunchy vegetable, perhaps it would stimulate my digestive system. Needless to say, that advice left me more confused than anything.

But I was also alarmed. Always one to worry about my inability to gain weight, the psychics made intuitive if not medical sense to me. Upon returning home to Seattle, I pestered my doctor to recommend medical tests to investigate the psychics' appraisal. Though obviously skeptical, the young doc did what he could with routine blood tests, a 5-day stool analysis for fat absorption, and even a referral to an internal specialist who offered a *laproscopy*—a scope to be inserted down my esophagus to detect abnormality. (I refused that procedure when I spied the internal specialist wolfing down a jelly doughnut.) It was just as well. The routine tests and exams failed to reveal any malady.

Nine months after the psychics' reading I tried to incubate a dream, asking how to get my physical system working—towards health and weight gain. Thanks to the psychics, I now had support for my long-held suspicion that my 78-pound body betrayed a pathological process. Incredibly, I was graced with a dream that proved to be prophetic.

A long boat floated by with white ivory discs held by people. Ancient, the discs had been saved from a war or destruction of their culture. (I associated the discs to white, ivory curio pieces of my father's.) I heard something about an *alimentary canal—if only I could get it flowing in the right direction.* Unbeknown to me, my dream held the diagnosis for the disease that was to swallow up the next five years of my life.

The alimentary canal refers to the tubular passage and organs through which food passes for digestion and elimination. Mine had long struggled to provide nourishment, sustenance and support. How fitting that the lymphatic system be involved—the network of vessels that transport fluid, fats, proteins and lymphocytes to the bloodstream as lymph, and remove debris from tissues.

And so it was that almost two years to the day after Cassadaga, a singular event occurred. It happened during a period of high stress. In the midst of being embroiled in my father's estate, I developed a physical symptom that seemed an uncanny reminder of his death. My throat swelled up like a toad's, as if in sympathy with my father's strangulation. Harbinger of ill health, my entire throat was enlarged, leaving me fatigued. Sluggish. As this symptom was unknown to me, I made the obligatory visit to a medical doctor.

My doctor was relatively new to the practice of medicine. While his youth had once been a bond between us, it was now a liability. At least he had the good sense to send me for a chest x-ray. I had previously complained of a troubling cough that he had diagnosed as a stubborn case of *post-nasal drip.* Never sick with so much as a cold, I found such a mundane malady dubious. But as this doc excelled at drawing pictures to decipher the mysterious workings of the body, he had drawn my sinuses specked with drops of fluid ... drip ... drip, for which he prescribed a cough medicine.

Little did I realize that a chronic, lingering cough was one of the warning signs of cancer.

Sure enough, the x-ray disclosed a large mass. It was located in the chest space behind my sternum called the "anterior mediastinum." The swelling and morbid change in those lymph nodes was termed "anterior mediastinal *adenopathy*." Ever the student, I looked up those technical words in medical dictionaries to alleviate my ignorance. But I simply could not grasp that a mass could be *inside* me, much less discern its function, its *meaning*.

During subsequent consultation with my doctor, he outlined the possibilities on notepaper, courtesy of a pharmaceutical company. By this time I had grown wary. In fact, I didn't believe a single word he said. Lymphoma was mentioned. But what did a *disease* have to do with my tender flesh? We would not know what the mass meant until a biopsy was performed.

Performed? On whose body? Surely there must be some mistake. But I was game enough to go through with the procedure, if only to prove to this doctor that he was wrong. After all, when it came to doctors, I was savvy. Doctors, I knew, were not to be trusted. My own father had failed me, and his colleagues had turned a blind face to his drug use. Still I prayed in earnest. *Only grant me courage.* If cancer was truly meant for me, I was in it for the long haul.

I was blessed. Never mired in the politics of affliction (*Why me?),* right from the start I sensed my prayer was heard. Surely I was watched over by someone during the biopsy—the angel of the operating room.

This gentle, good spirit was made manifest by a female medical technician. That she could bypass my fear and insert the dreaded IV with such ease into my tiny blue vein was the miracle I had been waiting for. I will never forget the care she graced me with, nor the concern with which she patted my arm throughout the operation. Though the contents of the IV ensured I would remain floaty and relaxed, her healing connection with me was a critical ingredient of the mixture. The operation was successfully concluded. I have the scars to prove it.

I had been through an initiation. The successful conclusion of *anything* relating to my seemingly blighted body was cause to celebrate. That I could emerge triumphant from so close an encounter with doctors was proof of my invincibility.

Diseased? *Hah! I would show them.*

*

Yet psychospiritual rebirth was three years in the offing. My virtual overnight cure from an eating disorder—due to a dream—was but a rehearsal for the main event.

I grew cocky. I approached the appointment with my surgeon for the outcome of the biopsy fully prepared to send the medical establishment packing. My partner and I had even done an intuitive reading. Tom had discovered that during meditation he could *see* writing that formed as if from an external, wiser source. Having pestered him for help from beyond, he quoted: *Your health is good. Don't worry. The bee can't sting people with needles under their skin.* I was thus woefully unprepared for the surgeon's verdict, delivered while his back was turned, as he scrubbed his hands at the sink.

"You're lucky. You have Hodgkin's lymphoma."

And so it was that two years after the dire prediction of the Cassadaga psychics, I received an official medical diagnosis. Assessed as a slow-growing tumor, no wonder it hadn't been detected before. This was hardly a vindication I savored. *Lucky?*

When my disbelief wore off, I was madder than hell. Where had I gone wrong? What about Tom's reading? We had assumed the cancer threat was nil. Even in the aftermath of the diagnosis, we could not shake our fundamental belief that this cancer did not toll the death-knell. Whatever its portent, it did not register as terminal in the subtle realm. Taking my cue from the realm beyond the medical establishment's reach, I assumed God was provoking me to grow. I only had to figure out how.

As if duly prompted, a friend gave me a copy of a *March 1985* interview in The Tarryton Letter: "A Yale surgeon Says Cancer Has a Positive Message for Humanity: Dr. Bernard Siegel believes feelings of loss and defeat contribute to cancer. He offers his patients a radically new cure—loving better and living fuller lives." I thus reconciled the subtle realm with the material realm in the form of Bernie Siegel, M.D.

The Bernie Siegel approach to cancer was that it was God's reset button, much like the reset button on the garbage disposal. His belief that *disease is a divine message of redirection* transformed my views about cancer. I did not need convincing that my life needed healing. But the flip side of accepting responsibility for my illness led me to believe that I could effectively heal my physical body. By what means, I did not yet know. But I resolved to enter the medical realm not as a victim suffering from life-threatening cancer. Determined to *do cancer differently*, I became someone with a *life-challenging* illness.

For the next five years, it was my primary identity.

*

The way I see it, I inherited daunting ancestral debt. I faced karmic fallout that made for truly toxic conditioning. After absorbing a legacy of shame, I needed a powerful awakening. At thirty, I was diagnosed with cancer. I date the growth of that tumor from the day I absorbed guilt over my father's suicide. Was I guilty, after all?

Like my slow-growing tumor, I too, was slow to burn. It took years of emotional healing before anger at my father surfaced, much less, forgiveness. It took years to forgive my role in my father's suicide. *I was not to blame.*

Skipping ahead seven years, past my cancer cure and into my graduate training in psychology.... *Shock.* The onus of my father's suicide lifted virtually overnight. It happened during a Process-oriented Psychology intensive. In attendance was a woman of no little psychic ability. Consequently, *Dr. Eliseo M. Colli arrived on the scene.*

Not everyone has the faith I do in contact after death. After-death communication (ADC), as it is called in the trade. But put yourself in my shoes when Colleen informed me that my father's death was no suicide. *Shock.* I remember collapsing to the floor. *Shock.* My father was the victim of a chokehold gone awry. A cover-up by two employees had ensued....

Suddenly the knot unraveled and all the loose ends got tied. My father had not been suicidal. Hypomanic, yes, even borderline delusional. But not despondent. Feisty, if anything. That is why the attendant had attempted to subdue and restrain him when he would not follow orders. *Good god, he was a physician! No one gives a physician orders!*

One enlightened teacher agreed. One enlightened teacher and one intuitive healer later, I had confirmation enough. Not a suicide; nonetheless, it had been the perfect death. No regrets. None. Though my father does regret his misuse of drugs, and their effects upon his mind, his present communication is clear.

Call me credulous, dub me delusional. But my father is overjoyed I'm writing about spiritual emergency and the dark face of heaven.

CHAPTER 4

JANET: DOLPHIN DOCTORS

For whosoever will save his life shall lose it; but whoever will lose his life for my sake, the same shall save it.

Luke 9:24

Cancer treatment is tailored according to how advanced the disease is. "Staging" refers to a variety of tests that determine that. One test scheduled to stage Hodgkin's, the *lymphangiogram*, involves injecting oil into the lymphatic vessels so x-rays can track the disease's progression. Only radiation would be used to treat Hodgkin's confined to the chest. This test would determine if the lymphoma had spread below my chest, thereby necessitating both radiation *and* chemotherapy. As chemotherapy, involving both nausea and needles, was unthinkable to me, there was no doubt in my mind that I would pass the requisite tests. For me, medical treatment itself was tantamount to death.

Little did I know that the healing I sought—the *psychospiritual rebirth* in store for me—involved death. Ego death, that is.

By now the medical procedures had become so difficult that I considered them not as *prerequisites* to treatment but *in lieu of* further treatment. I honestly believed that because I was doing my best to participate, the Hodgkin's would remit! The blockage in my lymphatic system that had somehow ballooned into tumors was surely melting in the emotional tumult that roiled in my body, and would be routed by the healing fevers that the medical threat had wrought. Thus I prayed.

I prayed especially upon hearing what was in store for me during a *lymphangiogram*. The special oil was to be fed through thin lines inserted into lymphatic vessels that lay exposed through *surgical cuts* made in each foot, the surgical cuts being made after *each toe in each foot* was injected with numbing substance. *Force-feed me through multiple IVs made ready through ten injections?* The whole procedure would take six hours, with me lying prone so as not to disturb the delicate-as-a-hair lines.

Six *hours?* I could not be trusted to remain in such a situation for six minutes. I was doomed to bolt just as surely as the first little piggy-of-a-toe was approached by needles.

My Father, Who Art in Heaven.... The very nature of my prayer, that is, its desperation in the face of a life-threat, ensured it would be heard. I myself had become an integral part of the prayer's equation. I thus embarked on a simultaneous act of surrender even while taking charge.

As soon as I checked in at the nurses' station, I started my campaign for survival. Talking about my fears to the appropriate party at each checkpoint seemed the only viable way to ensure my needs were met. By the time I found myself lying prone on the operating table, presumably ready for the injections, I had succeeded in establishing rapport with the medical team. This doctor proved himself to be a true healer by his response, at the very last second, to my final desperate measure. I can still see the white-robed doctor seated at the foot of the operating table, donned with special glasses that magnified lymphatic vessels. The glasses made him look goofy. The assisting nurse had already positioned herself by my side, holding my hand for support. Only then did I initiate my final condition.

The doctor had to be willing to wait *with my foot in hand*, posed with a shot to inject, until I signaled him to start. It was a simple act yet vital to my sense of control. It was also thereby crucial to my sense of safety. He agreed to wait for my signal. A compassionate response—in the unlikely form of a doctor—opened my heart at last.

And then the shots stung my toes *one by one* ... like ten angry bees. Little wonder the bee became a recurrent dream symbol relating to cancer throughout the course of my illness. But the lymphangiogram also provided the symbol of *me* keeping the angry swarm of bees under control. The six hours spent supine while the lines "fed" my lymphatic system "oil," no longer assumed the deadly metaphor of being force-fed. The same nurse, who had held my hands during my moment of truth, served me a piece of hot, buttered toast from the hospital cafeteria. Nurtured at last, a life-saving pattern had been established.

That I had genuinely communicated with a doctor was powerful medicine, as far as I was concerned. True communion. My emotional body was surely sending a message of complete healing, of body *and* soul alike. I was certain that my physical body would learn to respond to love—and heal itself. I was dead set on that.

*

When my oncologist told me the test results on the telephone, I was overjoyed. I had "passed" the test: the cancer had *not* spread below my chest. Alerted by my recalcitrant behavior, I was slated for an appointment with the head of the medical department. Naturally, the head doctor was downright horrified when I told him I planned to heal through "alternative means." That has got to be an oncologist's worst nightmare. And he only had that single appointment to try to talk me out of it. I will never forget the look on his face.

From my perspective, his stern look was meant to intimidate. Though he looked scared, for all I knew, he was bluffing. Yet even if he was genuinely concerned, I would be damned if I would let fear rule me. Least of all, fear *of him*. Having few symptoms, the disease was still abstract enough for me to dismiss it. I was determined to outlast his prediction. Without medical treatment, he predicted that the Hodgkin's would spread unchecked. Solemnly he declared that I would die without treatment.

That was enough for me. As far as I was concerned, I'd won yet another round. Clear of conscience and pure of heart, I bounded off the examination table. I felt positive that fear of the medical treatment was not the issue. I was simply choosing healing *through love* over their machines and toxic medicine ... and threats based on fear. Had not I had enough of that from my father, the doctor, when I refused to eat? This time, I was going to do it my way, or not at all.

My noncompliance with medical treatment, just like my childhood "failure to thrive," was basically a refusal to live under certain conditions, that is, without unconditional love. As a child, I had rejected the life force in its most basic form: food. The anorexia and phobias I developed as an adult ruled my life. Thus far, my life had assumed a stunted form. My ego-structure, after all, had been formed by being starved by my mother and rejected by my father. Yet the deep guilt I felt over that remained largely unconscious. It finally surfaced as guilt over having caused my own cancer.

Cancer is unconscious warfare. Certain masses of cells are at war with the body as an whole. Cancer is an entity unto itself. While the viability of my entire physical body was threatened from within, inner warfare was already raging inside me on the psychospiritual front. The first three years after diagnosis were largely spent becoming conscious of my pain. I spent thousands of dollars on workshops and therapies seemingly designed to put me in touch with it. After all, the substratum underlying my thoughts and actions was largely unknown to me. That is not surprising. Like fish, we are unaware of the water in which we swim. We awaken to recognize one level of awareness only by shifting to another level from which we can observe the former.

The first powerful shift of consciousness occurred in the state of crisis just after diagnosis. After dismissing my medical doctors, I entered the alternative realm of healing. Support groups, therapy, massage, acupressure and energy work of all sorts commenced. Sick enough to carry a diagnosis, yet not sick enough to be suffering, I had the leeway to pick and choose a strictly alternative team. *Transformational Psychiatry* is how Dr. Paul Tinker billed his work. It had a spiritual thrust complete with references to Ram Dass. I knew Paul Tinker was meant for me. Thus primed, I was ready and willing to be submerged under the waters of my own subconscious.

Immediately upon reclining on his couch, I entered a deep altered state. *Something* emerged from me—a dark, guttural cry forced itself up from my belly. My body inexplicably turned all pins and needles, the likes of which I had never felt before. In retrospect, it was reminiscent of Tom's intuitive reading: *Your health is good. Don't worry. The bee can't sting people with needles under their skin.* According to the medical perspective, hyperventilation—abnormally fast or deep respiration—and the loss of carbon dioxide from the blood, causes tingling of the extremities. From my perspective, surely I had entered another dimension where time and space collapsed.

In that altered state, I expressed my shame with the tortured cry— *I did it. I caused my own cancer.* Paradoxically, by expressing my guilt and shame, I released that bound energy. The healing process had begun.

Needless to say, this astute shrink tried to talk me out of my guilt. But having purged my admission of guilt, the force of it was no longer mine to argue. *Did I, indeed, cause my cancer?* It is not so simple. The complexity of factors—from genetic to environmental—belie that simplistic statement. To whom does the "I" refer, anyway? Surely the whole of me is greater than any given self-identity. Too often our assumption of responsibility over our lives is but a thinly veiled will-to-control. In actuality, we participate in a reality much greater than our ego-natures prefer to acknowledge. And it was *that* part that set up my soul's five-year growth plan, namely, cancer.

Yet speaking our hearts is a form of truth. On the psychiatrist's couch I spoke the simple truth. It may not have been absolute truth, but it was my truth, nonetheless. I have since learned to sense the energy of words. When we give voice to our inner truth—be that love and joy *or* guilt and self-hatred—we touch the heart of Creation.

Welcome to the world of healers.

*

Enter Richard Moss, M.D. Richard was known in healing circles for having united with all of Creation in a state of unity. *Enlightenment.* "In that moment, all of creation became a single consciousness, a state of indescribable glory and unspeakable peace."[1] And if that was not enough by way of credentials, he had been graced with an authenticated case of spontaneous remission during one of his 10-day conferences.

The woman in question had a grapefruit-sized tumor in her bowel from terminal liver cancer, after having suffered from diabetes for thirty-eight years. She attended one of Richard's conferences at full transformational tilt whereupon she had a genuine, bona fide *mystical* experience that initiated a complete physical healing.

> The next day her terminal liver cancer was gone. The grapefruit-sized bowel metastasis that she had supported with her hand was gone. Three days later she realized that for the first time in thirty-eight years she hadn't taken her daily insulin injections. In the ensuring weeks, all the secondary complications of her diabetes and cancer—kidney failure, fluid in her lungs, tumor-ridden lymph nodes, partial blindness, loss of sensation in her hands and feet, addiction to pain medication—healed. Even a few recently broken toes were completely mended within days.[2]

If enlightenment entailed spontaneous remission, *sign me up for the full treatment.*

And the full treatment is just what I got. The first night of my 10-day intensive with Richard, a woman with untreated, advanced breast cancer had a medical crisis. Not mincing words, Richard helped admit her to the hospital for some good old-fashioned chemotherapy. Scarcely a spontaneous healing! More likely another wimp drowning in the wake of the "natural healing" wave. All the more likely that I was *the one* destined for the one-in-a-million case of spontaneous remission. I was bound for glory.

Richard initiated heightened consciousness through 10 solid days of transformational exercises. We danced to *Flashdance* every morning, settled down to meditate and tone to Tibetan bells, only to whirl and spin like Sufi dervishes in the afternoon. One exercise involved each person, of a small group of four, singing in turn, *nonstop*—for hours if necessary, until each person passed through a *transformational door*. We vented, wept and shouted. We accessed overwhelming

67

group energies. On the eighth day a woman had a vision of Christ, who approached her and placed His Crown of Thorns on her head. Another participant sat communing with Nature as the local wildlife sat rapt at his feet. Blinding light briefly overcame my exercise partner. Such happenings became commonplace. On our three days of silence and strict fast, I watched the night sky for UFOs.

Much to my disappointment, no extraterrestrial visitation was in store for me. *Au contraire.* Instead, I was fast losing ground in my quest for mystical communion and spontaneous remission. I got nauseous during the Sufi whirling. My humiliation was complete when I found myself retching on the ground during the morning's exercise. Moreover, I was terrified of the dark and gripped my flashlight every night on the trail back to our cabins. My emotional agony grew as I compared myself unfavorably to the spiritually "advanced" people on the retreat. The altered states I entered with the express purpose of healing my cancer revealed nothing more than a vast inferiority complex. Though I had enrolled to transcend my physical body, I quickly learned that the body is the repository for unresolved emotional pain. Insecurities seemed to surface from my very cellular structure. Even Richard grew exasperated with me during one evening session. *Stop looking at me like I'm your daddy.*

Welcome to the world of gurus. Male gurus, that is. For the duration of the conference, I never recovered from that sharp slap. But my awakening continued. In truth, it would take more years of emotional development until I stopped searching for my daddy. Fortunately that slap catapulted me towards emotional healing to transform my guilt and shame.

Ironically, guilt and shame were exactly what Richard Moss was targeting. *Cancer is inner warfare*, according to him, created as our egoic consciousness generates discord within. In Eastern enlightenment traditions, the ego was to be conquered. In the Western mystical tradition, Richard taught, Christ's sacrifice was tantamount to forgiveness of our very nature. *Forgiveness.* Even our ego is part of Nature! As Handel's *Messiah* attests, all *"warfare is accomplished."* The end of the Old Testament's judgment and suffering had arrived. *Love* was the New Testament's message. Miracles of love were accomplished through the laying on of Christ's hands, a healing of the body not emphasized in the East. Likewise, energetic shifts or "transformational doors" usher us into a higher energetic. Healing cancer—fast growing cells not referent to the whole—meant subsuming cancer cells into a higher energy field. A heightened consciousness, such as Richard had realized. Energy not used becomes morbid, was Richard's dictum. His transformational approach provided a framework that guides me to this day.

But in those days, as Richard put it, I was a "hard nut to crack." My personal impasse continued to create an energetic bottleneck. When I returned home after ten days of hell, my physical body was in agony. The stress and tension in my muscles would have brought down an ox. Emotional work ensued.

Not that I ignored my physical body. But I sought therapies that had metaphysical underpinnings, such as Edgar Cayce's. Given that my childhood trauma with food was related to my cancer, Cayce's readings were nothing short of uncanny. As a medical intuitive, Edgar Cayce "saw" Hodgkin's disease as a lack of coordination between the autonomic nervous system in its digestive capacity, and the lymphatic system in its role in the assimilation of food.[3] The emotions could sometimes be the primary cause of this un-coordination. For our un-conscious mind—its anger, fear and grief—affects the functioning of our autonomic nervous system.

Edgar Cayce's readings, so perceptive as to seem preternatural, resonated deeply. Hodgkin's is a disease of the lymphatic system. Lymph has at least two functions: the absorption and assimilation of foods, and a cleansing or drainage system of the cells. Cayce called the lymphatic vessels of the intestinal canal (the lacteals), "that portion that makes for the ability of the system to take from the food values and ... revivify, revitalize, recharge the system itself."[4] Moreover, *lymph flows only in one direction*. I recalled my early dream about an alimentary canal *going in the wrong direction*. I read Cayce on toxic reactions in the alimentary canal: "*We wish to clear the alimentary canal and keep it clear.*"[5]

To that effect, Hodgkin's was one illness for which he saw the need for castor oil packs to stimulate better lymphatic drainage and liver function.[6] I added castor oil packs to my alternative regimen. I was happiest when applying a physical remedy that came from transcending the material realm. There were many such therapies based in the East.

My treatment plan included various forms of subtle energy work. I frequented a well-known healer with scientific credentials whose consciousness had expanded after being accidentally bopped on the head by a falling board. Thus "opened" to the subtle realm, biophysicist

Joyce Hawkes moved energy with her hands, and peered into my body with intuitive sight, while communicating with spirit guides. I was no skeptic. Such purported powers enthralled me. I only balked at being asked to use my own, such as when Joyce asked me to jump out of my body, turn around and look at myself lying on the massage table below!

Severe abuse or trauma (even a blow to the head as with Joyce) can initiate a propensity for leaving one's body. But I simply could not induce an out-of-body experience. These sessions did though expand the experiential base of my belief system. Previously I had only *read* of medical sensitives such as Edgar Cayce. Now I frequented them myself. Unfortunately, while I held their powers to be self-evident, mine were sorely lacking.

But Joyce had told me on our very first session that her guides wanted me to receive advanced knowledge. Joyce was thus instructed to relate how she had healed her own hand from a burn. So we humans were capable of self-healing. I just did not have a clue how I was supposed to manifest mine. But all the alternative practitioners I consulted agreed that I was destined to heal. My cancer was tantamount to a shamanic illness whereby an initiate is called into training to become a healer herself.

So I made the rounds to a varied and ever-changing team of alternative practitioners. In truth, I wanted healing only on my own terms. Still without overt physical symptoms, I relied mostly on emotional and spiritual healing. But my psycho-spiritual healing was not fully integrated on the physical level. I periodically checked in with a medical doctor the first year or so, and had no conclusive reports that my cancer was progressing. Those outside of the medical profession took my apparent good health as a sign that I was on the road to full recovery.

Indeed, my choices seemed constructive. Not a matter of ideology for me, I distinguished myself from other "medical non-compliants." I was not acting on some idea that radiation and chemotherapy were *unnatural.* Nor was I a vegetarian seeking to cure myself with massive doses of wheat grass juice. I recognized from my work with the transformational gurus that nothing less than being totally undone would do the trick. Deriving from a trauma in childhood, my conviction (and my fear) was rooted far more deeply.

Elisabeth Kubler-Ross, well known for explicating the stages of grief, came to town. In Dr. Kubler-Ross's intensive grief workshops, we beat phone books with rubber hoses on mattresses. We were told we were *externalizing* our pain. In truth, it was an exorcism of sorts as we verbalized—and shouted out—our pain with every blow. I was one of the first to work with a facilitator in front of the entire group of 100. They must have sensed I was ready to explode. Upon reaching the mattress crawling on all fours, I screamed with all the force I could muster—*I want to live!*

I thus kicked off the weekend. The energy that I released at such moments was astounding. At less than 80 pounds, my power could lead and transform a large group. Chosen to participate in the closing ceremonies, I drank a soupçon of wine in symbolic communion with another participant with AIDS. Truly, I felt like a movie star of the healing circuit. Sadly though, I attended Dave's funeral in the months after the workshop. Not everyone was slated to heal physically.

During the second year without treatment, my condition took a turn for the worse. Dr. Tinker, the psychiatrist, shared with me his fear of *mis*interpreting "the signs." He had taken a patient's vision—in which she was told she would soon be healed—for the literal truth. She "healed," just not physically. She died a few weeks after the vision. Did such a story apply to me? Not if I was to be miraculously healed. Still I clung to hope. Though fast becoming desperate, I could not bear to be pushed over the edge. I stubbornly (or obtusely) stayed the course and disregarded my increasing symptoms. One fateful day during the second year I realized that my fatigue was not from exercise. No amount of exercise could strengthen a body increasingly riddled with cancer.

At two-and-a-half years, I began to lose weight. My cheeks lost their habitual fullness. My face was beginning to hollow out, giving me a starved look. As I could brook no feedback about my deteriorating appearance, I retreated into isolation, determined to go it alone rather than face interference. I attempted to assuage a rattling cough with tea laced with honey.

Going on the third year without medical treatment, my condition deteriorated rapidly. Since diagnosis, a tumor as big as a fist had formed in my chest. Night sweats ensued, caused by a clogged lymphatic system. I awakened several times throughout the night soaked with my own sweat. I was scarcely able to walk the distance of a room, so weakened had I become. No amount of codeine syrup could touch the real cause of my cough. I frequently vomited to ease a cough caused by the pressure of my tumors. Eating was out of the question. Though not nauseous, I nonetheless had no appetite. A few grapefruit and a protein bar was my daily sustenance. Ironically, I was reduced to the very skeleton that I feared chemotherapy would make of me.

I had entered into the death process, a series of subtle and not-so-subtle changes whereby I lost all interest in external life. Close to death, consciousness shuts down. Unable to do anything but lie prone, the TV droned on. I was vaguely aware of a Spanish soap opera. I seemed to be reconciling something with the Cubans on my father's side. I had never before tuned into this television show, nor been able to find it afterwards.

Had I entered the subtle realm?

Still victim to my fears, in the winter of 1987, I lay dying. And my progression towards death was agonizing because I clung to life, powered solely by the regret that my life had been incomplete. I spent my days crying. In this state of crisis, another powerful shift occurred.

I had essentially recreated the neglect of my childhood. By not following my own body's signals that medical treatment was needed, I repeated a pattern set in childhood. But now I shifted my awareness—from my father—to my wounds from my mother. Shaman-like, I had dug a hole-in-the-ground and buried myself, ready to face my demons at last. Alone, my crying reached a shattering crescendo: *My mother never took care of me.* In that emotional release, I begged not to be abandoned again. I had found my way to my own broken heart.

Yet if a tormentor resided within me, so did a savior. Giving expression to my grief was a call for help ... a prayer. A door opened to forgiveness—for my parents, as well as for myself. And so my prayer was heard.

I had been in counseling at the Sacred Heart Family Center[7], housed in the first orphanage on the west coast established by a bona fide saint: St. Frances Xavier Cabrini. Symbolically orphaned myself, I was truly touched by her spirit. Having founded the Institute of the Missionary Sisters of the Sacred Heart in 1880, Frances Xavier Cabrini had come from Italy in 1889 to serve the immigrants of America. She opened 67 schools, orphanages and hospitals throughout the world, crossing the ocean 25 times to do so. An original photograph of Mother Cabrini hung on the wall in the counseling room, sanctifying our sessions and regarding me with compassion.

The Catholic Church's conditions for canonization include well-attested miracles ascribed to the religious in question. I was regaled with the story of how Mother Cabrini had healed a nun stricken with cancer. A deceased Mother Cabrini appeared to the nun, who was dying a lingering death in the convent's infirmary, in answer to her prayers. After the visitation, the nun slowly recovered her strength. She spontaneously started eating again ... *soup*. It was not so much a spontaneous remission as a simple recovery. How I longed for similar recompense. I was three-quarter Italian, after all.

Even so, my miracle came in another way.

One night, while meditating in the bath, I momentarily lost consciousness ... lost my ordinary sense of self. Seriously weakened and more susceptible to the subtle realm, I heard a voice speak to me. I believe it was Mother Cabrini. Whoever it was, she was simple and direct. She told me she would help me. And then I "saw" a black, tangled mass rise from my chest. I intuited that I had been delivered of *something*. Whatever that malignant something was, surely it was carried over from my childhood. By releasing that ancient trauma, my heart opened to new possibilities. Trust.

My partner, Tom, had stood by helplessly for some time. In a last-ditch effort, he convinced me to schedule therapy sessions with someone in the local community of transactional analysis. I cried in the shower, despairing over the swollen lymph glands in my armpit seemingly as large as hens' eggs. Exhausted by the time I was dressed, I was scarcely able to climb the flight of steps to the counseling center.

Carol Poole, ARNP, was duly alarmed by my condition, all the more because she knew Hodgkin's disease was curable by traditional medical treatment. Yet something about her "no nonsense" approach worked, especially as it was combined with gentle care and consideration. In a few short sessions, she applied to the situation at hand no little grace.

And something in me responded. I was beginning to soften. Still, I waited for a sign, an unmistakable call from beyond ... *to take the leap.*

Jump!

*

I remember an indoor swimming pool. I remember wandering up to a bulletin board. Tacked to the bulletin board was a notice. The notice announced that Janet Colli would be facilitating dolphin encounters with cancer patients.

I had that dream in the winter of 1987. I was dying.

For 3 years after my diagnosis at the age of 30, I had focused on emotional healing, avoiding allopathic medical treatment. Hodg-

73

kin's lymphoma is curable, but I simply did not trust doctors. My fears of nausea cut too close to the bone. After a bout of food poisoning and hospitalization at about 3 years old, I started refusing to eat. My mother, after all, had emotional problems that focused on food. She ate mostly bananas, cottage cheese and Milky Ways. My father was a doctor who threatened to give me "shots" when I refused to eat. Little wonder I developed phobias about nausea and needles that ruled my life. *What is chemotherapy but nausea and needles?* Not until I was dying did I choose to face my fears of chemotherapy. That choice ushered in a psycho-spiritual transformation and the healing of my cancer.

But dolphins? Not a single dolphin graced my dream. I had no conscious desire to make the connection. Yet in February of 1988, I decided to take chemotherapy. Suddenly the decision was simple. Bedridden and debilitated, I took comfort in my dreams. But the dream that saved my life was far from dramatic. Its significance was subtle. *Pleasant.* I awoke refreshed and consoled by its promise; for I took that notice on the bulletin board as *assurance* that I was meant to live. And that reassurance gave me the courage to fight.

My sheer faith in that dream enabled me to make the long-dreaded decision to initiate allopathic medical treatment. If I were meant to live, I had to do everything everything within my power—even chemotherapy and radiation. Suddenly chemotherapy was not such a threat to me.

I knew I would survive.

Others were dreaming for me, too. Like Carol, a facilitator at my support group for life-challenging illness. Carol dreamt she was in the passenger seat of a jeep that I was driving. As we fast approached a cliff, a wide chasm opened up before us. Carol despaired of surviving the breach. She turned to face me—in the driver's seat. But I had disappeared! In my place sat ... the *Water Saint.* Our dream-jeep, piloted by the newly-embodied saint, *shot* across the chasm. We landed safely—on the other side of the abyss. We had miraculously survived.

Surely this dream portended a miraculous recovery in store for me. But before, when various healers predicted my survival, I had banked on healing even *without* medical treatment. This time I was not taking any chances.

The key to survival was the transformation of my self-identity— formed by fear of my doctor father—and the engulfment of my ego by the sacred archetype of water. *Feminine fluidity.* Chemotherapy began to symbolize the water element cleansing my cells. Dolphins—embodying *bliss beyond ego*—were the perfect agents of transformation.

When I finally decided to take the dip, a suitable doctor appeared as if "on cue" from the cosmic corps-of-oncologists. Hardly able to walk across the room, Tom drove me to my appointment. And so I made my foray into what I had formerly regarded as enemy territory, now transformed into safe haven.

*

Dr. Milton faced us across his huge desk. He was a straight shooter. I liked his frank open manner, especially when he told me, straight from the hip, that with treatment I had only 50 per cent chance of survival. I blurted out, "I can do *that!*" No fear-based threats or emotional entreaties were used to manipulate me. He simply outlined the procedures I would have to undergo. It was a negotiation, pure and simple.

I remember the sunshine when Tom and I emerged from the meeting. We stood on a crowded street corner, waiting for the lights to change. Washed by waves of gentle hope, we looked at each other as if we shared a secret. Indeed, we did. We had just been given the secret of life itself. We were astounded at how simple that secret was.

"It sounds so easy," Tom said. "I can do it! I responded.

Yet my physical condition was so poor I was immediately scheduled for a procedure to remove the accumulated liquid from my lungs. Wracked with coughing and short of breath, I looked forward to simple relief. Amazingly, just two days prior, I had believed only death would bring a reprieve. But though it promised to alleviate some of my physical suffering, the procedure involved being punctured and drained *via the dreaded needle*. Only a passage through my personal door of fear would allow me to enter the promised land of healing.

My God, my God, why hast thou forsaken me?

Dr. Milton approached me from the back as I sat half-naked, readied with antiseptic and numbed with quick shots, virtual bee stings. Luckily I could not watch where the needle would enter my body. Though I had reluctantly signed a release form alerting me to the dangers of puncturing a lung, nothing could prepare me for that moment of truth. In that instant I fully faced my frail human body's vulnerability. Then the boundary of my tissue was breached.

I nearly fainted. But simultaneously relieved, I vomited instead. A plastic bucket was immediately produced and disposed of. I was amazed at how quickly and efficiently the disturbance was dealt with.

Nothing to be ashamed of, vomiting was a basic human function, nothing more and nothing less. We all watched, seemingly impressed, as a pint of yellowish fluid poured from the tube. Given that I weighed 60 pounds, perhaps it was a record of some sort.

*

Carol, my support group facilitator, played a significant role in my bout with chemotherapy. In short, I owe my life to her. The simplest of gestures can have the profoundest effect. The worst part of the chemotherapy was not the nausea I endured. It was the first IV injection that presented my ultimate moment of truth. Once the decision was made to commence with medical treatment, I did not expect to back out. But faced with the immediate prospect of a needle piercing my vein—to hook me up to a bagful of misery-producing poison—I nearly halted the procedure. Once again, it was my phobia about nausea and needles. Luckily, Carol was there.

Carol had offered to accompany me to my first treatment. Some instinct of survival made me accept. Having escorted me to the treatment room where an IV stand was readied to administer the "chemo," Carol sat down beside me. She sat on one side of me and Dr. Milton took his position on my other side. One look at my own meager, blue-veined arm, extended and held firmly by the doctor's, and I began to panic. My arm looked like a tiny twig about to be split or broken in two.

I had secured Dr. Milton's agreement to wait for my final cue. Shrinking, I muttered, "I don't know if I can go through with this." Carol took a deep breath, cueing me in the process. *Breathe.* But I understood by her attitude—her compassion—that even my fear was allowed. She did not threaten or cajole. Or urge me to proceed. If she had, I would surely have fought. If we had fought, I might not be alive today.

Instead Carol simply sat in full compassion. Not even actively waiting. But in so doing, Carol created a spacious enough passageway for me to walk through the door of transformation. And in our brave new world, this doctor was not incompetent. With one skillful thrust, the needle was introduced into my vein.

Carol got me through the phase with needles. Tom got me through the nausea.

First, the IV dripped a purifying water solution. *Purification.* That appealed to me. A nurse then changed the bag to the chemotherapy solution chosen specifically for my type of cancer, specific chemical agents found to be selectively destructive to the malignant cells of Hodgkin's lymphoma. This solution's efficacy was reflected in the disease's high cure rates. Even among chemotherapies, *this* chemo was deemed potent ... *toxic*. Only six doses would be given, over a period of six months. Yet the actual bag of chemotherapy was crystal clear—indistinguishable from water. I had considered visualizing the chemo as a certain healing color. Say, blue or green. But my chemo was simply symbolized by clear, pure cleansing water.

All in all, I was not unduly discomforted by the procedure. I sat tethered to the IV stand, reading or listening to music through my earphones. After several hours, I was safely ushered home by Tom to await the chemotherapy's effects. I felt completely in the dark about the nausea. When would it strike? And when would it subside?

*

Nausea invaded me in the early evening, overwhelming my senses as nausea is wont to do. But this nausea was different than a simple case of stomach upset or flu. Wave after wave hit, for hour after hour. About twenty minutes after each trip to the toilet, it steadily crept up again. At times, I lost control of both bowels and bladder, though each blast meant a respite that enabled me to crawl back to bed where I sat up and tried to rest. Lying prone only stimulated the nausea. This deadly cycle lasted 4-5 hours throughout the night, until I fell asleep, exhausted.

That this horrendous experience did not defeat me, nor trigger a recurrence of anorexia, I owe to a singular remedy. It would be an exaggeration to say that Tom never left my side. He was certainly not vigilant all throughout the night. In fact, he slept soundly when I could not. But at just the worst moments, I invariably felt Tom's steady hand upon my back. His gentle touch transmitted some vital sense of balance. As insular as nausea can be, I was not totally alone. It became a shared experience. Simple human touch—and the compassion it entailed—became the most powerful medicine to offset the chemical agents capable of destroying malignant cells.

Thus initiated, I learned to navigate during chemotherapy's altered state. My friend Ann had grown so sensitized to the sensory cues of treatment that she became nauseous immediately upon entering the doctor's office. It was the antiseptic *smell* that set her off. I got my own taste of Pavlovian conditioning when one treatment was rescheduled because of my low blood counts. It was an unexpected reprieve. Instead of being hooked up to an IV, I went home and happily ate a sausage sandwich. Nonetheless, I vomited like clockwork all throughout the night.

I had entered the private world of the chemotherapy patient.

The morning after my first nightlong bout with nausea, I was weak as a kitten. But the recovery process took no longer than a day, thanks to the steroid *prednisone*. By the second morning, I was ravenous. By midmorning I had eaten two breakfasts. The rest of my day was consumed by the needs of my increased appetite. And the steroids dramatically altered my taste buds as well. Overnight, I developed a hankering for foods both salty and sweet: significant slabs of ham; hefty pork sausages in buns smothered with hot mustard; hamburgers with pickles and deep fried mushrooms with a strawberry milk shake. Never had I derived so much sensual satisfaction from food, especially food of questionable quality.

Gone were the grated carrots, olive oil &lemon juice salad from my Edgar Cayce diet. Gone was my resolve to eliminate red meat and empty calories from carbohydrates and sugar. After all, doesn't eating such food increase one's risk of cancer? Thanks to the steroids, I threw caution to the winds. Without a care in the world, I gave in to my childhood cravings: angel food cake with a side of vanilla ice cream. I drank ice-cold ginger ale and cans of pop. Eating out, I polished off my chicken dinner and started in on Tom's. The waiter joked that I needed two forks. No more doggie bags for me!

And the steroids transformed my emotional body as well. Some say *red* signifies anger. But red also represents the primal energy of the Root Chakra, the *Muladhara*, where vital energy resides at the base of the spine. *Blood red* best describes the raw energy coursing through me after my first prednisone treatment. *Scarlet* signifies the vital energy that had long been denied. Dying, I had withered to 60 pounds. But with the cancer in check—and buoyed up by steroids— my health changed dramatically. I gained 10 pounds in a week. The steroids pepped me up with so much energy I just could not contain it. I started saying what I *really* felt. Words just popped out of my mouth. Angry words sometimes, but always words of passion. I was learning to speak my heart. Cancer drugs helped teach me a whole new way of being. While my physical body healed, my emotional body was restored by the raw shock of Life energy, raging unrefined.

*

After nearly a half-year of a highly toxic chemotherapy regimen—even by chemotherapy standards—I was thriving. But the medical treatment for Hodgkin's was only half over. Radiation treatment was about to commence. Unlike chemotherapy, administered only once a month, I was slated to endure being irradiated every weekday *for 3 to 5 weeks.*

The Director of Radiation Oncology at Swedish Tumor Institute had been assigned my case. I was convinced that my non-compliance with medical treatment was the reason I was given the red carpet treatment. Sure enough, Dr. Tesh (nicknamed Dr. Tissue) brought his full authority to bear to persuade me that anything less than the standard dose would endanger my life.

But how was I to effect healing in the inner sanctum of the radiation chamber? During the diagnostic phase of CT scans, I had seen panels of computerized equipment, manned by white-coated specialists. I had viewed this prodigious technology through thick glass that protected technicians from unwanted radiation. But the radiation room, built inside an underground tunnel, had an additional atmosphere of danger. The x-ray machine itself might as well have been a *cyclotron* or linear accelerator of charged subatomic particles. Instead of an atom smasher, it was a cancer cell smasher. The walls of the door enclosing the room were like a bank vault's. Among the warnings posted, I half-expected to see a skull & crossbones, the universal symbol of death.

I had already been quartered and sliced up with an indelible marker like a side-of-beef. Special blocks of cement were then formed to the exact size of my lungs. Placed directly above my lungs on a Plexiglas shelf during every irradiation, they thus protected my lungs as the x-rays bounced off the blocks. My larynx would be protected by a round shaft, little bigger than a pencil. Moving so much as a hair's breadth could expose me to an unseen, deadly energy bent on exterminating cells. How was such a death-ray to effect healing?

The first session acquainted me with the procedure that soon became routine—climbing onto the table while two technicians arranged the blocks, and positioned my body exactly below. Then, after warning me *not to move*, they seemingly both ran out of the room, pulling shut the steel vault door behind them. The emptiness of the room hit me with the finality of death. When the machine finally whirred on, I tried to hold my breath, convinced that by shrinking and stilling

79

myself, I would elude some of the rays. I desperately prayed as the machine emitted its invisible, deadly rays.

After that first treatment I knew I had to renew my consecration to Life. It was not the treatment that scared me so much as my own attitude towards it. I could not help but perceive the radiation as a deadly affair, and I did not want to face another session without a radical change in that perception.

It had become my touchstone that if I asked for help, Creation would see to it that someone suitable would arrive on the scene. Call it *bargaining with God*, but time after time, I had experienced the saving grace of surrender. This time was no exception.

I duly considered one of the two technicians intent upon adjusting my body on the table. I had noted a silver crucifix hanging on a delicate chain around her neck. Luckily, she was delegated last contact with me. So I took a calculated risk. When the time came for her to vacate the premises, I made an urgent request.

"Can't you say something ... *a little more healing?*"

And the young woman dressed in a white coat touched my forehead, marking out a tiny cross.

"*Christ be with you*," she said.

With her touch lingering and with a full heart, I proceeded with the radiation treatment. But this time when the technicians left the room, I was not alone. Thus my faith was ignited and my healing caught fire.

Henceforth, we ritually dedicated the radiation sessions to the radiant energy of Christ. Putting myself in the Hands of Christ was a cinch. I simply envisioned the job of subsuming cancerous cells, and protecting healthy cells and tissues, as overseen by Jesus Christ, Chief of Radiation Oncology.

Four years later, my art exhibit, *Aliveness Through Cancer*, consisting of 18 pictures and commentary, celebrated the re-opening of the Oncology Department of the University of Washington Medical Center. In 1989, Bernie Siegel saw it displayed at the American Holistic Medical Association conference, and drew a huge heart in my gallery book. Over 20 years later, as a psychotherapist, I believe that symptoms are a communication mechanism. Our total personality seeks above all to express itself. *Your biggest symptom just might be your greatest dream trying to break through.*

I see my cancer as a call to a deeper level of love. Though I had planned to forgo allopathic medicine and heal through "spiritual means," my dream of dolphins ushered in a path of *spiritualizing* western medicine. Chemotherapy, administered through a needle and causing a nausea like that which had tormented my life, proved to be the perfect healing for me. My very cells were informed. For when I transcended my fear, the waters of Life flowed into my veins.

CHAPTER 5

MONICA:
THE DIZZINESS OF FREEDOM

Anxiety is the dizziness of freedom....

Soren Kierkegaard

Monica comes to me deep in the throes of anxiety and depression. Daily, she struggles to keep her head above swelling tidewater. She is slowly slipping under. Chronic depression is like fighting an interminable tide—it comes and goes, with no conclusion. Until exhausted, the swimmer drowns. Drowning her sorrow in alcohol has hastened the deluge (glug, glug). Doctors have little to offer her except medication. Wellbutrin, Lexipro, Celexa, Prozac. She has tried just about everything. It is hard to keep a good symptom down. Her emotions are what doctors refer to as "labile." Volatile. Anger surfaces readily. She is so angry she'll "rip him a new one." She will "tear his head off." Every single session, she cries at the drop-of-a-hat. She uses so much Kleenex she offers to bring her own box.

> *Cry baby cry*
> *Make your mother sigh*
> *She's old enough to know better*
> *Cry baby cry.*[1]

On heavy medication for 15 years, Monica suffers not only from depression but also from Panic Disorder. A near-crippling series of panic attacks threaten to interrupt her days as a public servant, where she serves to manage the city's risk. She manages her own risk by popping "anti-anxiety" pills (such as Valium, Ativan, Zanex) in a vain attempt to keep her feelings at bay.

Her emotions are the enemy of her state-of-mind.

Her doctor, a well-intended shrink from a psychiatric community for whom depression is a "biochemical imbalance," says it is "genetic." Her morbid story does not matter in the least. Monica is destined for drugs for the rest of her life, not to mention a drinking problem. Monica, who washed the remaining tissue and fragments of her father's brains off the wall—15 years ago. Monica, whose beloved father blew his head off with a 12-gauge shotgun—a measure of his torment since he had returned from WWII.

Who wouldn't be anxious and depressed? Off balance. Out of sorts.

Bessel van der Kolk, the leading expert in the field of traumatic stress, recounts how he grew up with uncles who had returned from WWII, men who were symptomatic for posttraumatic stress disorder—long before he treated those similarly traumatized from the Vietnam war. His education growing up afforded him an early introduction into trauma's effect on the nervous system. War and its aftermath activate PTSD not only in its soldiers, but also sets in motion *secondary* trauma in the families of the war torn, such as Monica's. Each generation growing up in the aftermath is forced to confront these effects. That is the lineage of warfare. I serve the daughters of men who strangled Germans with their own bare hands. Little wonder their fathers drank to excess or bullied their families while in the throes of long-term untreated PTSD.

Laurel, another daughter of a soldier, witnessed s a singular account of her father's service in WWII. One day, apropos of nothing, he went into yet another low-level rant that Laurel knew not to interrupt. He had recently had a heart attack and told her that a minister had visited him "in hospital," proselytizing. Her father, unlike the rest of the family, was not a churchgoer. Well, he'd told that minister, "Don't waste your breath; there's no hope for me. You have no idea what I did in the war." Nonetheless he made an appointment to talk when he got out of the hospital. "I'll show him," he said to Laurel. "I have blood on my hands up to here," slapping his upper arms. The similarity to Shakespeare's Lady MacBeth, which her father had most assuredly not read, took her breath away. "He doesn't know what I did during the war." Laurel's father had been a tail gunner in a Boeing B-17 bomber in WWII. "I *saw where our bombs landed.*" Apartment buildings. Homes. Civilians. Laurel's father suffered from untreated PTSD his entire life; and her family, reeling from the shock of his symptoms, notably an arrested development, drifted into disorder. But after his meeting with the minister Laurel's father started attending church. Perhaps at last he felt some forgiveness for himself.

And Monica's father?

Both Monica and the ghost of her beloved father come to me, shackled together by the chains of their torment. Monica tells me her *bona fide* vision of her father—breaking free from those chains—immediately after his death. Indeed, only that vision sustains her. She *knows* he felt redemption from his suffering even though he committed suicide. As therapy progresses, we hear of his tortured life, and the burden Monica has shouldered.

Do I tell her that my own much-loved, bipolar father was said to have strangled himself with a shower hose? I too, am a daughter born of a disordered nervous system. No, it is not time for disclosure. But I can definitely relate.

Panic attacks are my point of entry. Whether cancer, bipolar disorder or depression, every person has their own secret door. The doorway to the garden of their soul.

In Monica's case, her physical body tells the story. *Fight or flight* is evolutionary overkill, in such cases. Her nervous system, specifically, her limbic system is over-stimulated. Over-firing. The human body is no dummy, as anyone with panic attacks knows. The human physical body under attack knows perfectly well how to handle itself. *Freeze!* The Deer-in-the-headlights Syndrome, before the Disorder of Blind Bolt. Monica is essentially numb—deadlocked—but for the blind urge to ... *flee!* Heart is off & running. Pulse racing, headed for hell-in-a-handbasket. But she is stuck, glued to one place. No matter. Whether airplane aisle or suspension bridge or tight corridor, there is ... No-exit.

Did you know that John-Paul Sartre's existential nausea is suspected to be unresolved *birth* trauma, triggered by a psylocibin trip? Panic disorder can be seen as a version of the second matrix of birth trauma humans routinely experience. And still hold within the nervous system as a template for life itself. Second matrix birth trauma is routinely kicked off by contractions when the neck-of-the-womb, the *cervix*, is closed. [2] Blocked. No Exit. Panic, par excellence.

The only way out of it is *through* it—through the birth process. Being reborn.

Panic overtakes Monica and an estimated 2.4 million *or* one in 113 Americans. Each year an estimated 1.7% (or 1 in 58) adult Americans aged 18 to 54 experiences a panic attack. Moreover, it is estimated that up to 15% of all Americans are very likely to suffer from a panic attack at some point in their lives.[3] The instant panic ignites, it is Monica's *one and only* sensory impression. She is aware of virtually nothing else but sweat heartbeat breath heartbeat *thought-of-death death-threat* heartbeat. Death itself, is seemingly imminent. Monica herself, turns bright pink. Shades of red. Does anyone (like her boss) notice? Does anyone care?

Be with me now.

In Terrence Malick's film, "The Thin Red Line," a WWII soldier focuses on a picture of his beloved fiancé prior to every battle. Another soldier, a sharpshooter, kisses a crucifix around his neck prior to every skirmish. *Be with me now.* Invoking their higher power—Love—only one is killed in combat. But both survive the destruction fo the soul.

Consecrate yourself. An awakening will occur. Richard Moss, M.D. recorded one such awakening. Richard was big on consecration. He facilitated several "spontaneous remissions" from terminal diseases by challenging cancer patients to higher-order consecration. In the 1980s, a woman attending one of Richard's transformational conferences had a mystical experience. Terminally ill as well as diabetic, Laura went into spontaneous remission and fully recovered her health as a direct result of her experience. Her healing was sparked during the transformational dancing exercise (each member of a team of four danced until they became One with the dance, and an energetic shift was felt by all). It was during that dance that Laura was challenged beyond her identity as cancer victim. Dragging, with a great tumor in her belly, Richard nonetheless told her, *Dance! You aren't dead yet!* [4] Her radical change of perspective—and consecration to full participation—propelled her *beyond* her ego identity. By continuing to choose radical aliveness, Laura entered unitive consciousness.

Laura as One with mountain and sky.

Laura ceased to be Laura.

Dying to herself, she become One with Everything. Even her cancer merged and melted away. Accept nothing but *the whole enchilada.* Death is a door.

For every panic-stricken person, there is a moment to take a stand. Stare down the danger. Or at least, stand with it. Allow at least some of the panic to take its toll. Take its measure with mind. *Be mindful.* That is what I challenge Monica to do. Eschew the panic-dissolving, anti-anxiety pill—its potent suppression of your symptom. Let at least some of the panic *be known.* Face it. Feel it. Monica takes a stand. She will not back down.

Monica's attitude changes. The shift is slow and subtle but real. She feels the anxiety of her panic, learns *firsthand* that it will not kill her. Embarrassment will not destroy her. Prior to this, she could not attend a business meeting without sitting in a chair next to the door, poised to flee. Nor could she fly in an airplane without drugging herself. Now she refuses to restrict her actions. She has a panic attack on a plane. *Allowing* it, she knows full well she is alive and well.

Monica takes a stand. A stance of allowance.

Noticing this, thanks to neuroplasticity—the ability of the brain to change neural pathways—Monica's brain kicks into higher gear. A higher-order intelligence. Watching, *witnessing*, talking her through it. This becomes her practice. This becomes her meditation: her prescribed medication. Like most medications, it has side effects. It feels like holy hell. But she does a good enough job. Her *life* kicks into gear.

A *meta*-position is a position or perspective above the problem. Taking such a position on the problem reworks the problem itself. Was it really Einstein who said that you cannot solve the problem on the level of the problem? Whoever said it really was a genius. Working with such a symptom will alter one's nervous system, one's physical brain. Something vital is being born.

A healing force within the nervous system activates traumatic imprints and brings them to the forefront of consciousness. A very determined force activates your anxiety. A spiritual opening is potentially in the works. As in homoeopathy, symptoms are not nuisances but repeated attempts to heal. In many languages, fear and anxiety denote some sort of "narrowing end." Panic is experienced *internally* as life-threatening though it is not necessarily externally real. But it must be dealt with internally. Your "inner healer" has put you in this place of panic. It has all come down to this. A narrowing and contraction. You are gearing up for expansion. Trust nature; this is the natural order.

So why not utilize your own timing to expand your conscious awareness?

Stay just a little bit longer, even a second longer—in conscious awareness. It may seem life-threatening. But go right up to that edge (the edge-of-your-known-universe). And come back from it. *Dance* backwards. *Even if you can't breathe?* Yes, even if you are scared to pieces. Your *inner healer* brought you to this edge, after all. Trust that. You will always be able to pull yourself back. Trust your inner self. Just go up right to that edge, try to maintain your awareness when you reach that place of panic ... and come back. Each time you go there, each time you approach that panic, you bring the light of consciousness. Every moment brings healing. 'Til you are lit up within. That is how to grow. That is how to heal.

That is how the brain "grows" new neural pathways. Neuroplasticity, in action.

While the tendency of the panicked person is to avoid situations that activate symptoms, and to suppress those symptoms with medication, their discomfort must ultimately be faced—and energetically transformed. And if I support the process behind the symptom, it may temporarily exacerbate the symptom. But the result will be self-healing, and the expansion of consciousness. According to Stanislav Grof, M.D., one of the founders of transpersonal psychology, an effective cure "does not come through alleviation of the emotional and psychosomatic symptoms involved, but through their temporary intensification, full experience, and conscious integration."[5]

Now that is an effective strategy for healing.

So when her face and neck get beet-red, Monica no longer runs embarrassed to the bathroom. Noticeable as a red beet at work, Monica even tells her concerned boss not to be concerned. It's *just* a panic attack. She thus finds out that boss-man suffers from panic attacks, too. Regarding panic disorder, they are simpatico, as are 4.2 million Americans. Calming, placating is Big Business. Pharmaceutical business, that is. Are our lives so fraught with peril that our nervous systems cannot be trusted? Even while overriding it with conscious awareness, Monica is learning to trust hers.

Such a consecration is profound.

In short order, her panic begins to subside; her neurophysiology is impacted. *Desensitized.* A relaxation response is naturally induced. Her nervous system is ... seduced. Before she knows it, Monica cannot remember when she last resorted to popping an anti-anxiety pill. On an airplane, she sits tight, but she is not under pharmaceutical influence. Instead of the vast suppression that was her pattern, her habit of keeping her feelings at bay, Monica now has access to their full energy. And more degrees of freedom to express it.

Monica is no stranger to consecrated change. She made a deliberate choice at great expense to move across country. She took a pay-cut and landed on relatively remote Whidbey Island—the perfect situation to focus on *inner* work. She knew her drinking threatened to subsume her. She recognized that she was *uber*-controlling and obsessive in relationship with her children. *Off.* That choice was critical, for sure. How many of us can "correct course," even without so much at stake? Do you see our collective energy policies, our financial structures changing? Monica is one in a million. How many will it take to offset those millions? How many will it take to chart a new course?

Even a symptom has a right to exist, will *fight* to exist, I remind her. There is energy to be found within that symptom. Like finding *gold* underground. Information abounds within that symptom, just below conscious awareness. An underlying principle, I tell her. *A raison d'être.* Dead right, there is. Just ask Monica's father.

Energy not used becomes morbid. Depression becomes a way of

life ... and a way to death.

Untangle me—from the ties that bind me. Unfetter me and free me. Just like the image of her father bound with chains—breaking free. Monica is learning to break the chains of panic and depression in a manner other than substance abuse and suicide. In so doing, she heals her father, moving backwards in time. She heals her lineage, *collapsing* time. It takes a truly great soul to heal a lineage.

Great soul, Monica.

CHAPTER 6

JUDITH: CANCER IN A BOX

Sometimes it takes a personal crisis to turn you on the spiritual path.

Joni Mitchell, *Both Sides Now*

Reflection
by Judith

I stand before a full-length mirror.
The reflection is unknown to me.
It is bent and emaciated.
The face is haggard and the eyes unseeing.

I watch in dismay as tears fall from those vacant eyes.
Lifting my hand, I touch my cheek.
This hand is wet, I see.
Like an arrow straight to my heart,
Comes the realization that this apparition is me.

Judith is in her mid-sixties, seemingly frail and undeniably conservative in her dress and attitude. *Seemingly* traditional and mainstream. Retired, she had a career in the airline industry as a Customer Service Representative dealing with irate and hostile customers, even downright threatening customers. Such calm in the face of threat bespeaks a person who has already remained alive *despite* a life threat, passed over the razor's edge, so to speak—and survived.

Yes, that is Judith. Survivor *par excellence.*

But she does not share that yet. Now she faces a more immediate challenge. Cancer. She has been on Hormone Replacement Therapy (HRT) for 16 years, creating (unbeknownst to her) the estrogen her particular type of cancer feeds on. But Judith does not seem to fit my psychotherapy practice where people readily talk transpersonal, or seek alternative "energy medicine." She does not spout spiritual beliefs, has never heard of Shamanism. Seemingly nothing whatsoever in her background or current life prepares us for what is about to unfold.

Nothing whatsoever, except that when she had buried her elderly mother, her mother's spirit "came back" the day after she died. And then again, two days later. Perhaps mom will show up again—as an inner resource for Judith. (My own beliefs about the afterlife initially do not matter, that is, whether Judith's dead mother is *inside* her or *outside.* Or so I thought. Judith's story will ultimately challenge my belief system about the difference between inside and outside.)

Judith is going to need every resource she can muster for she is anxious and depressed. Diagnosed with breast cancer, she is slated for

91

a mastectomy followed by reconstructive surgery. The loss of a breast, a vital part of her female identity, has devastated her, especially as her breasts had represented Femininity. Upon hearing the diagnosis, she had gone into a state of virtual shock, "suspended into nothingness." Hardly started on the long road to recovery, Judith is tired and out of hope.

Having survived cancer in my early thirties, I cut my baby therapist's teeth supporting people with life-challenging illness. My own dream about facilitating encounters between cancer patients and dolphins saved my life. I know the power of dreams.

Judith brings me a classic nightmare. *A polar bear, circling in icewater, clutches a small poodle in its jaws, about to drag it underwater to drown.*

Terrified, Judith identifies with the dog, "I'm being devoured alive." Judith can still see the stark terror in that poodle's eyes, the instinctive fear of death. (She does not realize that her own terror-stricken, brown eyes perfectly mirror the poodle's.) The image keeps reappearing in her daily life, torturing her anew each time. Her situation seems helpless. Out of her control....

In the face of such anxiety, dream analysis is beside the point. We begin straight away with Eye Movement Desensitization & Reprocessing (EMDR), focusing directly on that dream. EMDR is a form of bilateral stimulation. Right brain, left brain, right brain, back & forth we go as Judith's eyes track my moving fingers. As trauma or difficult material is "stored" in the right hemisphere, it is best "unstuck" or processed along with the left hemisphere—physical site of our analytical, thinking mind. The closest thing to EMDR is the rapid eye movement (REM) we experience during sleep that is indicative of dreamstates wherein our psyches process and integrate material. Even posttraumatic stress heals with bilateral stimulation. Thinking and verbalizing a narrative helps bring one out of frozen terror—to the safety of here and now.

Sure enough, Judith's polar bear dissolves. In a light altered state, Judith "sees" her mother approach, "beckoning," a smile on her face. But she is younger now, and what's more, she reads a poem, ending it by saying, "When you pass this way, I'll be there to say, Welcome Home."

"That's weird," says Judith. Weird stuff happens with EMDR. Most important is the effect it had on Judith.

"I feel free," Judith says, "like I'm floating ... like air."

In another EMDR session Judith images her surgery in detail. In excruciating detail, I might add. Judith has an uncanny ability to see herself outside of her body, as in classic out-of-body experiences (OBEs). She "sees" cutting and even blood, and swoops down to touch her own disembodied chest "to make it right, to put it all back together." Judith takes us through the surgery, all the way to her recovery and her husband's care. She even dialogues with her surgeon regarding trust. "You have to have faith in me. Or do you want another doctor?" Judith and her surgeon strike a bargain. Judith's trust level grows from 75% to 99%, from some doubt to acceptance, in a single session.

Though I recommend a course of treatment with EMDR to target Judith's anxiety-producing, cancer treatment, we never do complete it. To showcase her impressive powers of dissociation, something totally unexpected happens during our third session.

I ask Judith to imagine some figure of support ("resource-building"), real or imaginary, to bring into the scene. Like Judith's dead mom. Such supportive figures range from one's adult-self to Super- or Archetypal figures that "rescue," or help with difficult situations. With closed eyes, Judith promptly responds that "Mr. Eagle" has appeared.

Who? Whaaat?

What follows is her introduction to an authentic and seemingly autonomous Spirit Guide whose path of learning transforms her life.

Mr. Eagle is beautiful, calm and strong. She "sees" him soaring, looking down at her. Eagle lands. He is standing 10-feet tall, with commensurate wingspan, right beside Judith. Can she communicate with Mr. Eagle? Just like C. G. Jung did with his Philemon? This, I recommend.

Eagle is quite communicative. "Look inside yourself for an area of calm." A pool of water beckons, "Put your foot in; I'll make you calm and cleanse you." Judith is afraid of losing herself (like a poodle going under), but the pool itself reassures her, "No, I'm just going to cleanse you; you will remain the same."

"Do you promise?"

"I promise."

I listen, enthralled. Judith puts one foot into the water and she sees a white light. Eagle reassures her. He advises her to let it envelop her, let it "wrap itself around you." "Will it devour me?" "No, this is your place of calm, suspended in white light."

Suddenly Judith gets claustrophobic. "I've got to get out!" Immediately the white light parts, tree and blue sky appear, along with

Eagle. "See, you can do it!"

"I have control over what goes on in my head! That's what Eagle is teaching me. I was in a place I didn't want to be, and I got out." For the second time in our sessions, Judith feels free, hopeful.

So this was "a teaching," not about control, but about her ability to remove herself from discomfort, to place herself in a better place. "Keep looking for your serenity." One by one, Judith practices with her fears. Her first fear is that the tumor will devour her ("but it will be removed"). Her next fear is the mastectomy ("but it will be made right"). "Keep walking down the long road; there will be pain but you have to keep moving," Eagle says.

"I see the path. Control is out of my hands in a certain way, like with the physicians. But my mind can control what I think. I can put my trust in my physicians." Judith argues with herself out loud: "It's hard to have trust. But I have to let go of that—to control the fear." She even tries to get Eagle to dispense with her fear.

"No, I can't take it for you," says Eagle. "You have to do it yourself. But I will help."

Eagle even offers a distraction. "When you can't control your fear, come fly with me! Fly up in the sky, look down on the control you don't have, and see it's not important. What's important is that you feel free! You didn't have control in the first place. *Put yourself in another dimension.*"

In one fell swoop, Eagle has put his finger (or wingtip) on the function of dissociation. That is, removing us from danger or threat, even to the point of leaving our physical, material body.

Judith intones, "Move on down the path towards my refuge. But my refuge is learning to let go of things beyond my control—that's my refuge!"

Eagle admits, "It's not easy. But each time you walk down the path, and pass your fears, it will be easier. You can learn a new way. Now, practice walking past your fears. Come, walk with me down the path. There's freedom in letting go."

Eagle then proceeds step-by-step to teach Judith how to deal with her debilitating fear and worry. She is instructed on various imagery techniques, while I take notes. Eagle has Judith picture her fears "inside a box," and then "*slam* the lid shut!" It requires terrific self-control. Those wretched horrid worries just keep popping back up. Beware. Danger is afoot.

Shut it. Cancer. *Slam it.* Surgery. "Slam. It. Shut!"

"Compartmentalize your fear—*put it in a box*—and close the lid. Do you see the surgery? You can control that. *Take hold of the lid and slam it*," says Eagle.

"**No**," she responds fearfully. Judith has to learn to close the lid tight.

"Give me your hand, and we'll close the door together."

"**No**."

"You promised!" Finally, that promise hits home.

"Slam!" She's done it! Judith startles. Her ferocity surprises her.

"Now, feel the calm." And she could. She could even feel the air when the lid slammed shut!

"I can do this—one box-at-a-time—so my fears aren't controlling me! By compartmentalizing my fears, I'm on the path to wholeness. Eagle will lead me to wholeness, and *wholeness is wellness*. He says, "Follow me." He put his wing around me and we started walking. It's a power of mind to compartmentalize things and leave them. I can do this. So now, whenever I have fears about the surgery, I'll slam the lid shut. My psyche has control. I can slam the lid *damn hard!*"

Practicing a species of "active imagination" (à la C. G. Jung), Judith is instructed by Eagle to walk down an imagined path, to see the "boxes" lined up, and her fears safely contained. "Life will always hold more challenges. You must *practice* turning away from fear and worry." Wise words, especially for Judith, so prone to self-destructive worry. Privately, I ponder the relationship of such self-defeating, feeling-states to the development of cancer. Judith notes that stress weakens the body so the immune system cannot fight. She is fighting now. "I'm not allowing my fears to control me. I'm leaving them behind because there's nothing more I can do."

Eagle sometimes takes Judith flying, as a distraction from her fears. Exhilarating joy, unrestrained! She even "sees" his wingspread. Early on, we dispense with EMDR. Judith simply closes her eyes and calls on Eagle, who assumes the body of a fierce, giant eagle, standing 10-feet tall. She can actually "feel" that Eagle speaks from her right side; she feels "pulled" on *the right side of her brain*. Judith speaks from the left hemisphere, while Eagle speaks from the right. "He's meshing the two!"

Just like EMDR, which meshes two brain hemispheres through bi-lateral stimulation, that is, by alternating between the right hemisphere and the left. Speaking with Eagle, Judith says, "feels like being stimulated, like a magnetic field is stretching from the left to the right." Neuroscience teaches that traumatic memory is "stored" in the right hemisphere, site of our more intuitive feeling nature—as well as the site of Eagle. Healing involves the processing of that stuck material. By helping Judith control her fears, truly Eagle is "meshing the two!"

Judith can generally always sense her spirit guide. "Eagle makes me more aware of my inner life. He tries to show me the better path. We take it a day-at-a-time. But he's there for me whenever I want to chat.

We discuss and he says, *Follow me.*"

*

Surgery is one big "box." Can Eagle intercede if the surgeons make a wrong move? "No," he is only there to observe. But Eagle says he will be there every step of the way. Judith is to look beyond surgery to a positive outcome. Eagle ponders the surgery, saying he has "got to think about it," and promises to get back to her tomorrow(!) He wants to "make sure it's the right thing for her." Apparently it is, for Eagle gives explicit instructions in preparation for her surgery.

Judith is directed to take a plush, stuffed toy eagle with her into the hospital for Eagle's spirit to enter. She is to hold the toy eagle in her hand the night before surgery and talk to it, just like she talks to him. And his "spirit" will go into the stuffed toy! (Pure *shamanism*, I note. How does Judith, who is not familiar with the word *shaman,* know such things?) She wraps a "cocoon" around her. Thus insulated, she is prepared for surgery, accepting what has to be—her mind at peace. One hour before surgery, waiting for the team of surgeons, Judith calls on Eagle to come and help calm her.

"I can control my fear." The surgery is a success. Judith returns home to recuperate, victorious.

One day-at-a-time, we arrive at the stage of pain.

Oxycodone notwithstanding, Judith now knows pain. The drugs merely numb the pain and leave Judith feeling suffocated and drowning in the pressure. Surprisingly, Eagle again takes awhile to answer, "I'll have to think about this." We have challenged him again. "How about soaring away, leaving the pain behind? Temporary relief, soar and be free of it for awhile when it gets to be too much. Think of being with me."

Indeed, Judith finds that she does not feel pain when we use the eye movements of EMDR. But Eagle also tells her not to *actually* leave with him, as she needs to stay connected to earth. But she can fantasize she is floating with the wind, weightless. So she floats. Wonderful. Judith can feel the wind on her body. "Flap your arms," she transports herself _{up,} up, ^{up.}

Eagle says she needs to find other ways while on the ground (on earth) to transport herself away from her body. Like wind. Judith loves feeling the breeze, watching it stir and swirl things about. Eagle says she needs to transport herself away from her body, to remove her thoughts so she does not feel pain, or even the pain medication. Concentrate on something else, like nature, and use different mechanisms to distract herself. It is the same path but she is learning new coping skills, whatever "tricks" the brain into giving her respite, relief for a short time.

"The mind is a powerful tool." Until Judith started this work, she had no idea of her own capabilities. "Mysticism," as she calls it, "is a powerful way to disconnect but stay connected at the same time. And nature is mystical."

Nature is mystical. Spoken like a true shaman. I marvel at Judith's innate wisdom. "Open your mind to a multitude of ways to learn to deal with yourself. Once you learn to deal with yourself, everything else falls into place."

Judith is a quick study. "I need to compartmentalize *pain* just like fear. Each one has to go in a separate compartment, each situation I can't control. And shut the lid tight! Gently, softly, but permanently; otherwise they become bigger, more important than they are. If you're gentle, they won't become so important. *They won't metastasize.* Transport your mind to another dimension—of peace and serenity."

Functional dissociation. That is what I call that. Trauma engenders dissociation by virtue of the shattering of egoic consciousness. But when the skin-encapsulated ego is cracked open, our capacity to heal is thereby unfettered and unbound. Our capacity to heal, as in Judith's case, is given wings to fly. Trauma can initiate one into otherworldly realms that support healing. Eagle himself is proof of that. But so is Eagle's teaching to compartmentalize pain—with awareness—to foster peace and serenity.

Eagle teaches, "You need to stop concentrating on yourself so much. *Enjoy the things outside yourself.* Let the pain go, instead of holding it so close, dwelling within so much. *Use nature as a distraction.*" Every day, Judith is instructed, she needs to find a quiet place to think of something outside herself. Wind, boats, clouds. Anything to find respite from the misery that is eating her up—the perfect metaphor for the devouring cancer. She is learning to subsume its energy. Brilliant.

In due time, we arrive at grief for the missing body part. Judith's breast. "I am incomplete. I have lost a part of myself." Now Eagle takes a different tone. "Come here to me, little one. You need patience and acceptance, and time—to heal." Judith relates that she is to *embody* grief, let her feelings out and examine each one. "I have a perfect right to feel grief. If I didn't I would be holding things in, and not allowing the process."

Eagle says, "As you walk, the path will be clear. You need to embrace each obstacle and do what's necessary to contain that obstacle, do whatever to pass by that obstacle. Some obstacles will stay and some will become part of you. *They will become an extension of you, an acceptance of who you are now.*

"Embrace the grief. You need to let it walk beside you. In time it will become an old friend. Don't put it in a compartment, let it walk with you. Accept it. You *are* altered. In time, it will be incorporated within you, your new image of who you are becoming."

Judith says, "I need to let my feelings out—crying, talking. But each time I go through this process, it will be easier." There is hope. A profound advance for a woman who formerly was helpless as a drowning dog in the jaws of a polar bear.

There is hope.

*

Devoured
by Judith

The diagnosis was devastating.
Life turned upside down.
Was my mind becoming unsound?

Polar bears devouring blond dogs
With hopeless and empty pale eyes.
This repeated image muffled my cries.

Waiting consumed; nightmares eroded.
I felt trapped.

Life's fragile hold lapsed.

Determined cancer would not win,
Eagle became my guiding light
With advice and tools to fight the big fight.

"Where are you, Eagle?" One day Eagle comes from a long way off. Now begins a time of significance as Judith and I probe from whence Eagle comes, and the workings of his world.

Judith is to call on Eagle three times a week. "Just he and I, for at least half-an-hour." But Judith gets distracted, involved in taking care of other things. Thankfully, her spirit guide is savvy to our worldly ways. If she cannot manage three times, touch bases with him every day, just to say *hello*. Eagle understands that Judith needs that connection. She thinks nighttime might be the best time. But no! Eagle says nights are not good—for *him*. Mornings are better. They settle on 15 minutes. (Their negotiation is fascinating to me.)

Judith calls, "Eagle." He responds, "I'm right here."

Reconstructive surgery will take place in three months. Eagle teaches Judith to look beyond the reconstruction surgery to a positive outcome. Does Judith need the toy eagle again to connect with Eagle in the hospital? He says she will not need the stuffed animal if they communicate frequently. Traditional psychology would view the stuffed animal as a transitional object. Judith has negotiated her way from the transitional object to communication with whom, with what? I remember the difficulty we had before trying to ensure the plush toy made it into the operating theatre. Somehow Eagle believes he can find Judith if their connection is established?

Herein lies the difference between mainstream psychology and transpersonal. In the latter, an individual's expansion of consciousness is held to potentially inform us about the universe itself. What is the relationship between *the inner* and *the outer*? Jesus said: *When you make the two one, and when you make the inner as the outer and the outer as the inner and the above as the below ... then shall you enter* [the Kingdom].[1]

Given Judith's lack of familiarity with the spiritual subtle realm, she requires my reassurance—as the resident expert—that she has not gone 'round the bend. We sincerely consider the nature of Eagle's *ontological* status. That is, does Eagle exist only *relative to* Judith's own individual psyche? Does Eagle live just in Judith's head?

Listen up. Eagle informs Judith that he has been with "her family" for over 500 years. We ponder her European lineage and by virtue of her lineage, her golden tie to him.

Nevertheless, as a means of information technology, Eagle is not fail-proof. *Privately, we test Eagle.* Judith has mislaid her favorite wristwatch and fears it was lost, swallowed by ocean water while canoeing. We ask Eagle, was he aware of her losing it? Where is it now? Eagle agrees her wristwatch was swallowed by the water. (Judith's watch turned up later in her jacket pocket, bound for the washing machine.) So much for Eagle's omniscience. When we confront him with the discrepancy, he gets testy and flies off. When he does not want to answer, he conveniently fades away. It is clear that Eagle does not appreciate being tested. Apparently no one, material or non-material, likes to be wrong. Maybe other-dimensional beings are more like us than we realize.

Judith develops a practice of "checking in" with Eagle several times a week. After the initial, intense period of preparation for surgery, Eagle sometimes is more distant, telling her he cannot stay. He is "helping someone else." Once Eagle even appears with an injured wing, saying that he has been hurt while flying. *He flew into a tree limb!* Judith and I wonder if this Spirit Guide inhabits *physically material* eagles.

"When I'm not with you, I'm in your world." Judith and I ponder that. So Eagle *is* sometimes in our material world, after all. Sometimes Judith sees him, sitting in a tree, or flying towards her. "But when you call me, I'm in both worlds." "What's that like?" Judith asks.

"It's hard to explain. *It's like a suspended state. A dimensional state of suspension.*" But Eagle seems to vacillate, we note. "Basically, I am from the spirit world. You see me as you want to see me."

So he is mostly in the spirit world? Eagle grows irritated with Judith's queries. "Does it really matter what I am, as long as I'm helping you?" This spirit guide definitely does not want to be branded.

Judith and I ask, "Are all eagles capable of being guides?" "If you choose them, all eagles have that capability. They can become a part of someone if that person wants a guide. *But you have to call them.* You have to embrace it. Not all eagles are with someone. *I was with you because we are one. We are the same—because we both like to soar.*"

"We both like to seek."

Consider the Nature Spirits of the Tibetan Buddhist lineage. An ancient Nature Spirit has inhabited a succession of thirteen Tibetan mediums in the Bon lineage, which possesses a shamanic heritage. "Oracle" refers to the spirit that temporarily enters those men and women who act as mediators between the phenomenal natural world and the subtle spiritual realms. These special individuals are chosen by direct lineage, from father to son or daughter, or granddaughter.

Or the individual is revealed by special circumstance, as when Namsel Dolma walked across Tibet and showed up in public singing at the Dalai Lama's weekly address. *Singing loudly.* She was almost thrown out by the guards but for the Dalai Lama's intervention with a simple hand gesture.[2] Namsel Dolma, Medium of the Tenma Oracle, was formally recognized upon elaborate testing. For 400 years, in elaborate ceremonies only recently filmed for the first time, such Oracles gave prophecies regarding the prospects facing Tibetan Buddhism. But according to the Dalai Lama, "Tibetans rely on Oracles for various reasons. The purpose of the Oracles is not just to foretell the future. They are called upon as protectors and sometimes used as healers. However, their primary function is to protect the Buddha Dharma and its practitioners."

Unlike Judith, sitting calmly on my office sofa, these Oracles flail and stagger about—in profoundly altered trances. Lucky Judith is not a Tibetan Oracle. Their lifespan is limited, shortened by the physical intensity of the trancework. No doubt about it, Judith is channeling someone (or something) truly profound.

Just what is the subtle realm's relationship to material, physical reality? That is an age-old question. Carl Jung posited the notion of *synchronicity* as a meaningful coincidence of events that are not obviously caused by one another. Jung's famous example was an extremely rare Scarab beetle flying *smack* into his office window, while he was analyzing a dream about a *scarab* with a highly skeptical client. The relationship between the two realms—inner and outer—became conjoined. Our inner work can influence the weather, knew the shamans of old (and new). *Rain* dancers summon the rain by virtue of their inner state of mind.

Death is the constant companion of any cancer survivor. Death becomes Judith. Her fear of Death lessens, thanks to Eagle. Judith asks Eagle what will happen to her when she dies. Eagle promises that he will be present to escort her across the boundary between the realms. Eagle will be there to show her the ropes. Whereupon Judith will also assume the form of an animal, and act as Guide to others. He suggests

101

an owl—for flying, and wisdom. Sounds good to Judith. She is "glad I chose Eagle. They see everything."

"Animals are more spiritual than humans," she says, without hesitation.

Truly Eagle seems autonomous to Judith. Whoever, *whatever* he is, Eagle helps Judith negotiate healing with penetrating insight and wisdom. The Higher-order Intelligence shining through this seemingly autonomous entity *personifies* the ability to see things from a higher perspective, just as sharp-eyed eagles do. Judith will need that higher perspective as her healing progresses. For a powerful "negative" reaction within her psyche mobilizes to attack anew.

*

Dark thoughts assail Judith. Together, we talk to Eagle. Dark thoughts have had a depressing effect on her for as long as she can remember. The same theme plays over and over, with Judith feeling helpless in the face of it. She is attacked, raped, beaten, tortured in another realm, "brutalized" in every way. It runs in her family, you know. Now I hear about the fearsome head of Judith's family, her father.

Father was a bully. And Judith's docile mother just could not protect her. Though father's bullying was mostly verbal, shoving and hitting were not unknown. I hear about how Judith's own father beat her sister severely with his belt, even made her pull down her pants in high school to beat her. Judith herself was bedwetting until she was six or seven. Her father would wake her up in the morning by throwing a cold glass of water on her.

Not surprisingly, abuse runs in the family. Father himself, was beaten by his own alcoholic father. He left home at sixteen. Whatever had happened to her mother was unknown. Judith's long-suffering mother "kept everything inside," but it all came out in medical problems. (Dare I say, like Judith?)

Eagle says, "Call my name" to stop the evil thoughts. "And I will help you disperse them." Judith does not believe she can do it alone. "There's the path—like the fears you had. Together, we will put them into a box." Calling Eagle's name diverts her negative thought process to the positive. These are "old, black thoughts." A stronger, positive force is needed to stop them. Feeling safe and protected, Judith gives Eagle a hug 'round his neck. She can "see" his head. Eagle has a "presence, a large presence."

Now begins our serious practice of delving into Judith's inner space. We begin to consciously track her violent scenarios. They had become more frequent since her cancer diagnosis. "Once your body has deceived you," there's a sense of loss of control. We must break that pattern. Take control. Judith has an uncanny ability—born of dissociative trauma—to remove herself from the scene. "To see the big picture." But from that other, objective perspective, her "new me" has some neat new moves.

Almost every week she has troubling scenarios to report. "I'm tormenting you," says her (inner) brother, who had become a bully like her father. Judith's imagery is vivid, totally spontaneous.

Seemingly autonomous, lucid imagery.

But the turning point in a lifelong destructive process happens naturally enough. Again I counsel Judith to question, to interact with these autonomous, internal images. "What are you doing? Why are you tormenting me?" she asks her brother. "To get attention. And because I can!" Shock, shock. He has certainly got our attention now.

Judith responds, "I'm *not* going to allow this."

"How're you going to stop it? Nah, nah-nah nah."

She directs her *inner* self to turn her back to him—and his tormenting image fades. Nor does it return. Judith has hit upon an effective strategy. Previously her "inner" bro had shadowed her around her house, causing Judith to go into her bedroom and lock the door, whereupon he tried to "bust the door down" while she went out the window!

Each scene is more horrifying than the next. Judith is raped by an unidentified man. "Why are you doing this?" Her voice is not accusatory, yet forceful. "Because I can." "I'm not going to allow this," and she turns away. Very calm, cool as a cucumber. By now, Judith is actively intervening in the scenarios. She has become a part of the imagery, turning her back to the attacker. This image fades as well.

"Amazing!" I say. "I take your information to heart," she says, "to help myself!" She has plenty of heart, this one.

The third (inner) scene finds her husband robbed and killed. "Horrifying!" He went for a walk and never came back. She finds his body in the brush. Caught unawares and unprepared, Judith did not intercede. She was not expecting this from her own psyche. Next time she will be prepared. Gird your (inner) loins, take up your sword.

Another scene has an unknown man creeping about her house. Judith looks out, watching him. She manages to call 911 but is too fearful of her safety to confront him directly. She will intervene directly next time.

Now the images subtly change. Dangerous threats transpose into simple worries, such as her husband neglecting to do something or other. She deftly stops them before they gain strength, moving them about like so much furniture on a stage. Judith herself, is on the stage, and as she talks herself through movements, the violent imagery stops cold. Fades away.... Judith "puts the worries to bed," containing them to make them harmless. *Benign.* No cancer growths here. Changing the direction of her thoughts has helped her come to terms with "the new me."

No wonder Eagle says, "I'm not so concerned about you anymore."

So we ask Eagle why he appeared to Judith now and not sooner in her life? Surely she could have used his guidance when first diagnosed with cancer, not to mention, throughout her entire life. Judith speaks for Eagle. "I've always *been there. You just never called.*" Not until NOW did she call. Eagle was *waiting* to be called. That makes us think of calling him more often. The implications of Eagle watching, waiting to be called into action, are nothing short of profound. Eagle, the Witness.

What *is* this subtle realm of energetic connection that awaits us— whose entities spring into action when acknowledged by us?

According to Judith, Eagle claims he guided her to me, among the many therapists on her insurance list of providers. I cannot argue with that.

CHAPTER 7

JUDITH: DJ, MR. EAGLE & THE SNAKES

We need another and a wiser and perhaps a more mystical concept of animals.

Philosopher Henry Beston

So far Judith's process involved Eagle, a spirit guide. While Eagle's objective reality, ontological status or origin, remained undetermined, it was generally only his function that mattered to me. Given my role as the sole support and facilitator of Judith's psycho-spiritual process, I was delighted she had help. As greatly surprised as we were when he first arrived, Eagle provided such tangible guidance that we grew to rely on him. Nor was it a treatment goal that Eagle be absorbed or integrated within Judith's consciousness. Though she might question his relationship to herself at times, we never proceeded as if he was a dissociated aspect of Judith. Eagle gave ample evidence that he was autonomous. We took our cue from him.

Judith is quite adept at a form of inner "seeing" called Active Imagination by Carl Jung. But with Judith this is no deep hypnotic trance, not even a guided meditation. For I do not make any suggestions; nor is she highly suggestible. Judith sits with her eyes open for the most part, but she simply concentrates and speaks in a quiet voice. That is how it happens that one day Judith discovers a dissociated part ... of ... herself.

Even given Eagle, what followed was a development that frankly astounded me. Judith's psyche happened to encompass a movement of consciousness that had virtually gone underground.

Some part of Judith that she "sees" as herself, though at a younger age, appears to be in a "dark cave." Indeed, this young-ish woman has been living in a cave for much of Judith's life. She is apparently stuck, caught fast, ensnared *in a dark cave ... with snakes!* Obviously unschooled but with a native wisdom, I am reminded of Casper Hauser, the early 19th century German youth who grew up in total isolation—for as long as he could remember he spent his life totally alone in a darkened cell.

Dark Judith has this to say about her rescue, "It was overwhelming—the shock of the light."

Naturally I counsel Judith to begin the process of communicating with this vital part. But I confess I had no foreknowledge of how this process would evolve. I certainly had no agenda, not even a plan to reintegrate this aspect. First contact was surprising enough to us both.

So Judith begins to slowly make the acquaintance of Dark Judith, nicknamed "DJ," during short bouts of active imagination or inner work. It is truly a significant day when Judith manages to coax DJ out of her cave. And when DJ climbs a tree for the very first time, she lifts her face up avidly to the Sun. *Such glorious warmth and light.* It is another landmark day when Judith "sees" herself embrace DJ, who daily grows in trust.

Thus Judith, intrepid traveler in the subtle realm, embraces this segment of her journey.

But *snakes?!* Kundalini energy is that vital life force energy first delineated in detail in the Eastern spiritual traditions as lying dormant at the base of the spine—until called into action or activated, for example, through yoga. This vital energy is the wellspring of the energy of transformation, and ultimately, enlightenment. Awakened Kundalini may also make for spiritual emergency; I had already assisted in such processes. Proprioceptive (sensory) physiological symptoms can be very disturbing and even mistaken for a psychiatric disorder. But I had never known of a process involving the seemingly autonomous and *visual* enactment of this energy as symbolized by snakes.

Now, we both realize that Judith has suffered some deep trauma that caused the dissociation that was DJ. During one session Judith is able to directly perceive her own shattered psyche.

Split. Into. Pieces.

Judith "sees" shards. Besides Judith, DJ and the snakes, there are a few major pieces and lots of little ones. (She draws a picture.) During one memorable session, Judith engages in the process of collecting these pieces, the shards of her own shattered psyche. I suggest we direct them to be absorbed into either DJ or Judith. But Judith, as egoic consciousness, is really the centerpiece of our recovery efforts. So the "pieces" readily merge into Judith's core.

Like a shadow, DJ also comes into Judith, completely unbidden. But then she moves back out again. The integration does not last, nor was it repeated. Nonetheless, now DJ feels "so much closer" to Judith. Judith herself felt a delicious warmth, as did DJ. "Delightful."

As the larger pieces become integrated Judith "sees" movement. "I feel alive!" Judith declares. A part of her core energy— her life force— had been missing her entire life. Furthermore, it calmed the snakes down, DJ says, when DJ (and the snakes) merged with Judith. Now the snakes can freely come to Judith.

"They are with me now," she says.

There are five snakes in all. Slithering up her left arm, one snake wraps around Judith's neck. Three wrap about her torso. One settles on her shoulders. Judith experiences the snakes as COLD. "Yes, it will be like that for awhile, but it will warm up," DJ says, as all the snakes slither back to her. (DJ is their keeper.) Except the one snake around Judith's neck ... stayed. And her arm is not cold anymore!

Now DJ is almost like an essence rather than a discrete, separate entity. And that is about as far as the integration process goes. Only time will tell if integration will progress.

But after this integration process, for the first time in her life, yesterday Judith "felt physically strong." She enjoys her newfound strength and feels invigorated. Judith feels protected and safe with the snakes, especially with Jacob, "the fiercest one." He is her protector. She is not so vulnerable anymore. "My emotions are always on edge. It doesn't take much to send me over the edge to despair. Maybe now it will be different."

*

Judith has been sick and is now on antibiotics. "Are *you* ill as well?" I ask DJ. "No." Interestingly, DJ was not sick when Judith was sick. DJ does not carry the emotional or the physical aspects. But she is Judith's core stability. I suggest Judith ask DJ for help with her sinus infection. DJ says she will send *Judy*. The snake. DJ, who understands each snake's essence, will talk to her and intercede on Judith's behalf. While *Amy* provides emotional help, *Judy* "works on your body's system—to make it stronger."

Is Judy capable of effecting change in Judith's autoimmune system? Apparently so. Then Judith's ability to work with Judy could affect her overall health and even her ability to heal from cancer. That is a profound discovery, indeed.

Judith asks DJ how certain snakes have certain capabilities. "It's hard to explain," but there is a "flavor" she senses. Only a few have a distinct flavor: Amy. Judy. Jacob. Of the five snakes, *Amy* calms; *Judy* is for health; *Jacob* is the protective guardian, the warrior. The gatekeeper.

*

Judith hears DJ on the right side of her brain. Eagle is also mostly on her right. This makes meaningful sense as the right hemisphere is known to be the intuitive one. DJ perceives Eagle, too. She perceives Judith's spirit guide through Judith, as a kind of secondary perception.

109

Theirs is a complex layering of energies and consciousness.

Nor is Eagle completely out of the picture though the frequency of his communication with Judith has lessened. Eagle interacts with other animals quite well. For example, he is of assistance in getting other animals out of the way of Judith's car. Once Eagle sent Rabbit to her, "a novice in training." (Living on Whidbey Island as we do, the deer and other wildlife are in constant peril on the main thoroughfare.) Eagle spoke to Rabbit, "I'll go in front of you." Presumably to clear the way. What did Judith experience? She did not see a physical rabbit, but she felt an airy movement. She definitely felt a presence. After the drive, Judith called Eagle and told him he was not needed anymore.

"Thank you," she politely said. He appreciated this and disappeared.

"Can DJ talk with animals as Eagle can?" I ask. "No, but the snakes can talk to other animals on the level of feeling." It is a sensory communication that takes place with the earthly or physical level. DJ uses the snakes to communicate with animals but she herself cannot.

I ask Judith if DJ still goes out at night with the snakes. (Apparently DJ and the snakes explore outdoors while Judith sleeps at night. The wilderness of Whidbey Island delights the entourage. The implication of such unbounded consciousness delights me.)

DJ answers through Judith. "Yes. Tell her, yes."

*

Now Judith talks to DJ every day, checking in. Judith is about to take a trip to the Galapagos Islands. "The snakes are really looking forward to it. Where you go, I go," DJ says to Judith. I wonder aloud what the snakes are capable of. After all, snakes have been known to swallow their "food" whole. But Judith is adamant on that score. "They'd never hurt anyone. They can't hurt any of the animals, you know."

I express audible relief on that score.

When Judith returns, she reports that the trip was "out of this world." Judith herself was transported back in time. The snakes felt right at home. Animals were everywhere. The entire trip was "an enlightenment process." For her. For DJ. For the snakes. Truly, they felt at one with Mother Earth. Everyone was appreciative of nature, the environment, the stewardship they witnessed. Their Ecuadorian guides were so enthusiastic! Their sacred duty is to preserve the environment—for all time. By their full participation, Judith, DJ and the snakes partake in that duty.

*

A friend of Judith's had terminal breast cancer, and she died alone in her apartment, unknown to anyone. She was actually dead for one week before anyone found her body. Judith was horrified. Blood was everywhere. Eagle "knows" about Susan. "I'll do what I can" to set her spirit free. "I wished you'd called me earlier," Eagle says. Judith confides that she is not afraid of death herself. "Eagle has already told me he's going to be there for me." Judith accepts that with easy grace. Yet the implications of that are nothing short of profound. If only others could be thusly comforted.

We ask DJ if hearing about this death upsets or disturbs her. "No, it didn't upset me or the snakes." But DJ does feel an oppressive energy. We resolve to put salt on the floor for an energetic healing ritual. Salt is an energetic cleanser. After the salt, the oppression is gone. Dissipated. Peace comes.

*

DJ wants to ask me a question. But she cannot readily speak. "I feel incomplete," she says. Judith answers, "But I depend on you, and you depend on me." Nonetheless, DJ is fearful, fragile and unengaged at the beginning. There is clearly more work to do. And DJ does not want to "merge" with Judith because of Judith's "issues." At first DJ is scared of Judith's emotions, but learns to call on her for help. Communication between the two is the key to their mutual healing. If only they could sense each other's needs and act on them, "I'd be whole," says Judith, with an open pathway between them. But DJ's fear is that Judith's emotional weakness and her physical disturbances will be overwhelming.

Judith says, "DJ gives me stability when I'm depressed and sad. She gives me a hug and sends Amy, the snake. Amy *does* emotion. But DJ is not yet ready to take on that burden."

I follow *their* process instead of imposing one of my own. Integration of all aspects—assimilation of all dissociated parts—is not always in the best interest of the whole. It varies according to the individual psyche.

Nonetheless, "we've freed her," says Judith. Indeed, DJ is feeling more whole (while not completely). The two are independent yet more connected than ever. Still DJ does not feel entitled to ask a question.

She needs to project herself to Judith, instead of Judith all the time having to having to go to *her*.

"You have to come to *me*," Judith says to DJ.

Judith herself would like to feel more comfortable and complete instead of agitated. DJ does see Judith's negative images but she is not ready to work with Judith on them. "I really don't know who I am." She needs more independent time to find out who she is.

One day some months later, Judith says, "DJ wants to talk directly *'to Dr. Colli.'*"

Will she be able to speak directly to me? DJ speaks with another voice, a halting voice. One I do not easily forget.

"Dr. Colli, my name is Judith also. I have one question for you that is so important to me. *Why did I get left behind? I need to understand why I was left in the dark for all those years. Please don't think I don't appreciate what you and the other Judith did for me. You were so patient, and had you not been so determined, I would still be in the dark. This question haunts me, and I would appreciate it if you would answer it.*"

I ask DJ if she remembered when she first split off.

"Yes. At sixteen. Your father was violent and was hitting your brother's wife. (Judith says, "I remember that incident; it was *shocking*. I remember being frozen.") *It was like being torn apart. I tried to hang on, but I just drifted away. I called out to you* (Judith) *but you didn't hear me. And then everything was dark. Why was I the one that was sent into darkness?*"

Thus DJ speaks of the traumatic splitting when sixteen-year old Judith witnessed her father's brutal assault. DJ "split off," expelled into darkness. Until rescued.

I speak to DJ about emotional shock and trauma. I speak to DJ about her snakes—that they contain Judith's core energy. I speak with tears in my eyes. And I tell her that she needs to practice calling out to Judith for help. Until rescued. Time and time again.

DJ replies, "Yes, without the snakes I wouldn't have survived. I would not exist without the snakes. We seem wrapped all together. But I would like to feel myself separately from the snakes. I need more time. I am a work in progress. I know Judith and I need to be close. I didn't know that at first. *But I have to find me first. And feel comfortable with me. I'm not there yet. Judith has agreed to give me more time. As always, I'm appreciative. Now that she talks with me every day, it's good. I feel this will be resolved in time. I thank you for your advice. But it still doesn't answer the core of my question.*"

It is with difficulty that I speak because of the emotion I am feeling. "You represent the core that had to be saved. *You* are the core of Judith."

"It was dark for so long. But I did survive. I'll think about this. I know Judith needs me. I didn't know at first. I've come a long ways from the dark. *I thank you because it gives me comfort to know I wasn't thrown away as so much rubbish.* [At this point, I frankly sobbed.] *I felt abandoned. You've given me hope. We will make it right in time. I have to feel strong in who I am. You've given me hope that my essence is meaningful. I know I survived. No light, no sound, nothing. Until you and Judith, together found me. You saved me. Through your diligence and determination. I came out into the light and was reborn. It's so overwhelming, in the dark. I'm so grateful. That's really why I'm determined this will work out. But not straight away.*

"I don't want to talk anymore."

Judith changes voice and comments, as herself. "I didn't feel the fissure. But I always felt adrift. I never felt like I had substance. Floundering around all those years without purpose. Decisions, I made— yes, but I never felt grounded and whole. I never felt whole—like there was a hole in me that was empty. It's kind of removed now."

*

Next morning Judith called Eagle to her. Judith asked Eagle if he saw "the split" in her when it first occurred. Did he see the traumatic shattering of her psyche that created DJ and the snakes? "It's not my realm," Eagle said at first. But then Eagle admitted that he did indeed, see it. Eagle claims he was witness to the splitting.

"Yes, but there was nothing I could do. You didn't know I existed."

Sometimes conscious awareness is everything. Without it, often the hands (or wingtips) of other presences and entities are tied.

*

Judith had a landmark dream. A polar bear sat with a friendly expression and warm eyes. It approached Judith, running. But the bear had no inclination of violence. She did not have to be afraid. In fact, it was communicative. Empathetic. It was a reversal of her formerly devouring fears of cancer—also symbolized by a (dream) polar bear. When she tells me this dream, Judith says the polar bear was looking at her— just like me.

113

Truly, I have tears of compassion in my eyes as Judith tells me her dream.

Judith has had to contend with her fear of a reoccurrence of cancer. Thankfully, her cancer check-up reveals nothing. So she lets her fear dissipate. The polar bear is not dangerous this time around.

Even DJ remembers this dream. She was prepared to help if asked; she was prepared to intervene. But DJ saw something else, too. DJ "saw" Eagle in the dreamscape—as a Light moving towards the polar bear. And when the Light touched the bear—friendly or not, the bear stopped in its tracks. So Judith has a protector even in her dreamscapes!

Judith also dreamt of a rigid Gingerbread man lying on the ground. DJ saw how Gingerbread man got there, while listening to our session. Something created it out of snow! Lots of cold snow in these dreams, though warmed by eyes and friendly expressions. That same something turned the gingerbread man brown, then called Judith softly by name. DJ thinks the polar bear represents hope of resolution—of working through the *barrier* between her and Judith. She thinks Gingerbread man represents the chasm between them. It is "man-made, a barrier we put up to protect ourselves from everything that hurts us."

Judith is dealing with the possibility that cancer can come back. But she is stepping over that fear and moving steadily down her path. However, her fear of cancer resurrects her original trauma, the loss of part of herself. "I've created that barrier myself for protection." There is hope on the other side.

Gingerbread man is huge, ten to twenty feet tall. Judith is now being invited to come over to the other side of the barrier; she needs to cross over her fear. However, Judith does not like the taste of gingerbread! But not liking it is part of what she must overcome. She must reach across the barrier of dislikes and prejudices—to accept them and get past them—to become whole.

Amazingly, I have gingerbread men cookies in my kitchen. I excuse myself, and magically reappear with a plate of cookies. Together, we each eat one. "It's not so bad. The more I eat it, the better it tastes," Judith says.

No longer wandering aimless without direction, Judith is about to embark on a writing course. Writing, and sharing her poetry will help her find confidence. DJ says, "Let's get to work."

*

Gingerbread man still appears inert. Stilted. Surely that is symbolic of the part yet to be energized within Judith. She is still struggling, as if within an arctic wasteland. Trying to find her way, not yet comfortable with others, much less herself. In social functions she is still protective. Tight. "People don't find me approachable," Judith says.

DJ says Judith's dream struggles are based on their separation. She knows that Judith is lost. But DJ is steadfast. She is determined to make them whole. They are like Siamese twins—joined at the heart. DJ says the key to wholeness is the snakes.

"But you have to call me more." DJ can intervene in the dream if called. "Talk with me," she says, "and the snakes through me; they are part of me." Apparently they are a vital part of Judith, too, her life-force energy. DJ says to call on her whenever she has an emotional need, such as upset or confusion. So the next time Judith felt melancholy at the gym, she called on DJ, who put her arm around her saying, "Amy wants to come over." Judith could actually feel Amy Snake slither up her left arm, and she started feeling better. Her sadness disappeared.

Though DJ understands she is part of Judith, she is nonetheless very grounded. She even gives relationship advice. Judith's sister treats her as inferior, a person of little worth. She is demeaning to Judith. No wonder. Their overbearing bullying father beat her. Any sign of emotion was cause for ridicule by him. Judith is showing signs of emotion now. She is draining a reservoir of emotion. "Was she sad growing up?" I ask.

Judith answers. "Yes, oh yes." So DJ sends Emily Snake, and puts her own arm around Judith.

"I am your Soul," she says.

"This is just my opinion but you can change the way you interact with your sister. You allow her to dominate. You need to neutralize her. I understand your perspective but I look at it differently." So Judith tried a new approach. DJ says that the only way to defend yourself is to take control. Good advice for the meek.

DJ sent Amy Snake over to Judith at the gym again to help with her overwhelming sadness. Amy helps with emotional instability. She slithers up Judith's left side, and settles on her neck. I suggest Judith call on Amy before she intervenes in family arguments. Call on the snakes to change her entire demeanor.

DJ says, "You need to step back, take a breath."

If Judith persists with this practice, stability will come.

115

*

Judith rarely has negative images anymore. She talks with DJ every single day. But when Judith sees scenes on TV of children in Haiti with their limbs torn off, she is upset and calls DJ for help. DJ says, "Now, take a deep breath and calm down." "I always feel your turmoil but I stand back until you ask for help. I enjoy helping because it helps us feel more connected. Closer."

Judith says, "I want to work on emotions. Not to be so reactive, to absorb whatever comes to me and respond sensibly. Not to take it personally." Throughout her interactions with her husband, friends and family, the serene part is DJ. In the face of others' distress, such as Haiti victims, DJ directs her to send positive energy. DJ will help through the snakes but Judith can reach out to them with spiritual words of caring and support. "I can send spiritual energy; that makes me feel good," Judith says. After all, during her mastectomy surgery, she was above herself (out-of-body), talking to herself. "Everything is going to be okay."

I tell Judith the legendary near-death story of a passerby who sent prayers to the victims of a car accident. Little did she know that one of the victims had left their body and actually "saw" a pure white energy emanating from that onlooker's car. So, that NDEr memorized the license plate! After their recovery, they tracked down the car's owner and showed up at the house with flowers—in gratitude.

Yes, our prayers register in Haiti.

*

Judith's physical health has suffered. No doubt she had been weakened as a result of the fundamental shattering of her psyche that led to DJ's existence. Previously she had been prone to getting sick from flu's and asthma. She is very reactive, has environmental sensitivities and allergies galore. Now her vital energy is coming back. Though she feels it as *DJ's* energy, that is, dissociated, it feels lively and strong.

On the physical level, Judith has adhesions from scar tissue. Eagle had counseled, "Think of yourself as a warrior. Wear your scars proudly as a warrior's badge of courage." But Judith feels aching pain. Adhesions to the breastbone have formed. Judith is doing massage herself, but I suggest she talk to her scar tissue, and ask what might help. Judith so effectively dissociates her awareness that she just might get an answer. And she does. Talking to Breastbone works best. It seems that an organ is much more aware than undifferentiated nerve and tissue.

Q. Is there scar tissue attached to you? A. "Yes."

Q. What would help? A. "Don't know. But talk to me; call on me before you massage yourself tonight. We'll see [if it is beneficial]."

Can Judith talk to *my* tooth? Or my lower jawbone? "I'll have to stare at you," she says. But sure enough, my Jawbone answers through Judith. "[The tooth] *is infected.*"

Q. Does it need to be removed? "No." Jawbone says it does not know what should be done but "yes," it can be healed. It is "tired of this pain." Apparently it has been festering. Jawbone tried to bring antibodies to fight the infection but it was not enough. Judith easily locates the pain behind the tooth. If I do laser therapy again, Jawbone can feel the healing energy and direct it. That is a promise that denotes a fair amount of conscious intentionality—and agency. Still, Jawbone's a little muddled later. Jawbone does not readily respond and even becomes defensive, saying, "You're asking me things I don't know." So Judith makes it clear that it need not respond to what it does not know.

Judith is good at this. This comes as no surprise.

Judith's own pectoral muscle was cut four times during surgery. Pectoral is irritated and feels "abused." So she asks Breastbone to speak to Pectoral. But Pectoral's cranky and will not respond. Is it angry about being traumatized? Breastbone does not know. The nerves in her left breast respond though. Do Nerves communicate with Pectoral? Breastbone will ask. But Nerves' consciousness is "fleeting."

Judith does a "general body call." Breastbone says Pectoral is not talking. Nerves say, "We're so scattered." Judith will ferret out information as a conduit. Pectoral is "pissed." Angry! Judith tries to communicate with her right Pectoral muscle. "But it won't talk to me either." It is angry and snarling with pain. But the last massage was "wonderful," Pectoral grudgingly communicates.

Judith is involved in some remarkably complicated negotiations.

Interestingly, Judith was a shop steward in her union at work. She was a most tenacious go-between. In essence, she is doing the same thing now, in what I call "body talk." Finally Judith's giftedness is unfolding—the shamanic abilities that naturally result from the healing of dissociation and trauma. Judith exemplifies how dissociation can become highly functional. She even considers further training to validate and authenticate her abilities. "Where should we go [for training] *to better control the communication, to gain strength and clarity?*" Judith asks.

Naturally, Judith's "we" includes DJ and the snakes.

I once counseled a horse whisperer , who did energy work under-cover, covertly as massage. Susan could not only communicate with horses but diagnose and treat them at a distance. So I have worked with *interspecies communicators*, mediators between humans and other animals. And between humans and otherworldly species, sometimes known as aliens. I wrote the forward to a best-selling book written by a woman who believed herself an alien, who conversed with cats. For doctoral work, I helped interview an intuitive who communicated with weeping trees in Serbian war zones. Most assuredly, she said, trees *weep* for us humans. But as a communicator between dissociated, war torn parts of the psyche, or as spokesperson for ailing body parts, I would recommend Judith of the Snakes.

*

While we sit in session, the five snakes like to go to an empty lot quite far away. Once unconscious, unhappy and lost in a cave, this consti-tutes an outing, "an opening," for them. "Enlightenment." Judith's consciousness is vast.

But Judith is still not confident that she is not conjuring all this up. She has trouble believing that she has capabilities that are truly insightful and not made-up. So Judith talked with DJ, who reassured her that she, too, hears the various parts. Skin. Breastbone. Jawbone. Pectoral. "It's a real communication!" she excitedly reports to me. She is not imagining, making believe or conjuring it. She really *can* com-municate with her own body parts and those of others.

DJ says, "If we hadn't got split off, we would have been a force to be reckoned with—with the snakes as our energy source. We would've really made a difference. Now, we must deal with what we have.

"We are starting afresh."

CHAPTER 8

ABBEY: BAD TO THE BONE

We are all witches and shape-shifters and healers and gods and goddesses, and we must stay together and join forces to lift each other up.

Margaret Cho, *I'm The One That I Want*

Abbey is appealingly childlike in her demeanor and dotted pink tee shirt. She speaks with a southern twang. That and her soft-spoken, polite verbiage ("yes, Ma'am") give the impression of a ladylike, pink cushion of softness. In fact, she is *darling* (I do not tell her that) though she is overweight. Rotund, with full rounded flesh, Abbey weighs over 300 pounds. Her sweetness covers a solid mound of morbid obesity.

Abbey's pink tee is dotted with tiny, black Death's heads, and her hair is dyed an unlikely red. *Rad* red. Abbey has sought me out for my otherworldly expertise. She is self-selected for my psychotherapy practice. Acting on a hunch, she is drawn to me through her Google search of Close Encounters. Abbey brings a startling dream to our first session. She is in her own bedroom. She hears a loud noise and sees a HUGE object—a disk-shaped flying object that is an extraterrestrial spacecraft. In dreamtime, Abbey is too afraid to go outside. That dream ends.

Another dream begins when she walks through my door to therapy.

What Abbey has accomplished in her life so far is inspiring. Abbey has already quit her chronic misuse of marijuana, and other drugs. She is clean and sober now. That alone is impressive. Surely we can apply what she learned about self-control to her weight. Anyone that can quit a near-daily drug habit has got to know something about motivation, and willpower. Ultimately, when it comes to weight loss, surrender will prove more to the point. Hers is a spiritually transformative story about weight loss—with a twist.

As LSD is merely an *amplifier of the contents of the psyche*, I ask about her experience with it. Sure enough, Abbey relates valuable information. One past LSD trip revealed a fearful hurt "puppy" sitting in the corner. Cruelty to animals is anathema to Abbey. I surmise that Abbey has suffered some abuse that her psychedelic journey restaged.

Trauma recycles in the psyche until it is processed and integrated.

Poor lil' pup.

Yet Abbey is a profound teacher not only about the issue of weight and its correlation with childhood abuse, but about the power of the fractured psyche to heal itself, precisely through the growth and integration of its fractured parts.

Abbey's story is extreme. Abbey was born with jaundice. Her parents' religion forbade any blood transfusion, so the medical team was forced to use other means to heal her. As a result, doctors subjected Abbey to profound physical trauma for hours after her birth—as they intentionally and periodically *dropped her onto an examining table* to test her neurological responses. Abbey thus faced significant physical trauma during the first few days of her life.

During the course of therapy, Abbey will display shamanic abilities. She realizes she is gifted. *Gifted through damage.* Abbey relates two signs of a Celtic Shaman.[1] Red-haired, fair-skinned Abbey is Celtic to her core. One sign is a "fire in the brain." A neurological firestorm, no doubt. During the course of therapy, we will effectively re-wire parts of Abbey's brain. Deep-seated, habitually used *neural networks* that "work" her addictive pattern of overeating will be re-routed, as she learns other means of managing her distressing emotional states. It is no easy thing to cure an addictive eating disorder. Abbey will need every shamanic gift she has garnered. Healing will take place over time, neural link by neural link.

Abbey's healing is a miracle in slow motion.

The other Celtic shamanic sign is an injury to the foot. Disease definitely plays a role in the shamanic choice of vocation.

The initiatory call in which the vocation is revealed may come during an acute physical or mental crisis. This issue is discussed by Joan Halifax, who writes that the initiation often comes from a crisis of powerful illness involving an encounter with forces of decay and destruction. 'Illness thus becomes the vehicle to a higher plane of consciousness.' She tells of Matsuwa, a Huichol shaman, who did not receive shamanhood until he lost his right hand and *maimed his foot.* Only upon the impending crisis did he recognize his powers.[2]

However, Abbey has suffered from an almost primal sense of insufficiency, just like W. Somerset Maughm's clubfooted "Philip," in *Of Human Bondage.* The medical treatment for clubfoot was actually to break her anklebones—as a newborn—and reset them, naturally, without any pain medication. Abbey's broken infant foot was restrained in a cast. Such physical trauma has set the stage for a profound initiation into dissociation—the shaman's stock-in-trade.

Abbey also had an operation on her foot when she was a few years old. Having been told by her naughty brother that *she would die during the operation*, Abbey fought like a hellcat. She was physically restrained in the hospital.

One theory espoused by transpersonal psychology is highly relevant. According to it, such physical restraint would be sensed, experienced and *held* in her nervous system as non-verbal, physical memory. Physical trauma, including hospitalizations, are held by Stanislav Grof to be even more significant than emotional trauma. A multitude of cases taught him so. The traumas that were *first and foremost* spontaneously revisited—during Grof's decade of facilitating LSD psychotherapy sessions—were physical rather than emotional. That will likely hold true when any deep (altered state) healing work is done.

Until she was four years old, physical violence exploded in Abbey's family when her alcoholic father drank and struck her older brothers. She was told that her father hit her mother *in the stomach* when Abbey was in the womb. So Abbey had physical trauma in the womb—also held by Grof to be stored in the nervous system.

But neither was there any shortage of emotional trauma. At six years old, Abbey threw up for six weeks straight. Together, we will consider the cause of that mysterious illness, although Little Abbey healed handily. But that is precisely when her out-of-control eating started. Soon she wanted to eat ... all ... the ... time. Abbey's painful childhood gives meaning to the phrase *comfort food*.

Thankfully, when she was four years old, her father's drinking stopped. No more physical abuse for her mother and brothers. But somebody was always yelling, screaming. The noise of silverware, pots and pans clanging, things dropping, still triggers her horribly.

Abbey was her father's favorite. Speaking frankly, she says she was spoiled. She cries when she remembers her father singing to her.

Here's the rub. Abbey dislikes herself intensely. Enormously. She considers herself "lazy." "Stoopid." Considers her weight "disgusting." But when she eats, she is not tense. Eating (*over*eating, really) is Abbey's major release from emotional pain.

Trauma and the transpersonal go hand and hand. Abbey's entire family is naturally inclined to the supernatural and the metaphysical. Abbey says she is aware of her spirit guides, two of whom have been with her since birth. She has *eight* guides in all, including the animals—an elephant and a crow. ("A Netsilik Eskimo, regarded as a major shaman of his time, had no fewer than seven spirits—a sea scorpion, a killer whale, a black dog with no ears, and ghosts of three dead people." [3]) On occasion, Abbey gives psychic readings. Three guides work with her for readings. With eyes shut, Abbey readily goes into the subtle realm. That, besides eating, is her only escape.

With such an *adept* in the subtle realm as Abbey, therapy's greatest challenge is grounding her in physical reality. Abbey will readily admit that she lacks the ability to make healthy boundaries, either internally or externally. Internally, she lacks the ability to soothe or comfort herself. Neither does her body readily differentiate when she has had enough to eat. In short, she is *dissociated* from her own body. Bessel van der Kolk, trauma researcher *and* clinician, notes that virtually every survivor he helped heal utilized a physical practice such as yoga, exercise or massage to return safely *into* their body.

Hardly mindful, Abbey overeats while watching TV. She has been depressed throughout her entire life. *Sad.* Eating numbs her elusive depression but it never entirely goes away. "I start to numb myself when an emotion is overwhelming." *Stupid, failure, loser, inferior.* No wonder she cries "all the time."

And, oh yes! Abbey has a subtle (or astral) realm *love* relationship with a well-known musician. Jay and Abbey primarily meet in dreamstates and dreamscapes, or so she says. She paints his music and swears she is his "muse." *Can this be really happening?* I ask myself. Are their meetings conscious for him, too?

The plot thickens. Jay and Abbey actually have met on the physical plane. Jay had asked, "Do you know who I am?" When Abbey asked if he recognized *her*, Jay answered, "I would recognize your aura anywhere." When they both acknowledged what was going on, he told her, "It will have to be our secret." So they only meet up on the subtle plane.

"Visiting," she calls it.

Their relationship serves as an escape for Abbey. That is, until she, balking at being in love *with a married man*, decides to move on. Abbey draws a line. She realizes that their relationship needs to be on equal terms—in the physical world. She has been hanging out in the astral plane even as she neglects the material plane. Soon after we begin therapy, Abbey breaks (subtle realm) ties with Jay. That garners "three stars" from me—in my case notes. Focusing on Jay, she was ignoring physical reality. She has not "stood up" for herself until now. Typically, she has been "taken advantage of" in romantic relationships. Jay is no exception.

A secret relationship? Bound to go to hell-in-a-handbasket. And guess which handmaiden will be left carrying the handbasket.

Are subtle realm relationships *real?* So real that those adept at out-of-body travel have been known to make separate vows regarding monogamy (or polyamory) according to whether they are in—or out of—their bodies. Others maintain their commitment to their embodied marriage regardless. To many Westerners, they are out of their minds. But when trained in a systematic program such as the Monroe Institute's, one learns to experience these realms as having their own structures, laws and objective reality. Those skeptical should be apprised that the United States government sponsored and trained psychic spies to "remote view."

The U.S. government's involvement with psychic matters was born of the need to collect information about the country's enemies. Initial interest originated with the CIA in the 1970's, but the bulk of the research was conducted by U.S. Army intelligence, beginning with a highly secret project aimed at training some of their best officers.... While the CIA was enmeshed in its psychic troubles, the Army began creating a group of hidden or "black" units that would help solve some of its more difficult intelligence problems.... To introduce the general subject of altered awareness to the trainees, the team [Ingo Swann's military and civilian trainees, in what became known as "coordinate remote viewing"] was first sent to the Monroe Institute in Virginia, where they received formal training in out-of-body states.[4]

It is my job to help those with such sensibilities balance *the inner* subtle realm and *the outer* material plane, as well as engage in what I call "functional dissociation."

Unfortunately, Abbey's ability to dissociate has amplified to the point where it has become dysfunctional. Abbey is avoidant. She had "crushes" on TV characters and teachers throughout her childhood. Never dating in her teens due to her strict religion, she never even made eye contact. Her "whole world would fall apart," if those boys found out. Ultra-fearful of rejection even as a young adult, Abbey has been crushed by her crushes. She has a stay-at-home job and few social contacts. Abbey does not trust anyone, and because she assumes she will be rejected, does not give people a chance.

"I don't like people!" Abbey says.

Abbey's DSM-IV diagnosis? Avoidant Personality Disorder: a pervasive pattern of social discomfort, fear and timidity regarding people and interpersonal contact. Abbey does computer work from home, undisturbed by her fellow humans. In the face of conventional wisdom regarding the immutable and unchangeable nature of personality structures (and hence personality disorders), we endeavor to alter hers. After all, according to Buddhists, personality is purely habit, albeit long-standing habit. *Conditioning.* Even conditioning can be unconditioned. What is created can be altered.

Personalities are shaped by early life, their fabric and weave frequently warped.

The backdrop of her fundamentalist Christian upbringing was God-fearing. God seemingly rejected her as well. "Even God didn't love me." This was not a single incident but pervasive throughout her upbringing. Abbey's 1st grade teacher, who "didn't like" her church, *shamed* her whenever she did not celebrate holidays like her classmates. That reinforced her family's shame-based upbringing. They made fun of her when she wet her pants at five years old. That confirmed that whatever happened to Abbey was her fault.

Shame shame, double-shame. Everybody knows your name.

One's first dreams upon entering therapy may predict or foretell the course of therapy, or so Carl Jung taught. I always ask about opening dreams. Abbey dreams about a sick kitten she wants to bring into her childhood home—to nurse back to health and find a good home. Alas! Mother and father "freak-out" in their bedroom. I learn that Abbey slept in her parents' bedroom until she was three years old, while her father was still drinking. *Not good.*

As traumatic material rises to the surface of her awareness, Abbey's anxiety levels rise. So do her overeating and cravings. I try to reassure her that whatever happened was not her fault. But between her church and her family, her terror was reinforced. Abbey's habitual escape-routes (avoidance and dissociation) are survival-based. Not until later will Abbey be strong enough to forgo her numbing behaviors, to feel her pain, and recover from it. Now she eats and *overeats* to numb her pain. Meanwhile, her strength is expressed by her consecration—her dedication to healing.

Like the Biblical Jacob who wrestled an Angel down, Abbey will travel within the subtle realm to wrest her healing Daemon to the ground, and demand a blessing. Abbey, complete with a limp not unlike Jacob's, is a modern day shaman. Her consecration is profound.

"I wouldn't change a thing in my past. We're on this planet to learn."

*

Abbey's history of physical illness is substantial. Six-year old Abbey *just about to start school* became ill from "nerves" and vomited for six weeks straight. Developmental transitions like starting school often involve an impasse for a traumatized child. Not surprisingly, no diagnosis was ever found. Suddenly, unaccountably, she could eat without throwing up.

She ate a bowl of cereal. Frosted Flakes. *They're Greeat!* She ate another bowl of cereal. *Two ... are even Greater!* Unfortunately, she caught a tiger-by-the-tail. That is precisely when Abbey's overeating began. Now she cannot control her emotional eating. We go Time Traveling with EMDR, back to the first time Abbey remembers overeating.

She remembers a bucket, a *pale green* bucket for throwing up. Abbey's memory is very detailed. She sits on the bed in her PJ's, strawberry Pop Tart in hand. She is scared to eat it 'cause it'll make her sick. But she does eat it. She throws up—into the green bucket. She feels permanently damaged. We articulate her Negative Cognitions, negative "I" statements: "I'm never going to get well; I'm shameful; I'm permanently damaged, and I'm weak." It is happening again. Right NOW. Only NOW, we intervene.

NOW is our chance to make things right.

So before she eats the Pop Tart, Adult Abbey walks into the subtle realm, where the memory is still alive. She sits down beside her child self, and asks Little Abbey, "What's wrong? How did you get sick—in the first place?" Little Abbey replies that nobody knows. She points to her lower abdomen.

So I ask, "Who can answer? Who can help? Anyone?"

Adult Abbey calls *Indian,* her spirit guide. She has been aware of him for over 10 years. Little Abbey smiles at his feathers! *Indian* answers Adult Abbey's question about the origin and nature of her sickness. Indian answers that she got sick from a combination of things—nerves from her family environment, plus her body releasing toxins. It is a "cleansing" from the medicine—*the anesthetic she had when she was two years old*—that was trapped in her glands. Sickness was like a safety value, releasing hot steam.

And there is yet another poison Adult Abbey can "see" inside Little Abbey. A black, tar-like poison. It is everything she cannot speak that is detrimental to her. *Toxic fear.* As she sojourns in the subtle realm in an altered state, Abbey becomes aware that she took on her family's burdens *before she was born*. But even that amounts to merely a budding recognition of her true nature. Just a peek at her True Face, the face she had *before her parents were born*. The first seven years of Abbey's life brought trials that she is asked by Indian to see as a "spiritual gift."

It is not yet time to know more. Events will be revealed that she is not yet ready to acknowledge. Once she does, Abbey will have "accomplished a great thing." Her Indian guide pats the glands in Little Abbey's neck, and takes his leave.

Goodbye, Indian.

*

Another session. Though Indian's answers help progress our understanding, we return to Little Abbey to re-mediate the sensory feelings that cause her to overeat. Abbey asks, "What would my life been like without a weight problem?" With EMDR, we target her childhood experience of eating that second bowl of cereal: the turning point. We start with her Negative Cognition, her negative belief about herself: "I'm not satisfied."

But when we check with Little Abbey, she is not hungry for that second bowl.

"What if I give her an apple?" Adult Abbey asks. Little Abbey eats it really fast but wants something sugary, like Frosted Flakes. I suggest a piece of cheese instead. That seems to do the trick.

But eating got reinforced at home. *Cheeseburger cheeseburger cheeseburger* Burger King. Little Abbey got whatever she wanted, food-wise. Moreover, no one ever fought at the dinner table. Everywhere else but not there. Chaos ruled everywhere else. Dinnertime was the only time the house was calm. It was the only orderly time, with the same menu on weekdays. *Thursday was spaghetti night.* Adult Abbey is trying to order a chaotic nervous system. She tells Little Abbey that she can be calm without eating. "When the big folk are screaming, go into your room and listen to music. Don't be afraid. Make your own calm."

*

Again, we *Time Travel* with EMDR back to the beginning. Abbey hated school. In the 1st grade, she was just getting over being sick. She remembers the second day of school, being singled out by the teacher for her religious affiliation. She was made to feel something was wrong with her. All the kids made her feel nervous. The avoidant strain was starting to manifest. Cruelly teased at school, Abbey started to gain weight in 2nd grade.

Time Travel. Adult Abbey confronts her 1st grade teacher, telling her she shouldn't be a teacher—taking out her religious prejudices on little children. Abbey's going to tell her mother and the school principal! We find Little Abbey "split in half, and falling apart." Her psyche fractured under the burden of the pain. She cries at the memory. Abbey has never cried about this before. She cries now.

Little Abbey started believing she was "ugly" in school. She had a crush on her gym teacher in 1st grade, and some kid blackmailed her because of it. She was scared-to-death he would tell. Fear of rejection is an underlying dynamic of the Avoidant Personality Disorder. We go *Time Traveling* with EMDR. Adult Abbey approaches the kid who blackmailed Little Abbey to buy him paper ... *or else!* Or else he swore he'd tell the gym teacher Little Abbey liked him. Adult Abbey STOPS him COLD and "suggests" he walk away.

Little Abbey is super afraid of being rejected. Little Abbey associates *liking* someone with being *bad* and *rejection*. We reinforce that there is nothing wrong with liking someone; everyone feels that way sometimes. We will not let anyone hurt her.

We move on to a memory of her sister shaming her for eating a candy bar at the store when she was 10 years old. "Can't you even wait until we get to the car?" With Active Imagination, Adult Abbey intervenes. "You don't have the right to make me feel ashamed." She addresses Little Abbey, "You should never feel ashamed. Be good to yourself. You don't have to hide. Accept yourself exactly as you are."

129

In response, Little Abbey finds that she does not want to eat the entire candy bar, and throws part of it away. She only wanted a taste anyway. *She was eating to feel better.* Eating is a protection.

Abbey used to hide her eating. She has stopped that now.

Avoidance and protection go hand-in-hand.

After a round of bilateral eye movements in EMDR, the scene abruptly changes. Abbey is in high school; someone is "commenting" on her weight. Teenagers can be so terribly cruel. Bullying wounds us deeply and leaves lasting scars. Short Larry is insulting her. No doubt "short Larry" himself was teased. But his teasing hurts. Abbey tries to hide (just like Baby Abbey tried to "hide" from physical hurt). She tries to pretend it is not happening, to feign she does not hear it. She dissociates from her real feelings, from her true self. "I act like it doesn't faze me—on the outside, *while* inside *I'm really hurt.*"

I ask what would help her feel better. "I want to punch him in the face!"

What happens in the subtle realm, stays in the subtle realm.

Abbey grabs Larry's shirt and pushes him up against the wall. "You're going to get your ass kicked—by a girl!" His friends hear and laugh.

"It felt good to stand up for myself!"

*

Session. Sometimes EMDR initiates a unique altered state. Abbey utilizes it to explore her pervading sense of rejection that began even before grade school. Abbey finds herself standing in front of a movie screen. After a series of baby pictures, four-year old Little Abbey is "shown," jealous of her younger niece. Abbey is not happy now, watching Little Abbey's point of view. She is shown torturous pictures of her family of origin. *The Family.*

"This is the reason. It was not one thing that happened. *It was everything.* We were all abused. It's amazing one of us isn't dead. It was volatile! We were completely overloaded, all of us." Admitting this, Abbey says she has crossed a bridge. It is a relief. "It was terrible but I can move on. I survived it." Some part of her feels different—freer, more open. She can move forward and not be stuck.

"The more I heal, the more *they* heal. It's going to be okay. It's okay to admit that there was abuse in my family. I need to acknowl-

130

edge it. There was nothing I could do about it. *It was not my fault.*"

Abbey cries and cries.

She remembers when she was four years old. It was a particularly bad time—the root of her being sick. It compounded her later illness and became one big, bad thing. *The Big Bad.* "That man who drank was not your daddy. *He was not himself.*"

She always thought that if she admitted the abuse, she would have to forgo her love for her father. But she *does* love her father. And he stopped drinking when she was four years old. That is a matter of fact. As she got older, the violence went down to nothing. She also acknowledges the times when people laughed and smiled.

Abbey is smiling now. "I don't ever remember feeling this unburdened."

CHAPTER 9

THE FOUR FACES OF ABBEY

Getting to know you,
Getting to know all about you.
Getting to like you,
Getting to hope you like me.

Getting to know you,
Putting it my way,
But nicely,
You are precisely,
My cup of tea.

Oscar Hammerstein II

Abbey excels at active imagination, one of her shamanic gifts. In no time flat, we find three-to-four year old *Little Abbey* in a cramped, dark and dirty place with a few broken toys. We place her in a big beautiful, clean house with windows, next to the ocean even though she is afraid to go outside. That house is quite real to Abbey, as if in a lucid dream. But though she can decorate it and change it—*change* also happens independently of Adult Abbey. Little Abbey herself has a mind of her own.

Thus begins our work with Abbey's parts—fractured yet accessible aspects of herself that formed during her greatest traumas.

Abbey's inner child is alive and well. Little Abbey lives within Abbey's psyche. Still she is very real—seemingly independent—yet easily reached. Abbey is embarrassed to tell me that she sometimes gets angry with Little Abbey. And shakes her! Given her self-loathing, that is not surprising. And then Little Abbey ran straight off to Jay, her subtle realm paramour. "He put her on his lap. They've been together before," Abbey says. Little Jay, she reports, is in a terrible dark house. "He's a scared, sad little boy." I counsel her to call Little Abbey away from Jay. *We* need to attend to her and nurture her now.

Little Abbey grows. These split-off parts do that. Given our attention, developmental impasses are passed. Another client's infant self, Baby Sue, first came to our conscious awareness as a six month old. Within a few short weeks of attentive "nursing," Baby Sue "grew" to a year-and-a-half. Only rarely did she emerge after that. At four-to-five years, Little Abbey is talking to us *and* writing. We ask what had scared her so before? She writes a single word. "Dad." She resolutely refuses to tell us more. That is okay. But after that pivotal admission, she begins *going outside,* leaving her house beside the sea. She plays safely on the beach.

Little Abbey is healing at last.

*

Fearful Abbey-Face emerges during active imagination. She is another part, another aspect of Abbey that has been dissociated from conscious awareness. Not surprisingly, she is eating. At first, Abbey-Face is just a transparent face. Largely fearful, she feels guilty no matter what she eats. And she is eating "to fill something up." That alone is a huge self-discovery. Save for a numbing depression, Abbey is largely unaware of her feelings.

Avoidance personified, Abbey-Face is "scared to be noticed." We reassure her we will not take away her food. Deprivation is overwhelming to Abbey's nervous system. Eating functions to soothe her. Abbey-Face exists (or subsists) in empty space, like Infinity "without a lick of comfort." We brainstorm other means for alleviating deprivation, like shopping for art supplies (she is an avid artist). We plumb Abbey's artistic creativity.

Abbey-Face says, "I'm afraid I'll get blamed FOR EVERY-THING." Just like the Lynda Barry comic strip: "MISS FISK, OUR TESTS SHOW THAT NOT ONLY DO YOU HAVE CANCER OF EVERYTHING, YOU ARE ALSO A TOTAL FAILURE AND YOU *DID* LEAVE THE COFFEE POT PLUGGED IN AT WORK AND THE WHOLE PLACE IS ON FIRE RIGHT NOW."[1]

Abbey-Face is fearful that if Abbey heals, "she'll be gone. Disappeared." Reassurance is in order. With "parts work," especially when initially winning their trust, it is vital that their viewpoint be acknowledged. After all, these parts dissociated as a result of intrusive trauma. It is a splitting off of one's self-identity, resources *and* energy. Parts may present with a very real primal fear that they will be gotten rid of ... dispensed with ... eradicated. Terminated. So our Treatment Plan is *not* to integrate the parts—at all costs. I strive to reassure the emerging part that things happen in their own time. The energetic dynamics of the psyche are (and should be) beyond our control.

Nature is in charge. Sometimes full integration happens; sometimes it does not. The parts may continue to co-exist but with more communication and harmony. In many of us, the Inner Child is alive and well.

Surprise! A figure with a bloody ax emerges from the shadows, "the Chastiser." Abbey's life has been more hurtful than she has been able to admit. Like so many who have been hurt, Abbey managed to survive by dissociating. The Chastiser is a male, giant-sized figure with a black executioner's hood. When she encounters him the next time, Abbey decrees, "The only power you have is what I give you."

Thereupon he shrinks to the size of a normal man. She sees him as cowardly, a bully. Though the Chastiser says he has always been present, we wonder where all that judgment came from. Abbey wonders aloud if she was executed in some past life. Indeed, that scenario will later emerge. But whatever her belief system, some part of her is fearful. She relates this to her religious upbringing where she was virtually taught that as a sinner, she was not good enough.

Stairs and a hallway appear through which Abbey-Face goes. We completely remodel her vacuous Subtle realm Living Space—adding flowers, books and comfy chairs. *And* a little, white kitten. Abbey loves any animal, and has a plethora of animals herself. Physically material animals, that is, dogs, cats, birds, fish. The *im*material type "people" her garden: fairies, gnomes and such. Abbey is alive with a passionate love of all life forms.

Soon Abbey-Face is claiming her autonomy, saying to Abbey, "You can't just walk in. You have to knock!" Abbey-Face says she wants a BIG dog. An Alaskan malamute used for pulling sleds. Abbey had one as a child. As she cries, remembering, "Blue" comes running up.

"Blue, I missed you so much. You saved me. *Now I'm going to save* you."

Long-lost pets have a way of showing up in the subtle realm.

*

Little Abbey builds a sand castle on the beach. Abbey-Face has become a full-bodied adult in her twenties (instead of just a face). They both move in together—in the house by the ocean. The two hold hands. *Little Abbey smiles.*

Another adult aspect, AbbeyAnn, emerges. "I am the you that you don't know." She is a young adult, but without all the baggage. She is *not* overweight. She is smart and well-grounded, and can defend herself if needed. She gets things done. And she is not afraid of people. She says she wants Abbey to be *her*, not the other way around. She has always been in the background, so many others needed help first. She wants to take control of Abbey's body but Abbey will not let her, so she is stuck inside.

AbbeyAnn and Abbey-Face are split-off aspects that represent energies and capabilities. AbbeyAnn is sure mean and judgmental. Far from being afraid of people, she thinks she is better than them. In fact, she *hates* people. She wants to be in control. But she is confident and has courage and physical health—good characteristics. AbbeyAnn emerges when Abbey is backed into a corner. She is ready for a fight. She is also prone to blowing up in anger. That is why she does not want to be around people. (Yet I know her avoidant stance is a defensive posture.) AbbeyAnn is "the least broken." She just needs to learn how to stand up for herself. We can practice that.

We sit down with both AbbeyAnn and Abbey-Face. Abbey sees *cords of light* between the two. One wears a black pantsuit and the other, a white dress. Guess which one is which.

They agree to work together.

*

Adult Abbey connects with each part or aspect everyday. But there is another part that overeats who does not come out yet. Abbey can feel her. She is the part that has struggled so with addictions: alcohol, drugs and *eating.* Abbey still gets upset with herself about overeating but she is doing it less. And she does not wake up feeling bad about herself. Her child part has disappeared for now. Trauma does not come up, only the residual effects from it—*overeating.*

Finally, during our session, Abbey "sees" the Rock of Gilbrater, a huge impenetrable rock. She can feel it, rock-hard to her touch. Abbey first *felt* a presence. From the *proprioceptive* channel to the *visual* and *auditory,* her sensory channels open one-by-one with more information. We mediate and morph Abbey's internal environment until her experience is complete. Abbey goes to the rock, puts her hands on it and hears someone inside. Crying. But there is no way inside.

"Hellooo," she says.

"Go away! I'm hiding and I don't want to talk with you. Leave me alone. I don't want to come out," someone screams.

I suggest we introduce an animal—an animal can seem less threatening. How about a puppy? Shall we leave a puppy outside the rock? But it is raining, with dark, heavy and ominous clouds. Abbey conceives of a Golden Retriever puppy, "Happy." Virtually anyone can befriend a puppy. But Abbey does not have any way to get the puppy inside, so *they* try to carve out a tunnel with a pickax. Whoever is inside wants to see that puppy! But it is a long long way through that rock....

When Abbey bemoans, "I don't have any way to get it in" she hears, "Just put your hand through." But Abbey does not want to put the puppy in the long dark tunnel. So I suggest a *stuffed* animal instead. Animal-assisted therapy (AAT), as practiced at Green Chimneys, a New York farm for special needs and emotionally fragile children, is wonderfully effective. Children abused by humans form trust,

136

and learn to love more readily with animals. But supervision is always needed to ensure safety. Whoever is inside that rock takes the stuffed dog.

"Thank you," whoever she is whispers. *Puppy whisperer.*

*

Abbey names her "AbbeyApple," her deepest darkest part. At first AbbeyApple does not want to leave her solitary Rock. But she lets Abbey enter her private abode—just Abbey and no one else. Abbey has to crawl in through a 20-foot long tunnel. It took three long nights! Together they chisel the tunnel so a kitten can go through first.

Abbey connects with AbbeyApple on a regular basis.

"Yes, come in," and Abbey crawls in with a kitty. We declare to AbbeyApple that Kittycat will turn into a stuffed animal if she is mean to it. There she sits on the couch, with an ice cream drumstick in hand. "One day's pretty much like the rest of them 'round here."

Next time Abbey finds that Rock she crawls in through a ready hole. Not surprisingly, it is dark and depressing. AbbeyApple is twice the size of Abbey! She represents the distorted view of how Abbey sees herself. She is watching TV and it is messy, with clutter on the floor, an outdated kitchen, and un-hung paintings. Like an old lady's house in disrepair. She is irritable. Snippy. Snipping and snapping to release the build-up of pressure. Anxiety-prone, she is never just in-the-moment. AbbeyApple has a huge problem motivating herself to clean up. *Abbey-Apple took on Abbey's unfelt pain.* She eats and eats and eats....

"You're fat and lazy," AbbeyApple says to herself.

"But you could live anywhere!" Abbey tells her. AbbeyApple is not yet ready to leave her protective Rock. Finally, she says she wants to live "in a house, by a river in the woods." Abbey puts AbbeyApple in a new house, but the Rock is not gone yet.

*

Always able to feel compassion for animals, Abbey has never felt it for herself. She will develop compassion for herself through feeling it first for that hugely unloved, *huge* AbbeyApple. Abbey herself has lost a couple of pounds. She loses weight very slowly but steadily, pound by pound.

AbbeyApple is now in a big house that is no longer messy—with

Kittycat! She is dressing better though she does not feel great about her looks. She is not as big as before—she *was* 600 pounds! And there is no TV in sight. AbbeyApple agrees to allow the other Abbey's to stop by. Abbey introduces them in a big living room—with art and music and incense. But AbbeyApple persists in saying, "We can't let any other people inside."

She watches movies, sits on her deck.

When Abbey was nineteen or twenty, she lost a significant amount of weight with diet pills, and *anger.* She expressed her pain by drawing twelve hours at a time. Now, she feels numb as AbbeyApple has buried the pain. But she is losing weight as she releases it. Emotional pain has to be felt to be released.

Yet the Chastiser says, "You're not doing enough."

That is not true. Overcoming self-doubt "zaps" her energy. But it is the first time Abbey has admitted she chastises herself for bad behaviors that really are not so bad: TV, eating, not sweeping the floor. She talks badly about herself. "Ugly, disgusting, stupid, lazy, dirty." She has not cleaned her kitchen.

Nonetheless, she manages to "nail his big mouth SHUT!" But she still hears negative thoughts. He says, "I'm not the one doing it, *you are.*" Then he disappears.

She "sees" a crowd of people she recognizes—from church, teachers, her mom, kids who made fun of her at school. I suggest we utilize her shamanic powers. Abbey calls in a Big Brown Bear to defend her.

"You'd better leave her alone." Standing up, her bear is 10 feet tall. Together, they run away. Abbey hugs him and he pats her head. "Everything's going to be okay." Abbey is safe at last. She names him Big John. Big John lives in a meadow. "Everything's perfect. This is how your life is—whatever you don't like, paint it differently. It's in your hands."

"Can I apply this to not loving myself?" Abbey asks. "Repaint how I feel about myself?" As Abbey touches her stomach, a representation of herself is created. She is wearing a blue & white flowered dress. Too much like a grandma! So she sees herself in jeans—a perfect size 10. She looks real pretty. She smiles. We start with one positive thing: "My eyes are a pretty color."

She will call on Big John again. Animal helpers galore figure in both her inner and outer realities. Abbey gives a lot of love to pets, especially animals that cannot defend themselves. That is yet *another* characteristic she likes about herself.

Active imagination: In a scary wooded area, the Child Catcher from Chitty Chitty Bang Bang approaches. He is dressed in cape and top hat, with grinning Big Teeth. But she must face him herself, and not call any of her helpers. Abbey walks up to him. "You don't scare me. You can't hurt me.

"Yes, I can." Wicked smart.

The sun is going ^{down} down _{down.} She is frightened but pipes up, "You are my creation. I give you power."

"You figured out my weakness," he says, shrinking away. She turns him into a fluttery, white butterfly that flies off. She did it herself!

*

Soon enough that wondrous day comes when Abbey-Face, AbbeyAnn and AbbeyApple all merge into one. There they stand smiling. One **BIG** smile. Instead of a loss, they all stand to gain from it. And though Abbey's integration is not yet *stabilized*—they first come together then drift apart—eventually it is. *She* is. There stands Abbey, of one single mind. One big smile.

One big heart.

*

Abbey tries volunteering at the Humane Society socializing kittens, and joining a community arts guild. She really needs to get out of her house. Social connections form new circuitry in her neurophysiology. New neural networks bridge the gap between her and other people. *Energy not used becomes morbid*. The avoidant fear has structured her personality, so she will need to push hard to transform it. Her avoidance started at school. She did not like being around other children. Noisy, loud children like nails on a chalkboard! Her nervous system is easily overloaded. She cannot stave off others' energy.

"Some filter was blown off me when I was so sick as a newborn." To facilitate deep healing, we Time Travel to newborn Abbey, when her circuitry was first blown out.

Remember Abbey being "shown" a series of baby pictures before a movie screen? Or the scary monster with a Devilish face threatening Little Abbey? "Go away! Stay out!" So many of Abbey's monsters seem to have gotten hold there. Researcher Alan Schore specializes in infancy development and *attachment*—that golden bond of love between infant and caretaker that facilitates brain development. The fearful effect of Abbey's early trauma is affirmed by research into the integration of attachment, affect regulation and neurobiology. "The very rapid form of learning that occurs through the holding and smiling and vocal exchanges of the first months of life "irreversibly stamps early experience upon the developing nervous system and mediates attachment bond formation" (Schore, 2003a, p. 277)."[2]

Together we journey with EMDR to the first 21 days of her life. Can Abbey truly remember anything from infancy? Are the impressions that traumatized her infantile nervous system retrievable to her adult-self? Though Abbey's active imagination is likely a hybrid state of consciousness filtered through her adult mind, the answer is astonishing. *Yes, infancy can be remembered.*

I say, here comes a consequential truth: *I remember being born.*
Can't be done, you counter. Never happened.
Did, is my response.
I found out many, many years later the reason for my remembrance: I was a ten-month baby. Which means what? That snugged away from an extra twenty-eight or thirty days I had a serene opportunity to develop my sight, hearing, and taste. I came forth wide-eyed, aware of everything I saw and felt. Especially the dreadful shock of being propelled out into a cooler environment, leaving my old home forever, to be surrounded by strangers.
All because I had lingered for that extra month and sharpened my senses.
You must admit that gave me an advantage few other humans have had, to emerge with my retina in full register to recall from Instant One a lifetime of metaphors, large and small.
From that moment on I can recollect my life.[3]

Thus wrote Ray Bradbury, one of the most celebrated writers of our time. Among his best known works are *Fahrenheit 451, The Martian Chronicles, The Illustrated Man,* and *Dandelion Wine.* And though these works are fiction, Ray Bradbury's memories are not.

Memories from the first 21 days of life can also be accessed if one's state of consciousness is sufficiently altered. Psychiatrist Stanislav Grof spent almost two decades pioneering the most powerful form of therapy in the world: psychedelic psychotherapy with then-legal diethylamide of d-lysergic acid (LSD). Grof began in Czechoslovakia in the 1950's and continued in the United States at the Maryland Psychiatric Research center in Baltimore, where he participated in the last surviving American psychedelic research program with LSD. He spent many more years developing Holotropic Breathwork when LSD became illegal, mainly due to its unsupervised street use. Grof's extensive documented findings have simply not been dealt with by mainstream psychology, or for that matter, modern science.

Stanislav Grof's findings are revolutionary. Human consciousness can access memories from infancy; perinatal memories, that is, memories from birth; and even memories from the womb. Pre- and perinatal memories are a level of experience that would be integrated into the branch of psychology Grof helped establish, known as transpersonal psychology.

> I have been able to confirm the accuracy of many such reports.... [Subjects] have been able to recognize specificities and anomalies of their fetal position, detailed mechanics of labor, the nature of obstetric interventions, and the particulars of postnatal care. The experience of a breech postion, placenta previa, the umbilical cord twisted around the neck, castor oil applied during the birth process, the use of forceps, various manual maneuvers, different kinds of anesthesia, and specific resuscitation procedures are just a few examples of the phenomena observed.[4]

Grof's findings were initially based on thousands of cases during controlled drug therapies. However, such memories have also been *objectively verified* during non-drug-induced, altered states. Pre- and perinatal experience can emerge spontaneously during many therapeutic modalities, indeed, any work with the deep layers of the psyche, such as hypnotherapy or breathwork; or bodywork, such as Rolfing and acupuncture. Chapter 12 shares a spontaneous emergence from this author's case files during treatment with Eye Movement Desensitization and Reprocessing (EMDR). Veridical records have also been collected from two to four years old about their birth and/or life in the womb. Such ground-breaking research findings have expanded the frontier of human consciousness.[5]

During a relatively high dose of LSD (300 micrograms) one medical professional experienced the following regression.

I decided to close my eyes and observe carefully what was happening. At this point the experience seemed to deepen, and I realized that what with my eyes open appeared to be an adult experience of a viral disease now changed into a realistic situation of a fetus suffering some strange toxic insults during its intrauterine existence. I was greatly reduced in size, and my head was considerably bigger than the rest of the body and extremities. I was suspended in a liquid milieu and some harmful chemicals were being channeled into my body through the umbilical area. Using some unknown receptors, I was detecting these influences as noxious and hostile to my organism. I could also perceive the offending quality of the intruding substances in my gustatory buds; the sensation seemed to combine the taste of iodine with that of decomposing blood or old bouillon.

While this was happening, I was aware that these toxic "attacks" had something to do with the condition and activity of the maternal organism. Occasionally, I could distinguish influences that appeared to be due to alimentary factors—ingestion of alcohol, inappropriate food, or smoking—and others that I perceived as chemical mediators of my mother's emotions—anxieties, nervousness, anger, conflicting feelings about pregnancy, and even sexual arousal. The idea of astute consciousness existing in the fetus and the possibility of subjective awareness of all the nuances of its interaction with the mother were certainly contrary to my preconceptions based on my medical training. The reality and concrete nature of these experiences, as well as their very convincing quality, presented for a while a very serious conflict for the "scientist" in me. Then all of a sudden the resolution of this dilemma emerged; it became clear to me that it was more appropriate to consider the necessity of revising present scientific beliefs —something that has happened many times in the course of the history of mankind—than to question the relevance of my own experience.

When I was able to give up my analytical thinking and accept the experience for what it was, the nature of the session changed dramatically. The feelings of sickness and indigestion disappeared, and I was experiencing an ever-increasing state of ecstasy. . . .[6]

Trauma researcher Bessell van der Kolk jokes that "a few people in California remember being in the fallopian tube, but that never happens in Massachusetts. Basically, before age 3, unless you live on the West coast, nobody has memories for what happens to them."[7] That view is typical of mainstream psychiatry. Yet van der Kolk emphasizes it is not that there is *no* memory. Memory traces do get stored—not in verbal memory, but in *sensory-motor memories* stored in "vibes," for example, a sense of discomfort, anxiety or fear. A study of three to four-year old children, who said that they did *not* remember anything about having been hospitalized at 12-18 months, found that they actually could reproduce the event in drawings and amazingly accurate pictures.

With Abbey, that is, someone who readily resorted to dissociation due to early multiple traumas, and who developed shamanic abilities and proclivities, this level of regression is possible. What follows is Abbey's active imagination, likely a hybrid state of consciousness— filtered through her adult mind. Together, during EMDR we target Abbey's experience of the violation of being dropped on the table at *four days old*. Negative cognitions: "I deserve only bad things; I cannot protect myself; I am powerless; I cannot trust."

Abbey sees herself up close as a baby. She is crying hysterically. "They" pick her up and drop her on the table. Baby Abbey does not have access to words. A nurse wearing a mask picks her up and rocks her, trying to reassure her. But Baby Abbey does not believe her. She *knows* it is going to happen again. She's *without a lick of comfort*. Something *baaaad* is going to happen....

"What needs to happen here?" I ask.

Adult Abbey holds Baby Abbey—and imagines a *soft, pink light* around her, so Baby Abbey knows she is loved. She focuses green light, a healing energy, around the doctors. Baby Abbey seems to respond. Abbey makes the docs *unmask*. Unmask and *smile*. Baby Abbey is going to respond to that, for sure.

Taking the masks off the medical staff is quite astute given developmental research on the effect of the caretaker's *expression* on infants. Mother-infant interactions include baby's preference for eye contact, and attention to gaze-following activities; and baby's capacity to reenact parents' facial displays of emotion.[8]

Adult Abbey suddenly realizes the medical staff fear Baby Abbey is not going to survive! Though Baby Abbey cannot comprehend her tenuous hold on life, their concern makes a significant difference to adult Abbey.

We accompany Little Abbey at two-and-a-half into the hospital for surgery on her clubfoot. There is a little boy with red hair *crying crying crying* day and night. Little Abbey is trapped and cannot sleep. Her foot, up in a sling, *hurts* and she wants to go home. She is angry! Angry! **ANGRY!** Abbey never realized how angry Little Abbey was before. And how much loud noise bothers her! So we *remediate, morph* the scene and *move* Little Abbey to her own room where she can watch cartoons on TV.

We take Little Abbey through her release from the hospital, where she has to walk in a cast. Little Abbey is scared she will fall. We reassure her.

"If you do *fall, you will be okay.*"

*

Abbey is generally not in her body; she is disconnected from herself and her feelings, as if she is in a void. She is always thinking.... But she does *intuitively* connect with the pain of her foot in infancy. *Time Travel.* We journey to Baby Abbey when the doctors reset her ankle bone *11 days after birth.* Baby Abbey is on the examination table, her body stiff from fear. Now Abbey more directly experiences Baby Abbey's spatial feelings and visual imagery: her forehead and shoulder blades are tight, she's kicking her legs on the table. It is very bright and hazy. She hears voices but cannot understand them.

Slam bang!

A man with glasses and a wide face framed with grey hair touches her legs and foot. She senses something is about to happen and she is afraid. I suggest that it won't last long. She likens it to the pressure of a volcano building. Abbey (as Infant Abbey) actually feels horrible pain! And she wants it to stop.

STOP! The pain stops. The worst part is over. She does not want to feel like that can ever happen again. Everything is so scary all the time.

"Why won't someone help me? Why won't someone make it stop? Doesn't someone love me enough to stop this?"

Now she feels disconnected from the physical pain. They're wrapping ... wrapping (making a cast). It is wet, all the way up to her infant thigh. She hears a metal clanking. Someone's crying, *is it mom?* Someone (likely the doctor) pats her head, talking soothingly. The cast is tight and heavy. Her ankle still hurts but not as much. Infant Abbey's jumpy, ready for flight.

It is hard to stay in her body.

But the bad part is over. Somehow she is feeling everyone in the room. Leaving one's body repeatedly will most certainly expand one's perspective. *A Shaman is being born.* The doctor pats her leg and leaves the room.

"Mom picks me up, holding me. With a blanket over me, it's safer."

*

The root of Abbey's fear with people is a feeling of inferiority. "Something's wrong with me." It started with her physical ailments when she was born, and was reinforced by her religion and at school. With EMDR, we journey to the root experience: Baby Abbey was simply not able to process the physical pain when they dropped her on the table. Pain = Bad. "I must be hated. I'm being punished." Abbey "sees" the hospital room from an infant's point of view. There is an eerie green glow. She is wide awake, watching a shadow on the wall. Baby Abbey is tense with fear.

"Something's going to hurt me again. I don't know why. I'm so alone and helpless! *I see a Monster!*"

That is the way the medical team looks to her. Scary. She is trying to hide but she cannot. She cries and cries. It feels like she is *nothing*. It hurts. She just wants it to stop.

"Why won't anybody stop the pain? If they loved me they'd save me and take me away. No matter what I do, the pain doesn't change. *I have no control.* I just want to be alone, to hide. Not to be anymore. Someone needs to save me. I can't do it myself." Even as an adult, Abbey sleeps with her thumbs inside her fingers. She is doing that now, with her fists over her eyes.

The room becomes bright. *Bright.* BRIGHT. Blue-eyed Angel appears above Baby Abbey. She is holding her arms out and taking Baby Abbey up up up to safe light. They are not on the physical plane. "The blue-eyed Angel's petting me!"

Angel speaks. "It's okay, everything's going to be fine. You're going to have a beautiful life."

"But I'm not safe, and my life hasn't been beautiful. Why are you lying?"

"That's just how you see things. It's all in how you see it. Everything as a whole is what makes a life beautiful, not just one or two experiences." Abbey sees a shiny, sparkly, big silver ball—like a silvery moon—that represents her life.

"It's beautiful!" exclaims Abbey.

A radical shift has occurred. "There's something in me that is lighter. That's the deepest I've ever been without a safety net." After today's work, there is a new way she is going *to be* in the world. She experiences some modicum of safety and support, albeit, from the subtle realm, from a transpersonal level of consciousness. Now that Abbey has successfully negotiated her post-natal traumas from childhood, and her traumatic infancy, we turn again to Adult Abbey's physical body. Exercise and dietary changes continue, but now she can more effectively modulate her emotions. Will Abbey's weight loss continue?

Will Abbey stay in her physical body?

CHAPTER 10

ABBEY: ROCKIN' TWIN SOULS

There's always one who loves and one who lets himself be loved.

W. Somerset Maughm, *Of Human Bondage*

One of the most intriguing and provocative themes of Abbey's therapy is how a spontaneously recovered, past-life memory impacted her current life—and contributed to her overeating. C.G. Jung introduced the Archetypal level of consciousness, where universal symbols are observed in dreams and myth, where mythological gods dwell, and heroines such as Abbey awaken by the prince's kiss to live happily ever after. Awareness of the transpersonal level of consciousness begins *when skin-encapsulated, egoic boundaries melt or even dissolve.* As an integral part of her therapeutic process, Abbey will travel through time, following the cords of karma to another lifetime.

On the transpersonal level, we can tap into the Akashic archives and visit any part of history. Linear time is transcended as we relive our childhood and our birth, or relive collective and racial memories. Or get new information about other life forms; or fully experience becoming other *animals,* even animals of bygone eras, such as the Mesozoic Era of dinosaurs. Or trees. *Did you know that trees wept for the violence in Sarajevo?* Or so says one research subject of mine. I have known those who entered the transpersonal realm through childhood abuse and neglect, who communicated more freely with rocks than with their fellow human beings.

Stanislov Grof pioneered therapy with a form of crisis he termed Spiritual Emergency—a radical effort of the organism to restructure itself on a higher level of functioning. Given our global crisis, spiritual emergencies are increasing, making for the rapid transformation of humanity. Karmic memories and past life experiences may intrude; other historical periods may be remembered that eerily connect to one's present life and symptoms, such as phobias, attractions and idiosyncrasies. Such spontaneous episodes of non-ordinary states have remarkable healing potential for emotional or psychosomatic, even interpersonal problems. [1]

One of the manifold forms Spiritual Emergency takes is awareness of subtle realm relationships. This is particularly troublesome (as we shall see) when one's self is experienced as a *soul mate* or *twin flame* of another, but the other person does not share the experience. Some sense of reincarnation may be involved—an ontological hot potato in our current culture. When the nature of being is concerned, churches and science have definitely weighed in. As Grof notes, the Christian Church and science are in full agreement that reincarnation does not exist. The council of church fathers in the 6th century A. D. "voted out" reincarnation from the officially approved scriptures. "It has been a formal heresy since it was rejected by a narrow margin at the Second Council of Constantinople in AD 553."[2] The transmigration of souls was henceforth taboo.

Based empirically upon their personal observations, many who sojourn in the subtle realm would not agree. Nor would professor of psychiatry, Ian Stevenson, whose "extensive cross-cultural research of over two thousand spontaneous accounts of children claiming to be reincarnations of other people has been sufficiently rigorous and consistent to withstand challenge to date (e.g., Christie-Murray 1988; Wilson 1982; Rogo 1985)."[3] Stevenson traveled throughout the world, often in countries such as Thailand and Burma where belief in reincarnation is commonplace, investigating very young children who early on talked about former lives. He meticulously investigated their detailed stories, traveling to the people and places from "former lives" the children quite accurately and inexplicably named. The physical evidence was particularly impressive. *Birthmarks* and *congenital disabilities* marked the children and eerily replicated injuries of the deceased persons.[4] The Dalai Lama's own youngest brother, Tendzin Choegyal, was assessed according to such a sign.

The royal couple had recently suffered the loss of another son—a devout two-year-old who loved to go into the family altar-room and pay reverence to the statues. In March 1945, he had caught a fever—perhaps the smallpox which was raging in Lhasa and against which Kundun was vaccinated that year.

When it was clear that the child's death was imminent, the parents asked the Gadung Oracle to come, but he died just as the medium arrived. Gadung told the distressed parents to embalm the tiny corpse in salt, first marking it in an easily recognizable way, so that the boy could be reborn into the same house. So the servants put a smear of butter on the dead child's left buttock, before the tiny body was embalmed and taken down to the cellars.... When another child was born [exactly a year after the death of her last child], with the tell-tale butter-smear clearly visible on his left buttock, it seemed that the oracle was vindicated:

everyone was satisfied that the dead child had returned.[5]

The resolution of karmic memories of past life experiences that involve previously unfathomable fears, attractions, phobias, even physical symptoms, have remarkable healing potential. Abbey's story confirms that. At the time, I knew that Abbey was connecting on the subtle realm with "Jay," a musician of some renown. I also knew that she had no contact with him in the material, physical realm. Her past life recall began unexpectedly during EMDR. *Spontaneously.* Her experience unfolded as follows.

*

Suddenly, after a round of eye movements, the scene changes. Abbey sees a lake with flowers, lily pads and trees. She is alone, waiting for someone. Something *whizzes* by her head. A man with a beard and reddish hair is standing there. She knows him and "he wants to kill me!" But he is not the person she is waiting for; she is waiting for another man—in secret! She hears a horse. Sees a man she *knows* is Jay, though he looks different.

"We're not supposed to be here! This was the last time we were meeting!" Tragically, someone will be killed. From behind her, Abbey hears "Ruuuunnn!" She runs, but does ... not ... make ... it. She realizes Jay will not make it either. He is 50 yards behind her, and suddenly Jay is dead.

"Was it arrows that killed us? Neither of us made it." Abbey is looking down at the scene from above, presumably having left her body. She says that it was *supposed* to happen.

"That was the eventuality of our choices in that life."

We endeavor to process—with EMDR—her death in a past life. We enter the event again, this time with the foreknowledge of what is about to transpire. We take Abbey into the original scene before the tragedy occurs. Into the original scene she goes, seeing the man standing there, but this time her fear response is altered.

"It's almost a relief. That it's done. It's over—the fear of being caught, the secrecy."

*

Sometimes Abbey says she knows without a doubt that Jay is her *soul mate*, the other half of her. *Twin soul. Twin flame.* That I cannot validate. But I do serve to help her process and *translate* subtle realm experience into the material realm. Abbey believes wholeheartedly that when she and Jay get their problems figured out, they will be together. Like the universe gave them a taste of what could happen—a *carrot* to achieve individual growth. But for now, they are "not even close."

Abbey keeps up a wall, a barrier to intimacy in her marriage. We both know this is ungrounded, saving herself for the subtle realm. We experiment with taking the wall down. Given her proclivity for active imagination, she literally "sees" the wall, attached to her midsection. She strives to remove it. Abbey sees the metal things that unhook it. Handily, she images a screwdriver and unscrews them. She fills the empty space left within her with white light so nothing bad can get in. She sees her husband smiling and feels connected to him. Abbey is content.

"I feel emotional equality. I'm safe."

Together, we journey to the starting point of Abbey's addictive tendencies. Abbey follows a tunnel to her womb. She ends up in a medieval lifetime, the same as before. A man on a horse is ready to stab her in her heart with a sword! While *inside* that female body, she just gets a quick look. Nonetheless, it is a complete Gestalt, an entire experience to be processed. *She needs to understand this scene.*

Another person's body, a *dead body,* lies on the ground behind the swordsman.

"There is nothing left to live for, go ahead and kill me." Abbey can run away but she doesn't. She would rather die! The swordsman, she does not recognize; he is a messenger sent to kill them both. Abbey feels no fear. It is a relief and a release to die.

Eating is a relief and a release—into oblivion. Doesn't that just make sense? At the heart of every eating disorder is an attempt to calm or soothe a distraught nervous system. We overeat to soothe an edgy body, an anxious or fearful body. A traumatized body, in Abbey's case.

She goes through this mortal death of herself, the annihilation of the self she once embodied—into blackness. Yet oblivion is *not* the calm she sought.

She hears, "This is your fate. You deserve this." Punishment was called for, according to the historical period. The circumstances fill in....

She was married to someone else yet she fell in love with Jay.

But was such a punishment right and just? "Noooooo." I ask her to stand for herself, to fight resolutely for her right to live.

"I don't deserve to die." Abbey thus expresses a newfound respect for life—in an age when women were chattel and the honor-of-men superseded any woman's right, even the right to life. She is altering an age-old dynamic, an antiquated energy, with her words.

She repeats three times, "I deserve to live." That belief will re-route the morbid energy that results in her eating disorder. Self-soothing on a deep level is vital to her healing.

She hears a song, "I'll see you on the other side." Songs are a guidepost for Abbey, encouragement from the universe at large. She thought she would see Jay in oblivion. But oblivion is oblivion. *No one is there.* She starts to cry, missing Jay. Since childhood, Abbey's been aware that someone was out there, waiting for her.

Yet she also feels the guilt of forbidden love. She believes that there is an understanding on both their parts that it is just not possible to be together. She fears pulling him in closer, but also fears having him completely gone from her life. This limbo is surely not healthy, I say.

"How's this kind of thing supposed to be done?" Abbey wants to know. Who am I to tell her? Though not the first time I have encountered astral or subtle realm romances, no guidebook exists that I know of. At least not within traditional psychology.

"Just wait and it will come," an inner voice declares.

We both wait and see.

Changes in the physical plane usually come after the subtle plane sends her something she can *do* to prove herself. *Actions speak louder than words.* Their relationship is already becoming less numinous to her, less magical as Abbey becomes more functional in her day-to-day life. C. G. Jung trusted bringing the magically powerful numina of the unconscious into the light of day, thus redistributing and balancing the energetic wealth of the psyche. *Sounds like Socialism for the psyche.*

Abbey dreams that she is watching herself with Jay as they sit side-by-side. "Did you drink your tea?" he smiles. "Did you ever think we'd be sitting here having normal conversation?" This is different from every other lifetime they have had together.

"No matter what, I'm going to survive. No more dying."

No more oblivion or "little deaths" by overeating, I say.

*

Sometimes Abbey fears she is just one of Jay's female fans—a groupie—who projects onto him. She also believes they have had at least *three* past lives together. "Is it real? Is it the same to him, as it is to me?" She has actually spoken with Jay four times, for as long as an hour. There was no doubt in her mind when talking to him, or painting—that they had always known each other. She has even experienced other people "seeing" him in her (auric) energy field, and asking her, "Who's Jay?" In answer to her question, *Is it the same to him, as it is to me?* I liken it to what is known in mathematics as a Type Error. Jay's awareness of their relationship may not be on the same level as hers due to their different lifestyles and personalities. It is important not to mix up levels and assume too much.

How would she know if it were time to be together materially? "I'd trust the universe. I'd know if I were ready for that."

Abbey's guidance indicates that she is not to get obsessive about the energy exchange between them. Not let it keep her from doing anything, or allow it to bring her to a lower vibration. Don't keep trying to force it to be on the physical plane. "There is a timing for that."

She is to see everything from a spiritual or soul perspective. They each have to learn on their own. Though they only have contact on the astral or etheric plane, they are going through a transformation—of their relationship pattern. They made the same destructive, obsessive choices in *many* lives. They must consciously change, for example, how they resort to drugs and alcohol. But she is *not* a "crazy, deranged, obsessed fan."

Yet there is only one other person besides me with whom she has shared this. She fears "you'll think I'm making it up."

This is Abbey's story. She listened to his songs over and over. Certain words that he sings are doors for her. So she painted pictures of his music. She would sense him, "full-on" while painting—on the etheric plane. Sensing a deep connection, she went to see him in concert and took booklets of her paintings to give the band members. Standing in front while he performed she noticed that he *seemed* to look at her. But he did not come out to talk with his fans as usual. So she gave the other band members their booklets, and gave his to the tour manager. "He's afraid," she realized.

Another band member, the singer, told her he had looked at her art. Unabashed, he acts as go-between. "Jay wants you to grab his ass."

She replies honestly. "I'm married."

Nonetheless, after a concert, Abbey accompanies the band members and other fans to a bar. When she finally meets him she asks about his esoteric lyrics. "Is what you're writing about from someplace else?"

He answered. "Something takes over. Like a soft rape, while I write." She offered to give him a reading. When she touched his hand, a huge sadness came over her. As she looked at him, he transformed before her eyes. She "saw" him as a little boy about four years old. She wanted to cry. "Why, he's just a scared little boy! He keeps it well hidden."

He said, "I don't know what to do. *Do you know who I am?*"

She got scared.

"You're the one who knows who I am," he said.

"Maybe I'm too afraid to know," she answered. And she took her hand back. But she'd answered, "Yes, I know who you are." He grabbed her face and kissed her. "Listen to the song, 'Lost and Found.'" (The song is about seeing signs from the universe that the one you love is going away—the closer you get). "Always listen for the words, 'she said.' *That's your sign.*" He grabbed her arm and whispered, "For now, we can't tell anyone. This has to be our secret."

"For some reason, I trust you," she said.

She tells me they have met a total of five times on the physical plane. Once he called her house and left a message on the answering machine. That last time, he was pulling away. He was using drugs; it's in his music, sure enough.

She is not to shirk the physical plane of existence. One plane must not suffer for the other. Break down the wall between the two realms— the spiritual subtle realm and the physical. "Remove it!" she says.

"What will remain?" I ask myself.

*

Abbey is beginning to paint Jay's music again. She *does* want to be closer to Jay. "There's a door we each have that we open ... and close." That door has been shut since she deliberately stopped communicating with Jay. But she wants to open it again. Once it was life-transforming, having a "twin soul" relationship. *Once upon a time....* And she did move on, and marry someone else. She is not about to lose her head ... yet.

"I know if I sent a letter, he'd do it. He'd run off with me."

I have my doubts and gently probe. Abbey now weighs 315 pounds. Though down from 328 pounds, this is slow progress indeed. But blockages are being removed. Even past lives, like "cleaning a closet of old clothes."

I suggest she write a letter to Jay, whether or not she actually mails it. Tell it like it is—from her point of view. Tell it for the sake of speaking and acknowledging her truth—not to seduce or convince. Do the inner work first, I say. Process *her* experience rather than speaking face-to-face in the relationship channel. That is the most powerful way to bring whatever remains into the material plane. The deepest way, I say.

Months go by without a word from Abbey. No longer having sessions on a weekly basis, she is in that stage of therapy where she *integrates* what she has learned into her daily life. Sometimes I worry, remembering her vulnerabilities. But when she contacts me again she has startling news. She finally wrote the letter to Jay.

As I suspected, that act alone has a radical effect.

Abbey gave her letter to a mutual friend and fan who put it directly into his hand; he said he would read it when he was sober(!) As truthfully and objectively as she could, Abbey wrote about her experiences. Like when they had met in person and he told her to listen to a particular song. She wrote about their meeting on the subtle realm, and the synchronicities. Most importantly, Abbey wrote without his response in mind. *She completely surrendered her need to have him respond.* "I don't need anything from you. I don't need you to contact me. But if you want to, here's how."

What truly matters is what she has learned. By creating art based on his music, she released a lot of negativity. That introduced her, in essence, to herself. He was a guide in that way. But Abbey maintains, "I didn't just get something about me. I got *him*, too. His experiences, his emotions, his thoughts." With other artists' music, "I don't hear them; I just hear *me*." She says, "Other fans just feel what his music does for them." Abbey was thus assured that this was "something more than me being crazy." Frankly, I trust in Abbey's clairvoyance. I was telepathic with my own Teachers once upon a time.

Abbey still believes Jay will contact her. She will be okay with anything he has to say. "Even if it was only *me* that felt something, now I know what it is." It has been a soul search, for Abbey. If she can surrender *here*, where it was all consuming, *she can surrender anything*, any negative belief about herself. Now hearing Jay's music does not consume her. "Before I was afraid of who I would be without this." But she has achieved complete surrender. Synchronicities still happen, but she does not look at the signs as something about a future relationship with him—on the physical plane. "Don't limit this with words or concepts, even about past lives." That would be reductionist, I say.

"Don't limit the limitless soul," she says.

Any doubts about her conviction center around how she looks—her weight. Sometimes she is still a "bad, ugly girl." That is the core of her doubt. But Jay recognized her by her aura! When they met in person, he *said* he knew who she was. She had asked if he recognized her. Jay replied, "I would recognize your aura anywhere." He asked her the same question. "Do you know who I am?" Now she shares with me that when they met in person, and she saw him as a little boy of four years old, she immediately "saw" a *metamorphosis*. Jay transformed into a big bird, a crow!

Then the bird transformed into ... *her*. She saw *herself* when she looked at him; then Abbey saw Jay himself again.

"I am he as you are he as you are me and we are all together": The opening line of John Lennon's **"I Am the Walrus,"** written on an acid trip one weekend.[6]

"Let go of limiting beliefs," she says.

Abbey's next letter will be to herself. She awaits the power of the full moon, the lunar eclipse. Just be as completely honest with herself as she was with Jay. And she is going to a workshop on standup comedy! To get her *mojo* workin'—to let her love shine. She is going to stand up tall in front of people and let it flow—let Angels speak through her. Let her smaller self step aside, so Universal Self (within us all) can speak. For an Avoidant personality, that is tantamount to a revolutionary act. The world is hungry for what Abbey has to say. Pun intended.

*

Finally Abbey reports amazing physical change. She began by not eating so much processed food, nor eating in restaurants so much, not even a veggie burger with fries at Red Robin. She duly lost weight. But when she resumed eating comfort food, she did not gain the weight back—like before, she would inevitably gain back 5 pounds. You know, the dieter's *yo yo*: weight off, weight on. She is not *feeling* like eating constantly, so she is not overeating. She is not going back for seconds; she is not finishing everything on her plate automatically. Not eating to shut down feelings.

Two years ago when they first moved to their house Abbey weighed 328 pounds. She now weighs 305. That is 23 pounds lost and still losing. Frankly, I have not had another client that heavy who could lose weight consistently without resorting to a physical intervention like a lap band or gastric bypass surgery. How fitting that Abbey, so adept on the Subtle plane, should first make changes *there* before they manifest physically.

She is getting to "the root" and healing that root. "Unlocking who I am." **Not**, *I can't feel good about myself because fat people are ugly*. There is something to be grateful for in every emotion, even the negative ones. She is not feeling like a failure if she has a bad day. It is just a cycle, something that needs to be looked at. "The more we battle our weight, the more we create the ugliness we feel." Abbey is so full of gratitude for her many blessings.

"My reality is nothing but my perception. Life can never be what we don't already have within us. We can't receive anything that isn't in our mechanism. If we think times will be good, they'll be good."

Worrying has a snowball effect, she learned. She even gave up worrying about her family's skirmish with Bank of America. Like so many millions, the mortgage of Abbey's house is now worth more than its market value. Underwater already by virtue of the failed economy, Abbey's husband next lost his job. Abbey kept their family afloat but they lost their first house. Nonetheless, her attitude was what really kept them afloat.

The end result has not yet manifested, Abbey says. "I'm not completely healed." There is yet another layer but it has to be concrete. She has been so long in the subtle realm, something more has to manifest in the physical realm. A career change might be in the offing. Something more has to manifest in her physical body....

It is all about balance, we say, to have a complete human experience, not just in the spiritual subtle realm. Abbey finally honored the physical plane, her weakest aspect, by writing that letter to Jay. Finally, something concrete was done.

*

Epilogue. Abbey and her husband moved away. We formally concluded her sessions and said a tearful goodbye. Half a year had passed when Abbey contacts me again. She has been dealing with her feelings as they surface but she needs more support. One feeling in particular has got her attention. Anger has been so dissociated from her awareness that it seems an altered state. And she has been triggered by a familiar family situation. Only this time, Abbey has had enough.

She has always tried to protect her sibling's children from abuse. They have been vulnerable, prey to assaultive boyfriends. Now the kids are trying to protect their mom. Abbey must be willing to confront this latest "foul mouthed loser" alone. Confrontation is the final test, she says. This time Abbey will not run away. *Anger is your ally*, I say.

Many formerly abused people are terrified of anger, and rarely allow themselves even justified anger. Sure enough, Abbey thought something was wrong with her, she has been so angry. Good thing she has resorted to kickboxing to work this healthy energy, and release it. She has even got a physical trainer and works out three times each week. That's some workout she is getting. That Abbey can move at all, is testament to her healing. Even her ankle, broken at birth and reset, is healing anew, Abbey says. Before she hardly ever walked let alone exercised, so this is news, indeed.

And then she shares something else.

Abbey's pièce de résistance, the most impressive thing that brings her the greatest pride or satisfaction? She is twirling with delight—in my mind's eye.

Abbey has lost weight. She is down *five* dress sizes. She weighs 257 pounds and is continuing to lose. Compared to her highest weight of 328, this is extraordinary. And her weight loss is even more remarkable because Abbey did it without dieting. She has stabilized her weight loss through healthy eating, lots of fruits and veggies. So, her healing in the subtle realm has finally and truly impacted the physical, material realm.

Hallelujah, it is accomplished. Abbey-Face, Abbey Ann and Abbey Apple have coalesced into one. Time Travel has healed her unfortunate childhood; Little Abbey is happy and content. Abbey has revisited tragic past lives and survived. Jay has a standing invitation to visit, but only on the physical plane.

Abbey has virtually collapsed time and space in order to impact her physical reality. Abbey has bent light itself.

"I'm doing well with my eating," she says. "Hallelujah," I say.

CHAPTER 11

MARY & LORI: HEALING THROUGH DYING

No creature can attain a higher grade of nature without ceasing to exist.

Ananda Coomaraswamy

This chapter tells two stories of traumatic near-drowning to illustrate the ongoing therapeutic value of one of the most dissociative experiences known to humankind: the near-death (NDE) experience. Nothing has captured our collective imagination quite like the NDE. Fifteen per cent of people who come close-to-death report that "something happened." That "something" is the transcendental NDE where one has left the physical body and transcended the boundaries of the ego—and the confines of time and space.

Wake up, Dorothy, we're not in Kansas anymore.

This phenomenon has been reported throughout centuries, from many diverse cultures and manifold religious traditions. A 1982 Gallup Poll estimated at least 8 million have experienced an NDE, though it is now believed to be closer to 13 million in the United States alone.[1] Just imagine the energy coursing through our collective as a result of the cracking of so many "cosmic eggs." The visions, bliss and psi phenomena of the otherworldly near-death experiences are singularly transpersonal. This chapter follows the transformation that ensues when egoic consciousness is challenged in this specific way.

Just what constitutes a NDE is actually quite broad as no two NDEs are identical. But its most discernable pattern includes a life-threatening event (or an event perceived as such).[2] The 'self' seemingly leaves the body and hovers overhead. One might move through dark space or a tunnel. Deceased loved ones or relatives are often met, or beings of light. In the following, Lori will carry on a conversation with a disembodied voice. A life review may be experienced where every single event is relived—sometimes from the perspective of others.[3] *The answer to life, the universe and everything* is glimpsed, and information beyond our ordinary human capabilities is given. Finally, a boundary or barrier may be reached that may not be crossed if one is to return to earthly life. While the decision to return may be voluntary or involuntary, unfinished responsibilities may prove to be the deciding factor, as in Lori's story below. As we shall see, the integration of NDE learning positively transforms the individual. Ultimately, an NDE *permanently alters* one's perceptions of what is important, and what constitutes reality. It is a profound healing into life—through a death process.

161

At the International Association of Near-Death Studies At IANDS' North American conference in January 2003, I presented a talk on the powerful effect the NDE has on those subjected to childhood abuse.[4] One NDE so changed a child's sense of self that she became capable of enforcing a halt to sexual abuse. The first case study is compiled from my presentation; the second draws upon the clinical practice I developed to encompass trauma and its transcendence.

*

There are said to be two paths to transcendence: one is the path of joy, and the other is the path of suffering.[5] Needless to say, NDEs are encountered on the path of suffering. The person is almost always brought near-to-death by some extreme difficulty. Near-death experience can be triggered by a cardiac arrest or other type of severe injury. This story is about an experiencer whose life also held another kind of suffering—the trauma of childhood sexual abuse.

Such trauma may entail *dissociation* as one's usual identity with one's physical body is diminished or otherwise distorted. One's relationship to oneself is thereby severely altered. In the case of imminent trauma that separation or dissociation insulates one from the terror and physical pain inflicted on the body.[6] Dissociation, however caused, may encompass perceiving that one is *above* or *outside* one's physical body—in a classic out-of-body experience.

However, NDEs differ from such a psychic defense. For the dissociation involved in a NDE may also lead to transcendence. "An ineffable sense of peace and well-being accompanies this transition as the pain experienced by the body ceases.... Subjects note a sense of expansiveness, peace, relief and well-being at being out of the body, even knowing they are dead."[7] One's sense of self is not so much diminished as expanded. Thinking is alert and perception vivid, even hyper-lucid. A higher perspective is reached, a wholly different awareness or connection to one's life. The two types of dissociation thus may have significant differences.[8]

*

It [is] difficult to equate the clinical characteristics of depersonalization—emotional detachment from the body; loss of meaning, intensity and emotion; distortion of time; and the sensation that

162

one's own thought processes seem strange and unreal—with the expansiveness, lucidity, joy, assurance, and better-than-normal well-being of NDEs. The two states share a degree of detachment, but depersonalization diminishes experience while NDEs enhance it.[9]

Even though induced by trauma and involving dissociation, an NDE usually encompasses a *transcendent* state.

How does that transcendent state affect someone who has been affected by long-term trauma? What happens to the psyche when both complex trauma *and* a NDE are experienced? That question itself is revolutionary. The field of near-death studies is only a few decades old. And it has taken 100 years to more fully comprehend the effects of chronic abuse. Their combination is only as old as a few good cases. There is one such case in my files.

We know in conventional clinical psychology that trauma can arrest the course of normal development. Yet when the *transcendent* experience of an NDE follows—even by many years—the arrested or repressed development can be dramatically ameliorated. When *both* occur to one person, the effect on that person's development is profound. One case in my research population illustrates that.[10]

Mary was only seven years old when she had a near-drowning accident. She was dead for at least two minutes, with documented cardiac arrest. She required close to three weeks in an oxygen tent in the hospital. Mary writes:

At that time in my life I was a very confused, frightened little girl, who did not believe in God, or that there was anyone else who could help me out of my abusive life. When I was under the water, I pulled on another girl's bathing suit to try to get up to the surface. But the girl kicked me down, which sent me to the bottom. The only way that I can describe what happened next is: I had my thoughts that I was drowning; then I had my life flashing before my eyes, very fast [a life review] then I was aware of a place that seemed like a huge tunnel, with a very faint white light at the end. I seemed to be moving towards that light. I just couldn't believe that I was dead. After all the horrors that had happened to me, now I was surrounded with a feeling of unbelievable love and peace; a feeling like one I'd never felt, and have never felt since. I knew the feeling was pure love, loving me, the wretched soul that I was.

Now, why would a seven-year-old think of herself as a wretched soul? Since the age of one and a half, Mary had been subjected to abuse. First, her baby-sitter repeatedly knocked her about and pulled her hair. A year later, Mary began to be sexually molested by an uncle and an older cousin. This continued until her near-drowning at seven. To continue Mary's telling of the latter experience:

I was aware that there were others there. I could hear other people's thoughts in my head; they were telling me to go back, it was not my time. Yet I loved this place: for me, it was the feeling, the thoughts, the unconditional love emanating from those beings. I felt more loved there than I have ever felt in my whole lifetime.

I realized then that I was important in this world—that we all are. I did indeed have a life to live that would be different from the one I had known.

I heard words of encouragement, words of love and praise, giving me great strength, to believe in myself, to believe in my heart and not let it get any heavier. I felt better after dying than I had living, for years. I know that sounds really terrible, as my mother and father did their best to look after me, but they did not know about the abuse.

My abuse had started when I was so small; I guess I'd never felt loved as I should have. And the NDE gave me that love and assured me I was okay, it was not my fault.

That love and assurance—a crucial component of her NDE—made for significant change in Mary's behavior:

One thing I knew afterwards that I did not know for sure beforehand, is that it was not *my* fault that they were abusing me, as the abusers had kept wanting me to believe. This helped in my decision to make them stop. After I was revived, the confusion concerning that part of it no longer remained. The fear still stayed, but I knew within my heart of hearts that I could not let them touch me again. And I didn't care what the consequences would be for me, figuring that if I could die and come back okay, I could probably survive the consequences of telling them to stop.

Also, during my life-review my parents' love for me was apparent.

There is that crucial isolation the abused so often take as a given. Mary had not ever *felt* her parents' love because of the abuse that was happening *unbeknownst* to her parents.

I'd always had my doubts, really, about whether they loved me, because of the abuse. But during the life-review I could feel their love for me, and how they wanted me to have a better life than they had had. This was another manipulation by the abusers, saying my parents wouldn't love me anymore once they found out what I had done, that they would send me away to a bad-girls' home.

To escape accountability, the perpetrator often says things like that—to ensure secrecy and silence. The child's self-blame gets integrated into her core identity, particularly so if she is still in an early stage of ego-development. The child assumes her own *innate badness* is the cause of the abuse. But Mary's stigmatized identity was fundamentally challenged by her NDE: "It changed my life immensely. I went from being withdrawn, and uncommunicative, to talking to everyone, feeling able to be truly myself no matter what. For the first time in my life I felt the same as my peers."

Mary's self-identity underwent a profound healing after the NDE, and it enabled the following dramatic intervention.

Mother took me to my Gran's, where my abuser [her uncle] stayed. When I saw him, I started feeling the same feelings of apprehension, nausea, shame, disgust, and panic. He cornered me, took me to his room, per usual. The whole time I was thinking, 'I'm not going to let him touch me; I can't.'—*I couldn't go back to being that fearful little girl again.* The adrenaline must have been coursing through my body: I felt sick, totally on edge, I've never felt so scared, even in death. The scene resembled a duel at high noon, him in one corner and me in the other, facing each other, the obscenities shooting out of his mouth. But I ignored everything he said, and concentrated solely on his movements.

Mary aptly describes a form of dissociation where the traumatized

165

person's perception alters so she can hone in and focus very keenly on what will keep her safe. "I ignored everything he said. I was cornered, like a frightened animal. I'd been there many times before and had suffered so much because of it. He came towards me, threatening to hurt me, calling me names. But instead of staying in the corner like usual, I jumped on the bed, and out of the room to safety."

This very significant change of action was facilitated by the changed feelings for herself that Mary first experienced during her NDE:

> I had found hope for my future. The next time we went to my Gran's, I didn't even wait for him to come to me; I went to him, to his room, and I told him the sexual stuff would have to stop, or else I'd be telling someone. And I didn't care if I got into trouble about it because so would he. Except he was an adult, and he would get into so much more trouble than me. He had constantly manipulated me into thinking the abuse was somehow my own fault, which I now knew was rubbish.

The NDE thus broadened Mary's perception to include the wider context of her situation.

> I pushed him away with a strength I never knew I had. And I walked nearer to him and said, 'If you ever lay another finger on me, I will tell whoever will listen what you've been doing to me for years.' Then I left the room.
> Every time I went there afterwards, I would always be very careful to never go anywhere near him. My turnaround had been completed. He did not sexually abuse me any more.

Mary's case is, admittedly, quite dramatic. However, it did require a few more encounters for her to confront both abusers. At first they did not want to believe her. But she says, "I held my ground. That's when they changed their tune. I took away their power over me by not believing their vicious lies anymore, but believing my feelings, believing in myself. This was the second happiest day of my life," (the first was her NDE), "tinged with so much sadness, so much regret, so much shame still inside—but I was free."

> Now, I'm the mother of three children, and I will campaign forever for the rights of children to have a decent life. I will work

tirelessly to alleviate the suffering that children endure in this sometimes cruel and harsh world. I feel so very lucky to be alive, though. I still need help with the child abuse I suffered, but surviving the abuse and the NDE, plus surviving this long a time afterwards, gives me great strength to carry on.

If I had not had my NDE, I do not truthfully know where I would be now, or if I would still be in this world. Knowing that someone cared for me, even if I would never see [God], was enough for me to carry on.

Mary wrote this in her mid-thirties during flashbacks of the abuse. She had always remembered that she had been abused but she started remembering it in excruciating detail. Such are the symptoms of post-traumatic stress disorder (PTSD). A near-death experience, however miraculous, is not a miracle *cure*. Mary will still have to deal with her symptoms, hopefully in a therapeutic context. But her healing was facilitated greatly by her NDE—and possibly years of further abuse were prevented. A higher level of psychological integration was certainly reached.

Mary exemplifies how a breach of the psyche, a far-reach of the soul, so to speak, can ultimately restore us.

*

My next story begins with Lori's NDE that seemingly had nothing to do with her traumatic near-drowning that happened years later. I know Lori's history and telling some of it is crucial. For Lori's initial NDE happened in her early twenties—in the aftermath of childhood abuse and neglect. Still waters may run deep, but the deep river of Lori's life ran turbulent.

The physical and emotional neglect Lori suffered in childhood will always be encapsulated for me by a single image. Living, as she did, on the wrong side of town, she rarely brought any friends home from school. But one attempt was memorable. *Pitiful*. Her rundown house was bad enough. Nervously, she opened up the refrigerator door hoping to share something to eat. But to her great embarrassment, her refrigerator was completely empty. *Nothing in it*. She could scarcely contain her shock. Now, I had already heard how Lori never had enough to eat, how her stomach rumbled and she *salivated* just thinking about the food other kids ate. But for a refrigerator to be completely bare, bespeaks a bleak house, indeed.

That sad start set her adrift in life. But it also set in motion a spectacular "save" from the spiritual subtle realm. "It is as though NDEs temporarily open the door to the transformative powers of Transcendent consciousness for people who normally function at lower levels of awareness, perhaps altering a part of their neurological system permanently."[11]

This next NDE is more extensive than Mary's and more ... *otherworldly*. Ever wonder why they say Jesus is the Light of the Earth? Read on.

I was in my early twenties, I believe around twenty-three. I was living a rather out-of-control life at the time. I'm not making excuses for my behavior, but I was neglected as a child. I spent my previous three or four years struggling to stave off homelessness and even was a squatter in a dilapidated building for a while. By this point, I was working as a waitress and recently married to a physically abusive husband.

Anyway, the fact of the matter is, I had taken some amphetamines which preceded this event. Evidently I took too much, because the result was I couldn't sleep. This went on for two days. I was beside myself trying to sleep. I went into the bedroom and tried listening to a meditation tape that I had, hoping that would help. I listened to this tape for hours, but still couldn't sleep. I would occasionally get up and move around, but I was exhausted and overwrought. Eventually, while I was lying on my stomach trying to sleep, I suddenly had the distinct sensation that a trap door just slid open at the top of my head. It felt as if there was a clear opening at the crown of my head, and then I heard a male voice say, "You can come if you want to." I didn't know what to make of this.

As I continued to lie there, I felt my body separating into three separate parts. My physical body felt like inanimate dead weight, and I felt a second body that was vibrating like a battery. It was pure energy. The third body seemed to be my higher, knowing self. I was still *in* the second body, but aware of this higher consciousness.

I had a conversation with the disembodied voice. I remember I asked about the Lotus flower. I was shown an enormous, beautiful violet flower about 6 feet tall that expanded out in all directions. I understood that we are like the lotus flower in that our souls expand outward. I asked about time and was shown that time was curved. I saw the Earth history like a repeating circle. First, the mythological realm in the heavens, with gods and creatures of all sorts. Then, the birth into the world. Then, the development of civilizations, resulting in a cataclysm that caused all the earthly souls to inhabit the heavenly regions again. It was like a repeating pulse. I began to feel that I was as large as a planet. I felt that I had a huge soul at that time (though to be honest, I don't feel like such a great soul anymore).

I was excited about this information and went to tell my husband about it. He was very disinterested, especially when I mentioned that Jesus was the Alpha and Omega, as in Genesis in the Bible. I went back to my room and lay down again. I then became aware that there were people in the room. They surrounded my bed. They were smiling as if it was a surprise birthday party! I suspected that I was having some kind of out-of-body experience, but I hadn't actually left my body. I became aware of a man sitting on the edge of the bed. He had a goatee and seemed to be wearing an artist's beret. He was someone that I felt I knew. He was smiling joyfully at me. At the end of the bed was a woman with blonde hair I didn't seem to know. She was sitting next to a lanky 12-year old boy, and said, "Your son is waiting to be born."

It was then that I realized that I might be dying. I was shown my husband sitting with his face in his hands, in tears, saying to paramedics, "I didn't know." I felt great personal shame and remorse at the thought of putting him through that. I didn't want to die that way. At that realization, it came to me that I was dehydrated. I probably hadn't drunk or eaten anything for two or three days. In a panic, I got up and began drinking water, a gallon or two. I didn't know if I could get the water in my system fast enough, but somehow it worked, because I survived.

Years later, when I became pregnant, I never chose a girl's name. I always knew that I would have a boy and I did.

I am not proud of the mistakes that I made in the past, but this experience has never left me. In my opinion, when you die, it is like a reunion or birthday party on the other side. It is a celebration because no matter how well or how poorly you live your life, you are recognized for having tried. I'm just thankful my life didn't end in that way.

I am not sure about everything that I was shown. But perhaps the circular drama is just the great Earth play that we choose to incarnate into, in this realm. Perhaps at some point, we graduate from the Earth and the stories associated with it. I think there might be more than one heaven and that we graduate to other realms of glory when we leave the Earth system. Some have theorized that eventually we become stars. Well, maybe the star is a physical or symbolic representation of those truly evolved spiritual beings. Perhaps that is why they say Jesus is the light of this world. Perhaps Jesus is a spiritual star. My life has not been an easy one, so I do not know if my soul is still the size of a planet. It may have shrunk down to mortal size again.

Anyway, that is what happened to me. That is what I have learned from it.

Nor do I know if Lori's soul is still planet-size. But I do know her soul is *vast*. I am truly impressed with the high teachings imparted to her. When that "trap door" (her crown chakra) slid open, she entered realms of cosmology and evolution, as well as the future. What a whirlwind tour of the subtle realm! Thankfully, she rallied on behalf of her husband and unborn son. A common indication of precognitive material is information regarding children yet to be born,[12] and survivors of NDEs with previously little or no history of paranormal capabilities report an increase in precognition and clairvoyance.

But even if their neurological system *is* altered, "these new pathways may be disturbed by time and disinclination."[13] *Not so with Lori.* Though Lori's initial NDE happened early in her life, its therapeutic value, specifically, the availability of otherworldly guidance, continues to this day.

In the next serious situation, Lori hears another disembodied voice that directs her. Again her life is saved.

I hadn't gone rafting for 30 years, but here I was climbing into a raft with a very dear and old friend. She'd rafted this part of the river just the day before, so I knew she at least had an idea of the severity of the rapids. I'd been on the Clackamas years before but it is only classified as a Level 1. More like a floating waterway with a few mild, rocky rapids. This time, my friend wanted to tie a second raft to hold a cooler with our drinks and sandwiches. She said the raft had turned out to be cramped with the cooler the day before. So we put the cooler in the second raft and tied it to the back of ours. Well, instead of a nice relaxing ride down the river, we ended up paddling most of the way to keep the rafts in alignment and to keep ourselves off the shore and out of rough spots. The raft would have naturally floated with the current if not for this second raft.

We had life jackets, but neither of us wore them. It wasn't required and it was a hot day, so we never put them on. For the most part, we navigated easily along the river, except once we went too close to the shore and rushed through an outcropping of downed tree branches. These could have been quite bruising or even have caused some injury, except we ducked low in our raft. I used my feet to push the branches away. Another time we had a close call with a tree trunk that was jutting out into the river. Again, due to that second raft, we barely missed hitting it. For sure, we weren't acting like experienced rafters.

After about two hours of floating, I'd assumed the position of sitting on the back of the raft with one oar, while my friend crouched in the front of the raft with another. My mistake was that I was not actually *in* the raft, but seated on the rim of the raft. We approached what looked like large boulders, but soon saw that they appeared to be pilings of an old bridge that once crossed the river. Man-made rapids were thus created, where the water rushed through two concrete piers at a much greater speed than the rest of the river. There was also a change in elevation of the water through this opening.

It was too late for us to steer to the slower side of the river. Instead we drifted directly towards the concrete structures, picking up speed on the way. A young man stood on the side we were heading towards. Evidently, swimmers were able to reach that part of the structure safely. He yelled at us to go ahead and come through the two concrete structures. But again, our navigation was impeded by our attached raft.

We slammed directly into the first piling. I tried to push off with my oar, but the raft slammed and then tipped with such force that I bounced right out of the raft. I had one brief moment to see that I was hitting the water and took a deep breath upon entry. I know I had very little time because I normally always plug my nose when I jump into water, as I tend to get water in my nasal passage. I didn't even have time to do that. Luckily, I was able to take that deep breath. I expected to sink about 2-feet, but I was dragged deep down. I didn't hit bottom, but I know it was dark as no light penetrated the depth I was in.

I immediately began swimming upward. At this point I felt really foolish for having gotten into the raft to begin with, and especially for not wearing my life jacket. But when I reached the surface I was blocked by an object. I had my eyes open and could see a light blue object that I realized was probably the second raft. I touched it with my fingers but wasn't able to surface to catch my breath. Suddenly I was pulled down again and away from the raft. I found myself against a concrete wall under water.

Again, I tried swimming upward but did not make any progress. I had my eyes open and could see water rushing down on me from all sides. I was trapped in the current and going nowhere, no matter how hard I paddled. My hand was against the wall while struggling in a stalemate with the downward force of the current. I began to realize that if I didn't get out of this situation, I would inhale water. I now understood how people could drown so easily and that there was a real possibility that I was about to drown myself.

Then I heard someone say, "Go with the current." Since nothing else was working, I realized I had no choice but to trust the current and let go. I felt myself whooshing forward and it seemed like I was moving upward, but I was very disoriented so I didn't really know. I only knew I needed air and fast! I'd been under quite a while by this time. Just at that moment I breached the surface and inhaled with a great gasp, sucking some water into my lungs as I emerged. After coughing up some water up and gasping while I tread in the river, I located Tracy in the raft about 10-feet downstream.

Thank God I could breathe again! But I wasn't out of trouble. I had to get to the raft. Luckily the current worked with me and I was able to swim over to the raft though I didn't have the strength to climb in. My friend managed to row us over to the shore while I hung on. Eventually I was able to touch ground, *heavenly* ground.

I asked Tracy if she or the kid on the rocks told me to go with the current. She said no. I don't think I would have heard them down under the rushing current anyway. So the voice came from somewhere else. It was the best advice I've ever gotten.

Surviving this experience was nothing less than a baptism for me. Or a rebirth. I was really born again into a new life. I came away with only a scrape on my arm where it had rubbed against the concrete pillar. When I returned home that day, both my husband and my son showed visible signs of relief on their faces. I never told them what had happened, but on some subconscious level, I believe they knew anyway. My actions were foolish and irresponsible, but I thank God for my deliverance.

*

Lori is not alone in believing herself reborn. A significant proportion of near-death experiencers change dramatically in ways that indicate an evolution in consciousness. "Moreover, the joyful assurance of such experiences carries over into life for many.... Changes [include] a virtual loss of the fear of death; greater zest for life; preference for relationship—including increased compassion and tolerance—and self-development over material things; self-confidence and independence; strong sense of personal purpose; and an interest in contemplative pursuits."[14] Indeed, given the sheer numbers of such experiencers, the evolution of global consciousness may be well underway.

Remember Dr. Kenneth Ring, whose research linked certain subtle realm experiences with a higher incidence of childhood trauma? *The Omega Project* found that experiencers (of NDEs and UFOs) reported more abuse and trauma as children than the control subjects. Dr. Ring argued that childhood trauma plays a central role in promoting sensitivity to NDEs. Such experiencers may have developed a dissociative response style, which in turn, promotes "tuning into" other realities. Trauma, according to Dr. Ring, seems to stimulate the development of "an extended range of human perception beyond normally recognized limits."[15] He even hypothesized an encounter-prone personality, with the quality termed by psychologists as "psychological absorption," as its hallmark. Psychological absorption is the ability to focus attention on one's inner reality to the exclusion of the external environment, such as Lori's focus on the underwater voice that guided her to safety.

Furthermore, the literature suggests that the degree of psychological growth may be a function of the *depth* of the NDE; for example, near-death experiencers are compared to those who survive life-threatening conditions but who were not considered clinically dead. Consider the profundity of Lori's initial NDE, complete with a cosmic "download" about the nature of time, Christ consciousness and Earth evolution. My own research provides compelling evidence that we must additionally consider the traumatic childhood of subjects.[16] Lori's ultimate break with life gave rise to a radical initiation into the subtle realm—as if entry had been vouchsafed by the dissociation engendered by childhood trauma and neglect. Lori's childhood most certainly facilitated her entry into the spiritual subtle realms and the subsequent growth of her personality, if not the evolution of her soul.

CHAPTER 12

NICK: FLYING & DYING

One does not become enlightened by imagining figures of light, but by making the shadow conscious.

C. G. Jung, *Alchemical Studies*, Vol. 13

Key traumatic events, if unprocessed, will be repeated in some form or other throughout one's lifespan. That is an established tenet of clinical psychology, particularly trauma research. Five year old Nick is thrown against a wall by his mother. "I'm flying!" he believes. That is, until impact. The pattern of Nick's life unfolds with startling parallels to that central theme of his early childhood. Nick relives this defining incident multiple times throughout his life, most notably when he crashes in a hang gliding accident. Thus does his healing journey unfold. So, traumatic events are relived throughout one's life until the pattern and information contained within is processed and integration occurs. Thus are we restored to health. In a word, healed.

By the reliving and transformation of key traumatic events, psychospiritual transformation itself is attained.

Transpersonal psychology has furthermore advanced that tenet by adding novel stages or aspects of life during which traumatic patterns occur, namely, the perinatal stage (childbirth). Nick almost died when he was born with the umbilical cord wrapped around his neck. This dynamic pattern is relived yet again—during a traumatic intubation during an adult hospitalization. Transpersonal psychology also includes the karmic realm of past life experience, as Abbey illustrated, as well as near-death experience. Some people such as Nick exhibit repeating traumas from more than one stage of their soul's journey. One client with a similar traumatic birth, that is, with the umbilical cord wrapped around her neck, was literally strangled by an abusive boyfriend—with his hands wrapped around her neck. Asphyxiated until she passed out, Laraine left her body and flew into the waiting arms of the Divine Mother. After her revival from that near-death experience, Laraine straddled the material and the subtle realms, and became an ardent devotee of the Bengali sage Ramakrishna—Paramahamsa or Great Swan, who worshipped the blissful Divine Mother.

Sheer coincidence? Or synchronicity, born of the subtle realm?

I refer to Stanislav Grof's COEX theory (Systems of Condensed Experience): the constellation of experiences with a central associative theme—from perinatal to postnatal, to transpersonal experience in otherworldly realms. During the course of transpersonal therapy, Nick will re-experience key elements of his birth trauma as well as a near-death experience (NDE) that eerily reenacts his "flying" into a wall.

*

"What went wrong? I didn't die." Nineteen year old Nick had been in a hang gliding accident. Some months later, he awakened in the hospital after a near-death experience. By virtue of that extreme altered state, according to NDE research, his very neurophysiology was changed. But what triggered Nick's near-death experience? Had he almost died on the operating table during an emergency operation? Hardly. Twenty-four hours prior, a well-meaning doctor told Nick that he was going to die. Despite his great shock(or because of it), Nick duly prepared himself for death. That great shock ushered in his NDE. Yet it was Nick's own psyche that called Death to him.

Let me explain. Nick's internal injuries from the hang gliding accident were so extensive that he was not expected to live. Aside from a concussion, broken ribs, a collapsed lung, and many other broken bones, his kidney had been severely injured and he was bleeding internally. Nick's parents were called as emergency surgery was performed. He had many blood transfusions because of the internal bleeding. Afterward, he was in a coma for three weeks. Surviving that, he spent two months in the hospital.

That part alone was a miracle.

Yet he had been on 100 per cent oxygen for weeks as the oxygen levels in his blood failed to return to normal. Ultimately, the oxygen caused pulmonary fibrosis or hardening of the lungs and Nick again faced a life threat about five weeks into his stay. Even as he was on a respirator and could not speak, his doctor entered his hospital room and informed Nick that there was nothing more they could do—he had only hours to live. (According to the numbers, Nick says, his doctor was not inaccurate. Even now Nick harbors no enmity for that harsh death sentence.) Again his parents were called. "It's okay," he indicated to his family and girlfriend in the room. And he entered a state of total acceptance of death.

What happened next was almost predictable. Nick had a vision of a tunnel. This phenomenon appeared as an opening, more real than his physical surroundings. A place where the veil between this world and the next is paper-thin. And then a sensation of giving up all worldly attachments and moving through that thin veil to the world beyond.

It was a most powerful experience—moving into it.

Then he was gone.

Nick does not remember how far he went into that tunnel. Twenty-four hours passed before he tenuously regained consciousness. He sensed his feet first. He then felt his body and opened his eyes. His immediate thought was, "What went wrong? I didn't die."

A nurse who later came back on duty and entered his room did a double take. "You are not supposed to be here!" He was (again) not supposed to survive. Christian at the time, he chalked up his recovery to Jesus ... and prayer.

*

Every near-death experience is crisis turned into sheer opportunity, no matter if the result of a doctor's faulty prognosis. According to Buddhism, preparing to die is the ideal exercise. Apparently just thinking about one's death can greatly evolve the soul. Facing ego death is every spiritual aspirant's task at hand. In this therapy story, Nick claims the death card as his own.

Now Nick is in his fifties. This chapter includes our Eye Movement Desensitization & Reprocessing (EMDR) sessions, starting with Nick's attempt to process his near-death experience. Negative Cognitions: "I have no choice. I am going to die." Positive Cognitions: "I am an eternal soul; I will live." Each new paragraph describes Nick's response to a series of bi-lateral stimulation—generated as his eye movements track my moving fingers.

Immediately Nick "sees" a white field that he likens to white Lotus petals. "Spirit." He thanks his spiritual Master, Ajaib Singh Ji. Abruptly, he is looking down the barrel of a gun. That explosive content and trauma will be processed only later. Death might just be Nick's most viable connection to Life.

Nick all of a sudden has a remembrance of the tunnel of Light. The white Lotus he "sees" is made of the same material as the tunnel. Clearly that stuff is real—perhaps not materially—but real nonetheless. Consciousness researchers such as myself believe that consciousness precedes matter. Over twenty years ago, Deepok Chopra, then the medical director of the Lancaster center and former chief of staff of New England Memorial Hospital, referred to a system of medicine thousands of years old: "The fundamental promise of Ayurvedic medicine is that consciousness is primary, matter is secondary." Perhaps that white Lotus, tunnel material is the substrate itself, of matter.

That Nick is capable of accessing that memory says a lot. Altered state memories work best with altered state awareness. That is, being in a mental state similar to the mental state it was recorded in, best facilitates its memory. If you were inebriated or high, the memory is coded to that. You will access it best when you are inebriated or high again. Or down, whatever the altered or mental state. So technically speaking, every time Nick is capable of remembering the tunnel of Light, he is essentially there again. Nick is one pure dude.

Upon closing his eyes, SHOCK registers on his face. Nick remembers that the crash was his own father's fault. His father's design for the hang-glider was responsible for almost getting Nick killed. That is not something a young man can easily forget. Nick had been sewing the sail at a table in their shop when his father directed him to do it a certain way—against Nick's intuition. "No, make it like this." Another memory comes to mind. His father had even tried to teach him to steal. We veer off into his family dynamic.

Nick had been unwanted by both his parents. In fact, throughout his life, they had actively worked towards his demise. This was a startling insight. I cannot over-emphasize just how vital this awareness is to his healing. Anything less would be projecting mightily onto his parents—out of his own need to be loved. Unfortunately, that we were loved can be a lie. Our history, our personal story of our past, had best be accurate. From the perspective of the East Indian philosophy of Advaita or non-duality, enlightenment is just knowing what is. Sahaja, means "natural," enlightenment means seeing clearly.

Now there is acceptance—represented by a stony area by the ocean. A white granite material has appeared to Nick. A more material substance than the tunnel or Lotus, to be sure. Nick so obviously needs grounding in his life. Having faced the truth about his all but murderous parents, Nick can now move past the trauma. But for someone who has had an NDE, transcending trauma can entail shifting to a transcendent level. A Cosmic overview is in the making.

"Break on through to the other side." Jim Morrison's epic song was generated from sexual abuse and substance abuse and his own particular brand of genius. For someone who has had an NDE—the ultimate insult to the body—breaking through to another realm happens au naturel.

"I can see how my life is orchestrated." In an altered state, Nick "sees" the event in a much larger context: a karmic chain of events.

Balanced by his own ignorance, he had done the best he could do. He didn't know not to listen to his own father's advice. "I just didn't know better." That is an enormous life lesson about acceptance.

Back at the table sewing the sail, Nick wishes he had not been so ignorant. But life was, after all, unfolding step by step. Stay in the moment, Nick gets. If that moment has Cosmic overtones, then so much the better. But one does not have to know what orchestration is going to be produced. Level of Disturbance : 1 (scale = 0 - 10). Nick finally finds himself in a rainforest populated with ancient cedars. The trees hold the wisdom of a very long time.

Nick's EMDR session was profound. With a single movement of consciousness he circumvented shame. So often abuse victims spend precious years feeling guilt and shame. Yet when we "see" our essential innocence, a protection is afforded. "I was doing the best I could!" "Put yourself in my place." Moving out of shame is moving one step closer to our true Self.

*

When Nick was five years old, his mother threw him against a wall. He hit hard and high up. No comfort there! Crying, he hides but still wants to be comforted by her. But no! She's not safe. She's a dangerous person. As Nick describes this, SHOCK registers in his body.... He's flying through the air!

Nick is clearly disoriented even in our session.

Nick's parents were crazy. His mother was raised as a Christian Scientist and came to regard Nick as her "evil son." Something was wrong with her. She had a nervous breakdown when Nick was ten years old. Nick had long ago diagnosed her as a dependent personality: "she'd change her story depending on who was in the room." She never worked outside the home but sometimes sat in the car all day long where his dad worked. As an example of his neglectful home life, when Nick was somewhere between six and eight (his memory is notoriously vague), he got on his bike and rode five miles to a shopping mall. His parents did not even know where he was. That is the impression Nick was left with: a lack of concern ... neglect.

The dysfunction of his home life is appalling. Unfortunately, his perspective as a child has persisted to this day. EMDR's Negative Cognition: "I made her hate me." Positive Cognition : "I can fly!"

Upon closing his eyes, Nick "sees" a white sculptured shape—

181

where the wing of an airplane meets the fuselage. A thing of beauty. He always built model airplanes as a child.

Our entire lives are built on pivotal moments; they are the foundation of the story of our life that gives it meaning and purpose. That his significant experiences are dark is not to be rejected. Nick now "sees" this. Flying became a spiritual thing. Like many of the traumatized who have become spiritual adepts, Nick has had more than one out-of-body experience (OBE). Once during a sitting meditation, he simply floated away from his body.

Upon closing his eyes, he "sees" a glass of water with a green leaf in it. One touch of the water has a rippling effect. One experience causes others. He must see the far-reaching nature of it. Reclaim it in a new way. His story was laid down before birth as a life event. Karma. It is a familiar story—people flying and dying. To keep it "stuck" as trauma is to lose its full extent. Nick understands this now during EMDR.

Nick cycles back to getting thrown against the wall. He "sees" himself roll up just as tight as he can in the corner of the room. He wants to go to his mother but cannot. He has a sense that there is no one to blame but himself. He blames himself for this break with his mother. All children do. Only capable of regarding themselves as center-of- their-universe, beaten children believe they deserve it. Bad to the bone. But it is only a stage of brain development, or lack thereof.

Upon closing his eyes, Nick is reminded of the Greek Pantheon, wherein gods made mortals do things. Mortals could only partly exercise free will. Only the gods had access to full awareness and free will. (I am reminded of Julian Jaynes theory about schizophrenia, namely, that it represents an earlier stage in the human development of subject-object consciousness—and a non-egoic frame of reference. Not having an ego identity with which to make decisions, we more readily heard voices, perhaps mistaken as gods.) Naturally, only part of Nick was conscious at that age. But partially as a lasting effect of such early childhood trauma, Nick demonstrates startling poor judgment at times as an adult.

After throwing him, Nick's mother said, "I just meant to throw you on the bed." Obviously she had lost control of herself. I ask Nick, "What should have happened?" It is a psychotherapeutic intervention made possible by "time travel" with EMDR. Asking such a question can go a long way towards re-mediating trauma or abuse. His answer is telling.

"It should have been a place of holding." He should have gotten the message that the world is a safe place. Pursue it with full confidence. He should not have had to hold so much in reserve to protect himself. She should have been able to relate. She should have had a grounded caringness, instead of a false exuberance driven by anxiety. Nick contemplated meeting the world and pursuing his business interests with a relaxed confidence, with the social skills to forestall anxiety. EMDR's Positive Cognition: "I meet a safe world with confidence." From a more centered place.

Nick later reported a newfound confidence as he formed social connections. Our therapeutic work is a form of re-parenting, after all.

*

The Flight of the Phoenix. Nick was nine or ten years old, sitting in the drive-in movie when his dad told him that the stunt man (Paul Mantz) had died during the last landing during the actual filmmaking. Nick was struck dumbfounded. That actor was known to him. He had actually met Paul at a flight museum and shook hands with him. Paul Mantz even gave Nick a plastic model airplane. In shock, Nick wondered if anyone else watching the movie knew he had died.

Death was making a premature acquaintance to Nick. As if to acknowledge and process the unthinkable, he built model airplanes constantly afterwards. Incredibly, learning to see and think in 3-D would stand him in great stead during his later shamanic travels and visualizations. But that awareness comes only later.

EMDR's Negative Cognitions: "I can't meet the moment. I'm not big enough to understand or hold my father's feelings." Positive Cognitions: "It's okay to be young like a child." In time, Nick will grow to understand death as an adult.

Suddenly Nick smells a disgusting rotten egg! Smell plays a special role in the retrieval process of traumatic memories. One study asked how memory retrieval processes took place. When subjects thought most about the trauma, how did it come to them? Out of all the sensory modalities such as sight, hearing and touch, subjects smelled it seventy-five percent of the time. The neurobiological explanation has to do with the synapses between the olfactory lobe and the limbic system's amygdala.

That smell is his father's life, frustrating and miserable.

Dad had a flying jacket he loved. Even the jacket was evidence of failure. He had wanted to be in the Air Force but ended up in the

Navy instead. Nick took on such miserable things, thanks to his father. At ten, he worried about his father killing himself.

A "triangulation" existed between Nick, his father and Death. Dead people haunted his childhood. Like the haunted house (a porch enclosed with white sheets) Nick had tried to build at fourteen.

One's first childhood dream is said to predict a pattern throughout one's life.[1] One's dreams at the time of entering therapy are said to predict the course or prognosis of treatment. Such dreams are good prognostic tools. Though I often elicit their recall, without being bidden, Nick shares such a dream with me now.

Nick had a dream in early childhood of walking in a graveyard. He "knew" that if he walked on a grave, he'd spin like a top, spiraling down into the ground. Luckily he had a dream sash with an emblem that would save him, like the safety belt of a school crossing guard. Wearing the safety sash would prevent Nick from being spun and pulled down if he was so careless as to step on a grave. He has always hated whirlpools of water. Even pictures of whirlpools give him a sickening feeling of an abyss.

Suddenly, Nick gasps!

AAAARRRGGG!

It is a sound unlike any I have heard in my sessions and I have heard more than my share of primal sounds. It is a primitive cry of pain and fear. Awareness dawns on me. Nick is being born! Sure enough, he reports he is stuck headfirst in "a pipe." Yes, Nick is being born. The umbilical cord is wrapped around his neck. Death is closing in....

Seconds later he is safely head-down, with the water behind him. His emotions ease up. "That snuck up on me," he manages to gasp. Nick wonders if he nearly died at birth, at least in his subjective experience. He was unwanted, that much he knows. He was a blue baby. The umbilical cord had been wrapped around his neck. (Our traumas tend to be repeated. Nick endured an emergency entubation in his throat after his hang gliding accident.) Now Nick has a sense of vomiting. Feeling deep body states is sometimes required. The material in the psyche dictates.

Again he is a child sitting by himself, making airplane models. "Nobody ever helped me."

Nick is about to get help.

Now Nick is in the hospital after his accident. His girlfriend at the time actually stayed with him throughout his ordeal. She represents a new archetype in his solitary life: The Ideal Woman. The ultimate companion. Truly "she" ushered Nick into the world.

"That's how the energy got unstuck!" A new awareness transforms Nick's traumatic experience. He ultimately processed the stuck energy of his birth—with this archetypal relationship. (He and I are playing out the pattern yet again—from traumatic "stuckness" and near-death—to the appearance of a helper who ushers Nick into a brave new world. I am one such helper in a long lineage of women who heal. New circuitry and neural pathways are thus being forged.) His ordeal and subsequent healing obviously made a great impression on his girlfriend as she later became a truly exceptional doctor herself.

Nick's trauma has been significantly desensitized. EMDR's Level of Disturbance: 1 (scale = 0 - 10). Positive Cognitions: "Even if Death is at hand, I have other relationships that usher me in, other relationships more important than Death."

*

At four, Nick suffered his first traumatic head injury, which happened even before he was thrown against a wall. He was standing up on a backyard slide reaching for an orange on a nearby tree, when he fell. He remembers his hand loosening. The slide tipped over, his sister later said. A scar over his right eye attests that his head hit the brick planter around the tree. His right hand failed to support him. No surprise that he feels unsupported when it comes to doing in the world. Finances, mainly making a living, particularly eludes him.

EMDR's Negative Cognition: "Being ambitious brings me close to Death." A child was hit by a car and died on the same road Nick's school bus traversed. Another time his dad warned him of the dangers of taking a jar to school with an embryonic specimen—an octopus—in formaldehyde. "If it breaks, get away!" Given that warning, it is a wonder Nick did not drop the jar on the bricks with a dull thud. Death looms large in Nick's life.

An image of a soup can appears in the kitchen of his childhood home. A soup can without a label. It should have a label, it should be nurturing, he says. The kitchen—the mother's domain—should be nurturing. Nurturing is necessary for ambition. "There was none in my family. That hurts." He cannot open the can with a fork, and at that age he cannot manage a can opener. Cannot do (or say) anything right. His mother's father died at that time. He remembers sitting at the table when his family first found out.

"I can't believe it," Nick said.

"You shut up," his father said.

As no human being, no parent or relative or friend repaired that wound, Nick has been forced to transcend his own nervous system for healing. His consciousness readily, unfailingly goes to the animal kingdom. Children thus isolated from nurturing humans do learn quickly to transcend the human nervous system. Animals, nature, even rocks take over the function of nurturing. Our nervous systems are indeed well made. Transcendence is the name of the human game. Nick's ten years in a shamanic training program—given the neglect he suffered in childhood—came quite naturally to him.

A thick tree canopy is overhead. A large Mountain Gorilla is now cradling little Nick, applying a cold pack to his head. We have arrived back at the original traumatic head injury. That injury alone was enough to interrupt Nick's development. But Gorilla is a good healer with dexterous hands, building models with sticks to represent the world—the structure of things. Something his neglectful parents could not do. Molecule by molecule, atom by atom. Another animal, Buffalo, holds the space. Buffalo sneezes. "That's nothing to sneeze at." Nick laughs. A gentle reminder that he is always loved.

"The gorilla caught me!" and at the same time, "But I hit my head as if he didn't." It was Nick's first initiation. A traumatic experience and a transpersonal bridge to ego death. There is no real danger. "What am I worried about? It's a passage through space—a doorway." However, after this head injury, Nick could not read well. He was left out in school, finally reading at only a sixth grade level in Special Education. Nick hates not being able to engage with the outside world.

Now Nick reminds himself not to just look at his loss—not being able to read. It was not just a trauma but also a transitioning to another place. That moves him to tears.

An initiation of sorts is at hand.

The dark void. Suddenly Nick is in the car after his fall, being taken to the clinic, with the wind blowing on his head. How strange! His blood is dropping all the way to the clinic. What a dangerous place to be—so close to the road. The wheel, the spinning tire is right there. He remembers his mother holding his head out the car door! Face-down, with the car door slightly open, he watches his own blood streaming out. (This face-down trauma is oddly similar to the traumatic birth experience we had processed earlier. Can Nick's memory be other than materially real? Either this is extremely negligent care, or

186

an image from the active imagination—demonstrating how key traumatic events are relived throughout one's life span once the template is established.)

"I should be wrapped up in dad's woolen U.S. Army blanket ... held and swaddled tight, to a mother's breast ... with the door closed." Mountain Gorilla's thankfully sitting next to him on the car seat, pressing a green leaf to his head. Nick is gently passed from his mom to Gorilla. During active imagination, Nick "sees" his mom slip out the door! With every bone in her body broken, his "impersonal" mother tumbles head-over-heels down the road. It is a violent image but Nick steadfastly does not censor it. All the supporting bones of her (imaginal) body are broken—a sort of shamanic dismemberment. It is an impersonal violence, I say, to match her disconnected, impersonal role. His mother is simply "not one who can connect." Not one who can support.

So Nick disconnects, however violently, from her.

EMDR's Positive Cognition : "Ambition leads to initiation!" Courage leads Nick to the final leap, the complete loss of control so necessary to, and that precedes, the transpersonal. Something else is in control. Not oneself.

Shamanic animals.

A higher perspective obtains. Nick can now "see" his entire life process from the beginning to the end. Gorilla can.

Gorilla can do.

*

Nick recently made two "slip ups" with money. His rent check bounced when he did not make a necessary deposit. And he neglected to enclose an overdue invoice in a mailing. Nick dreams he is floating on his back with alligators in dark, bottomless water. A cold reptilian death is just beneath the surface—like the near-death, hang-gliding accident. EMDR's Negative Cognition : "I'll always be unsuccessful and never have a life." Returning to his dream imagery, he pulls his feet in cautiously as one alligator relentlessly turns towards him.

Upon closing his eyes, a series of round shapes appear: a silver dollar ("you can't take it with you"); a steering wheel, a solar eclipse. Finally, his Celtic family crest on a shield. A past life battlefield in the mud, complete with swinging swords even as Nick demurs, "But I'm not one to have past life experiences." There is a large round moon over the battlefield, and finally someone there to help him over Death. An old wooden coffin is pulled on a cart. A burial, a priest, old shrines and chapels.

"But I've got to have money to survive!"

Nick experiences a dissociation between the world of money ... and death. Complete opposites. Yet they are the two essentials of life, on par with each other. He wants to resolve his death trauma without pressing money issues; he feels depressed at the loss of what seemed like a monastic cell.

The alligators represent to Nick "all the things that could go wrong." It would almost be a relief to be eaten. Indeed (during EMDR), the alligators are slowly picking away at him. Half an arm and leg are already gone. Then no arms or legs are left, only a torso. Nick has no mobility at all. Almighty alligators push him along—providing direction. They do not want him for food, after all. Nor do the alligators intend to drown him. Nick is completely disabled. Yet they swim in unison, resigned—to a spiritual purpose. As if in an organized shamanic process of dismemberment and rebirth.

Incapable of direction, Nick is pulled from the water's surface down to the sea floor where a City resides. Breathing underwater is surprisingly not an issue.

Breathing underwater in a dream or active imagination is highly significant. Such a feat makes one truly master of two realms. In Nick's case, an underwater City neatly conjoins a spiritual world, represented by flowing water and a world of everyday life and finances. I look forward to improvement in his daily functioning.

*

Nick had a lucid dream in which he knew he was dreaming. Once again in a flying machine, he was in the control room on his belly with hands forward—to control the airship. On a soft fleshy part, a round mound, like a breast. (Infancy is a safe bet, although Nick was not identified as such in the dream. Dual awareness, the juxtapositon of higher-order awareness, is more Nick's forte.) When he landed, a toddler, another aspect of Nick who "couldn't connect," ran around on the ground.

Not connecting is a recurring theme. Nick's mother could not connect. Nick could not connect with his first wife. Nick himself is disconnected. Dissociated. He never received nurturing, guidance and support as a child. He has, nonetheless, a profound consciousness that has been nurtured, guided and supported—within the spiritual realm. Nick has truly led a non-ordinary existence. Abundant evidence of that is everywhere, from his NDE to his OBEs, and his resultant spiritual practice.

And his lucid dream capacity, that is, the capacity to recognize he is dreaming within his dreams. I henceforth hatch a plan—a treatment plan—to connect Nick with his inherent power. I outline this treatment plan in the next few sessions. Connectivity is the key. Follow the Tao, and his everyday life will harmonize with his ability to access the Universe as a whole. Connect him more to what he is already naturally doing. Such as the following.

"It's just a dream," he informs the toddler. "If you get into trouble, just wake up."

His dream self is already teaching him how to awaken from this dream we call life. His instruction to the toddler within the dream is uncanny. So, Nick himself (or his higher Self) can wake himself up during his everyday life before "slip ups" with money occur.

When Nick was fourteen, he had his first out-of-body experience. He had simply been following a meditation instruction. But by focusing his attention on his crown chakra, he went flying through space to an unknown planet. "It was easy to get there." Apollo 14 astronaut Edgar Mitchell, the sixth man to walk on the moon, was astounded when a Tibetan lama he met completely and accurately described Mitchell's experience. An adept at out-of-body travel, the lama said he had been there himself. Dr. Mitchell accepted that explanation without question. Having been initiated into unitive consciousness during his own space flight, he was no neophyte to extraordinary experience. However, adolescent Nick was a neophyte. Flying, he made a giant arc around the planet. But he was out of his element and paranoia began to take hold. He was fearful that he could not make it back to Earth if he completed the arc. It is generally known that OBEs can arouse fear in a novice. Somehow, to his great relief, Nick dropped back into his body. Fourteen year old Nick swore he would never do that again.

Nick's next OBE occurred during junior high school when he went to Pentecostal service. Church members surrounded him and prayed, some in trance, speaking in tongues. A powerful energy enveloped Nick. While he stood transfixed, he lost all sense of time. But he was fully aware that he had left his body.

Thus began his spiritual practice a year later of Surat Shabd Yoga

(Sant Mat, "the true path"), a practice of connecting with energy and vibration ("Naam," light and sound).

Nick's next experience of leaving his body was the most intense—during his hospitalization when the doctor erroneously announced he was slated for death. A Light had appeared. Fully conscious of the implications (imminent death), Nick surrendered and moved into it.

Hearing all this, I conclude that the challenge for Nick is not leaving his body. His growing edge, so to speak, will be to ground those spiritual energies. Given his early childhood disturbances, it is only natural that he has been tending towards disembodiment. One study found that in the aftermath of trauma, posttraumatic stress disorder (PTSD) was more likely to occur in those who dissociated or left their bodies during the traumatic event. What is dissociation, after all, but leaving one's body to a greater or lesser degree—the ultimate dissociation being the near-death experience. Disembodiment and dissociation go hand in hand.

Near-death experiencers often live a large dichotomy—between physical reality and the subtle spiritual realm. Nick's financial problems speak to that, as if he cannot keep body and soul together. He has trouble making money, sometimes seen as anathema to the spiritual aspirant. Such problems are symptomatic of that fracturing of realities; it is the experience of dissociation on a daily basis. In his daily life, Nick is forgetful and has little sense of priorities. He is simply unable to choose what is important. Yet life is only partially experienced without being able to build and create.

EMDR's Negative Cognition: "I don't know what's most important to do." He feels sad, pathetic. But there is more to this. With two traumatic head injuries, both left brain and right, surely Nick experiences a loss of what psychology calls "executive function." Such functions include getting organized and planning ahead; resisting impulses and staying focused; persisting with tasks; using time wisely. But when we target this in EMDR another startling life-threatening event surfaces that also affected his brain.

Suddenly, a gun. Nick had yet another trauma when he was twenty-five. A hold-up. Afterwards he could not sleep for several days. An intruder with a sawed-off shotgun stepped inside his apartment (the wrong apartment) and demanded to know where "the drugs and money" were hidden. Lying on the ground with a gun to his head, Nick literally thought he was going to die in his next breath. Now Nick has a graphic, detailed image of being shot in the head. "I would be released from this body." And part of him readily admits, "That wouldn't be such a bad thing."

It had happened only months after he had made a bad marriage. It is telling that though they were both in their twenties, Nick secretly believed that his wife was destined to die before him. At the time of the hold-up, that conviction (or desperate hope) was shattered. The truth was, he did not even like her. He knew their marriage was a horrible mistake on their honeymoon. They had met after his accident, and her brother's sudden death. Their mutual relationship to death attracted them to each other. Death is a compelling strange attractor for Nick. It had been wishful thinking that she would die and he would get out of the marriage. (Though I do not say so, there is a certain poetic justice in his near demise. Right back at ya.' Karmic law prevailed and his misguided death wish, boomerang-like, rebounded back to him.)

What a mistake! Nick hated misperception, not knowing what was important. Not putting two things together rightly. Marrying the wrong woman. Believing his dad about the hang-glider. At the hold-up, a big chunk of his soul split off. Shamans-of-old did soul retrievals. Psychology shamans use EMDR and other such interventions to bring souls back—to make one whole. That trauma almost ruined his life. Nick developed a full-blown case of PTSD that was acutely triggered whenever he had to open a door.

He hated opening doors for years.

*

Nick attended a workshop on spiritual living, death and dying. "Those are my people," he says. He continually nurses thoughts of disaster, like, what if the plane overhead crashes? The workshop participants were asked, what would you do if you had three days to live? For other spiritual aspirants, having death as a constant presence is an excellent practice. But not for Nick, I offer for consideration. Right on cue, Nick's latest dream gives me much-needed information to buttress my case. It is a particularly canny dream, even as dreams go.

Nick dreamt about a "cutter" whose forehead and arms are covered with scars and blood. His forehead (above the third eye) is an active wound, bleeding as if he has been shot in the head. (Nick's shadow figure has appeared, a same sex figure that represents an unconscious aspect of him.) Like sexuality, the cutting is a craving, a drive. It ener-

191

gizes him like thirst. But Nick yells at him, "You fool, look what you're doing!" The cutter says, "Cool! Talk to me some more." Somehow Nick has "the cutter's book," his bible of self-torture with instructions on cutting. In an ambiguous ending, Nick gives the book back.

The dream scene changes to a large hangar, with people practicing rescue for a plane disaster. But they are setting up in the wrong place. The rescue is not going smoothly.

Now Nick confesses that he comforts himself by "drifting off" to disaster scenarios. Nick has become addicted—attached to tragedy. For a time he was even a firefighter. He has thus worked out his own chaotic method to alter his hormones and give himself a cortisol rush, especially if he is depressed. Cortisol is a steroid hormone secreted by the adrenal glands during a stress reaction. Adrenal depletion and fatigue can result from its overproduction, a common symptom of the traumatized. He admits he uses this habit "like a drug" to wake himself up. At this point, it happens without plan or conscious choice. Not good, I say. At this point, such a "rescue" is not going smoothly. My role is to help people access more effective ways to function, preferably without drugs, drama or trauma. After all, the essence of spirituality is efficiency.

Without a pattern for nurturing guidance, Nick will need to improvise help. Sometimes help comes from the spiritual subtle realm. Though she was physically real, his archetypal girlfriend was one such helper. But his effort to marry "a real girl," failed drastically. And Nick's multiple traumatic brain injuries make life difficult on a daily basis, what with his financial misdeeds. We move forward with our treatment plan to initiate brain changes for Nick with lucid dreaming.

Can lucid dreaming actually help heal traumatic brain injury (TBI)? Can guidance from the subtle realm materially impact the human physical brain?

CHAPTER 13

NICK: IF I ONLY HAD A BRAIN

Lucid dream strategy for brain change. I first consult with consciousness researcher and lucid dream authority, Dr. Ted Esser, whose collaborative research study examined specific transpersonal experiences through the practice of lucid dreaming.[1] Research participants incubated lucid dreams in order to initiate Kundalini awakening, experience non-duality, or invite the Divine into their awareness. Eighty-five percent of research participants had what they considered sacred experience. Virtually all participants had life-changing experiences.

The lucid dream protocol to initiate contact with The Divine feminine (Sophia) is fairly simple. Incubation phase (from 20 seconds - 2 minutes): Call on intuition for a lucid dream experience of the Divine. Let go. Meditate, or mindfully go to sleep. The razor's edge is to be unattached to the outcome. Repeat the incubation *within* the dream with eyes open: "I want to experience the Divine *now*." Witness the dream with detachment. Do not wait for results because any dream material *is* the result. One hundred percent of the time, the dream reacts *instantly*.

To improve Nick's "executive functioning," we target his poor sense of remembering what is important. For example, he has trouble prioritizing tasks. He often sabotages himself, like not mailing an invoice. Can Nick practice skill building during lucid dreaming? Commitment building? "Am I fit for life?" he asks. That question itself comes out of a framework of having experienced multiple traumas. We plan to chart the increases of his executive function. *Have the software alter the hardware of his brain.* For accelerated healing of traumatic brain injury (TBI), Dr. Esser recommends that Nick specify during his lucid dreaming that his actual *physical* brain be healed. We decide to leave the actual brain changes up to the Divine.

As part of his lucid dream protocol, Nick is to repeat before sleep, "Experience the Divine healing my physical brain—to put my hands to efficient work."

Nick easily attains lucidity: "I can control this," he thinks during a dream. He hovers in a chair, a few feet above the ground, hopping over bodies encased in mud or clay. Apparently they had died and then been "prepared." Not yet fully in control or buoyant, he accidentally

195

lands on one body with the back legs of his chair. Nick is not yet fully consciousness, while the mud-encased bodies represent particularly unconscious aspects of him. But his conscious intentions ("prepara-tions), and movements show promise.

Nick dreams (though not lucidly) about a family of owls outside, hidden in the bushes. Then the baby owls, "owl-ettes," are *inside* his house, in an open kitchen with owl droppings on the counter. Owls, I note, are notorious portents of death *and* denizens of the subtle realm. A "familiar, " or helper spirit with supernatural powers often takes the form of an animal. These baby owl-ettes may represent a delicacy of seeing. Inside the house, they seem more integrated within Nick's various life functions. And the kitchen is the site of nurturing. Their droppings on the kitchen counter are processed food, after all. Good work, Nick.

Nick emails me about his lucid dreaming progress:

"Sleep... Oh! how I loathe those little slices of death." Author unknown, commonly attributed to Henry Wadsworth Longfel-low and Edgar Allan Poe.

I've discovered an important element in the process of lucid dreaming. Most every approach I've seen frames lucid dreaming as a "skill to be developed." But perhaps the reason more of us do not lucid dream has to do with fear. We simply do not want to encounter the material within our psyche. Just as the subcon-scious is a good place to put things we don't want to see, dreams contain even darker material that we naturally prefer to avoid. I suppose this is why people don't more readily remember their dreams and need to make a conscious commitment to do so.

Now consider the viewpoint of the dreamer. Dreaming is es-sential—we die without it. So what's the best way to avoid the material in dreams that we don't want to see. *Forget the dream.* Or hide the ego-self in the dreaming process so the ego-self doesn't have to actually encounter the dream material. This way we only need to deal with the dream material through the filter of memory once we have awoken from the dream.

However, in *lucid dreaming* a fully conscious ego-self is stand-ing there in the dream environment. I maintain that this is actu-ally a frightening proposition. Just imagine your lucid-self placed in a world where absolutely anything goes. And everything around you is not only the product of your own creation, but that very dream material is the core of your psyche. It *is* you.

I imagine that the way to moderate this potentially frightening dark material is by taking control of the dream. I read reports where people love to fly over beautiful landscapes. These are dreams of light and fun. But what if your objective for lucid dreaming is not to play but rather to confront the dark material for self-discovery and personal development? Now the lucid dreamer needs to form a strong commitment to face the fear and endure whatever may be discovered.

Lucid dreaming is probably much like the death process where our ego-self, hopefully consciously, steps into an unfamiliar landscape of its own making. There, we must face the sins / karmas of our own making. *I can think of nothing more akin to death than lucid dreaming.*

I realized that "fear" is the obstacle to lucid dreaming after considering the dream where I "consciously" floated in a chair and punctured one of the clay burial enclosures. The clay enclosures neatly concealed material I would like to consider dead and entombed. But there are many bodies. Each has their own unique pose—each one had been engaged in the normal activities of life that might produce thoughts and actions I prefer not to realize—to "entomb." These are literally part of my psyche that I prefer not to see.

If my ego-self is not present in the dream then the entombed personas can be ignored. But I am "consciously" hopping around puncturing the clay enclosure and getting to the yucky material. It's my lucid encounter of the material within that is the problem.

Lucid dreaming is the willingness to practice the death process and engage this potentially frightening material. It takes courage and trust that other powers will moderate the experience for my ultimate benefit. Definitely a good reason to believe in God! Once I realized that *enduring fear*—not developing skill—was the path to lucid dreaming I had a full lucid dream that very evening.

I realized in full consciousness that I was dreaming. I said, "Oh, this is a dream. I clearly see that I am lucid dreaming. Shall I *control* the dream? No, for this first dream I'll just see how it plays out." The dream content was gross and sickening. Two sickening, yellow fleshy spiders crawled around the end of a small hollowed out log. Then they quickly crawled inside. I looked inside to see a "hive" of sickly yellow spiders clogging the log. You see—ugly material.

*

Spider imagery appeared in Stanislav Grof's work with LSD psychotherapy as well as Holotropic Breathwork. Spider imagery arises during the replaying of a specific birth matrix—the second matrix—when the birth contractions have begun but the cervix is closed. No exit, no escape is the theme—the loss or termination of unbounded freedom. Nick's difficult birth might be repeating itself. Spiders are also an expression of the Cosmic Feminine. Kundalini awakening can involve dreams associated with spiders.

Shakti, the Divine feminine, comes in the form of spider.

Nick's insight about fear and the death process—with regard to lucid dreaming—is astute. According to Dr. Esser, out-of-body experiences can also be quite fearful (just as Nick had been terrified during his first OBE at fourteen). But then, Nick is no stranger to death. His consecration to healing will be crucial to the transformation of such "ugly material."

Nick shares his dream log as he strives to lucidly dream the healing of his own traumatized brain. "I had a remarkable and illuminating night of lucid dreaming. I had at least a dozen lucid dreams."

How It Started

I found myself driving down the road wondering if the dream was really photographic. Upon closer inspection I noticed that the visual image was more like an impressionist painting. Any painting, no matter how realistic, will look like small blobs of colored paint if you get close enough. So my thought process led me into lucidity. From this experience I decided that I was dreaming and I became aware within the dream.

From here I slipped in and out of the dream, and I quickly caught on that I should tend to the dream's sensory experience to remain within the dream. I consciously focused on colors, shapes and activities and did not drift back to awakening.

Lessons from the Dream

I begin to explore the limits of dreaming. I wanted to record these dreams *within the dream* so I pulled out my audio recorder and began manipulating the buttons (using the dream recorder). After some fumbling I finally decided that this was never going to work. This experience showed me a paradoxical relationship between dreaming and reality.

I saw a couple kissing tenderly, sensually. She came over and gave me a soft kiss. Then I went looking for someone else to kiss. Just then a heavyset woman in a minivan pulls up and tells me in so many words that "dream time" is not so different from "waking time" and that I need to follow the same moral guidelines within the dream as I do within waking life. I have a partner so I should not be kissing other women in the dream.

I learned that there is a balance between being receptive to the dream experience *versus* being expressive and choosing what I'd like to control. I had to pay close attention to the dream experience in order to remain there. Then I could willfully express what I wanted to do, for example, choosing to fly. Something like 80% receptive and only 20% expressive.

Finding the Brain

I decided to try my hand at flying. I flew to an intersection in a small town but on the other side of the street it opened up to huge buildings. Imagine buildings the size of the Boeing hangers where planes are built. The center of this huge complex was covered with intricate pipes running every direction and emitting steam. Other buildings attached to this complex: large hangars that held innumerable boats as in a dry dock with many levels. Large cranes carried dozens of different types of boats in and out these hangars. I'm sure this whole building complex of pipes and bowed hangars was my *brain*. I'll be going back to this brain experience again to do more lucid dreaming there.

Nick is a prolific lucid dreamer. He quickly discovers significant keys to conscious dreaming. Focusing on sensory experience within the dream does help with lucidity. In fact, the paradoxical relationship between waking and dreaming is such that it is one popular technique for lucidity. That is, if pushing a button does not give the expected response, then train yourself to think: This must be a dream. That thought alone can serve to awaken you to lucidity.

But this barrage of lucid dreams is not necessarily an indication to ditch his protocol, notably, asking the Divine to heal his physical brain.

Having "found the brain," his resolve is being tested. Nick needs to consecrate his dreaming (not to mention, consecrate himself to his partner). That is why we decided on a dream task. Furthermore, it is precisely his inability to resist impulses and stay focused, to persist with tasks and to use time wisely, that we want to remedy. It is conceivable that by persisting with his protocol in dreamtime, his physical brain will experience the greatest effects of neuroplasticity. Keep coming back to the protocol within the dream, I say. If he truly wants to go flying, then make that a part of his protocol. But do not deviate from it.

Regarding monogamy: Dr. Esser has said that lucid dreamers or those who practice OBEs often make conscious decisions to extend (or *not* to extend) their marriage vows to the astral or subtle realm. Nick and his partner have decided on the former.

Out of our work comes Nick's business plan for a healing practice he can market that encompasses years of Shamanic journeying, Polarity work, prayer, visualization and Pranic healing. As far as his predilection to move *within* and *without* the subtle realms, and his challenge to remain grounded, he remembers his guru advising him that *the spider easily goes up and down.* Nick's remembrance contains tacit permission to embark upon our journey to learn lucid dreaming—a practice that involves moving freely within states of consciousness.

However, we agree that his initial mantra ("Experience the Divine healing my physical brain—to put my hands to efficient work") is unwieldy. He consistently fails to remember it within his dreams. So we shorten it considerably: "Help my brain heal."

Nick dreams (non-lucidly) that he is 2,500 feet below the Earth. This mine shaft, the deepest on the planet, opens into a *white stone corridor.* But language cannot be discerned due to layer upon layer of distortion and echoes. To talk, a cylindrical chamber must be entered, much like a decompression chamber. This opens to a hospital, where patients receiving a "special treatment" lie on stretchers with their heads protruding into the hallway. They must avoid some radiation or energy emitted above Earth. Nick is a reporter doing a story that will take *30 x 4 days* (120 days). He will live in a quiet monk's cell without the echo effect. There is an initial oppressive feeling having the weight of so much rock overhead, but he will get used to it.

What does this dream communicate? Again, a white substance is manifest, presumably the stuff of consciousness. (Nick has formerly dreamt of white lotus petals of the same substance as the tunnel of

Light; white granite; and white sculptural shapes). The mineshaft heralds a reach deep within his physical brain, far beneath his skull, "the Earth's crust." And the dream points to Nick's inability to have intra-brain communication due to distraction. He deepens his meditation practice—in order to reach "the special chamber."

Each dream detail is significant. The hallway and cylindrical chamber likely relate to specific brain structures but we lack the expertise to follow up on that. According to this dream, our lucid dream treatment may take as long as four months—with a good prognosis.

A month or so later Nick emails the following.

I finally accomplished the objective. I entered a lucid dream and repeated my mantra for healing of my brain. And here's how it went.

I found myself looking at what appears to be a bag from a retail store shelf. It could have been something like pancake mix or cat food. It had the normal color graphics with text and pictures you would expect to find. I was looking at this when I realized that I was lucid dreaming, and I thought to myself, "What should I do with this? I guess I'll open it." So I tried to open it but this didn't work. Very quickly I remembered that Janet would want me to repeat my mantra and "stay on objective." So I repeated my objective/mantra.

And just then the picture on this colorful bag began to disassemble itself. Color would disappear from one spot; another geometric shape would slide off the edge of the bag; text disappeared; more color would disappear from another shape before that shape itself would slide off the bag and disappear. And in this way—each element of color, shape, text, image—disassembled and disappeared until the bag was completely blank. Then the bag itself disappeared.

Nick is finally able to "stay on objective," a milestone of sorts. Can such repeated efforts truly help his brain heal from traumatic brain injury (TBI)? A lot is at stake. Right on cue, his psyche throws up obstacles. It is a common occurrence in lucid dream practice that dream landscapes will shift and transform upon attaining lucidity, as if trying to stymie the mind's grasp of reality. But this is something different. Dream reality is literally deconstructed—into color, shape and text— dream element by dream element. *Then the bag itself disappeared.* Nick has been close enough to the Light of pure consciousness during his NDE for this deconstruction to take hold. All reality, especially dream reality, is relative to the Light of pure consciousness. Another example from my transpersonal practice:

According to Hayley, within six months of her spiritual awakening, *she saw with her own eyes* her stylish living room furniture dissolve into a myriad of dots. Momentarily, the illusion of physical reality yielded to the underlying matrix. *White light.*

Thankfully, Hayley recovered her furniture from the void. But she herself, will never be the same.[2]

Nick's narrative continues.

I was no longer lucid dreaming as the scene changed. I was walking up a gentle grassy slope towards a large tent. The tent was quite large and could house a small church service or small circus. It had broad pale yellow and white stripes. It sloped up towards the front opening such that you might expect to find a church steeple there. The wind was blowing the large fabric shape so it would move and flow. Upon entering the tent I noticed the white concrete floor. And *dividing the two sides of the tent was a row of empty boxes* a few feet deep and a few feet high [italics added]. To move past these boxes I had to stack smaller ones into bigger ones and fold some up to make my way through.

On the other side I saw large filing cabinets full of folders and files. This was interesting because the other half of the open space where I entered was completely empty. I returned to the open space and found a small wooden footstool that was familiar to me from my room here at home. As I picked it up I saw that it was moldy and dirty. I decided to discard it and looked for a paper bag to throw it away in. The bags were also moldy and dirty as well and I tried to find one clean enough to put the bags on the footstool in. The bags and the dirt were a mess so I couldn't quite accomplish the task of discarding this neatly.

Interesting dream! Of course I noticed the white stone floor; the bifurcation of the tent; my difficulty in getting to the files on the other side of the tent; the movement of the tent like gelatinous material perhaps like the brain; religious overtones. These are just a few first impressions.

Finally Nick's "dreambody" crosses the threshold of his own physical brain! Presumably the tent's bifurcation symbolizes the hemispheric bifurcation, and his stacking and folding of boxes may indicate some very real change in the *corpus callosum*, the thick band of nerve fibers that connects the two hemispheres and allows them to communicate. Those actions that enable him to make his way through "to the other side" could indicate some very real intra-brain communication.

Filing cabinets full of folders and files may indicate the language-oriented *left hemisphere*. If so, he returns to the "empty" *right hemisphere*, which contains moldy and dirty things. Interestingly, both Nick's brain injuries—from hang gliding and the fall from the slide— were mostly on the right side of his head. His helmet was fractured on the right front, and he has a scar above his right eye from his childhood fall.

Again, he tries to reorder dream objects and "couldn't quite accomplish the task." Practice, Nick, practice. You show every sign of being able to make conscious repair. *Yes, the software of the brain can alter the hardware* for accelerated healing of traumatic brain injury. While I contend that the tent's moldy footstool and dirty bags are not arbitrary but have symbolic meaning, we need physiological and anatomical data to proceed in our analysis. Interesting dream, indeed.

Another month or so passes before Nick again initiates his intention: "To have a Divine healing of my brain so that my hands can do efficient work. *Help my brain heal.*"

Three Dreams:
I decided to reinstate my lucid dreaming practice once again. I find that upon waking in the morning I can put myself back to sleep and that that's the most likely time to have a lucid dream. I did this the night after our phone conversation. I woke up and stated my intention and found myself lucid dreaming. At first I was just goofing around in the dream and then I reminded myself once again about my task. But the dream ended very quickly and I did not record any details.

"Goofing around" quickly resolves into consecrated intention. Nick is duly rewarded by the Divine Feminine in his next remembered dream. His next dreams reveal the Divine Feminine at work—helping Nick's brain heal.

The Crow and the Nun

A crow hangs upside down held by its feet, held gently and kindly by a feminine hand. A Nun holds the Crow. She is dressed in white with a blue sash that hangs around her neck and down her front. She wears a head covering and glasses. Holding the Crow, she brings her arm in front of her and gently releases it. The Crow flies around in front and overhead in erratic patterns. Clearly the Crow is injured and confused. It lands on a wall made of bricks, the kind of wall you would expect to see in India. The setting *is* India.

The Crow flies back down from the wall, and flips upside down, placing its feet in her hand. Her hand grasps the Crow's feet again. I can see the face of the Crow with its eyes facing forward—humanlike. But there is a crazy look on the Crow's face. This Crow has been sick and injured, *likely a head injury.* The Nun has nursed the Crow back to better health, although it's not completely healed. The two rely on each other. The Crow needs to be cared for and that Nun needs to care. They have a deep bond and relationship.

Note: *After this dream the next day I saw a painting of this same Indian Nun at an art show a gallery on Vashon Island*—a deeply emotional experience. *A well-known Vashon artist, Pam Ingalls, was the painter.*

Remember Nick's connection with Gorilla, who sat next to him on the car seat, pressing a cold pack and green leaf to his head? Gorilla "can do" by virtue of his prehensile hands. One of Nick's unconscious healing strategies was to build model airplanes as a child. So too, does Crow use a large variety of tools, plucking and bending twigs and grass to get hold of a variety of food.[3]

Crow though is a notorious denizen of the subtle realm. As far as symbolism, a myriad of cultural references are relevant to Nick. In Cornish folklore and Irish mythology, Crow is associated with war, death and the 'otherworld.' According to Australian Aboriginal mythology, Crow is a trickster, hero and ancestral being.[4] Crows are also considered ancestors in Hinduism. Crows are mentioned often in Buddhism, especially Tibetan Buddhism. *Mahakala*, protector of the Dharma, is represented by a crow in one of his earthly forms. Chenrezig, the embodiment of compassion, who is reincarnated on Earth as the Dalai

Lama, is often closely associated with the crow.[5] It is believed that crows heralded the birth of the current Dalai Lama, Tenzin Gyatso.

Another thing I didn't mention in my autobiography is that after my birth, a pair of crows came to roost on the roof of our house. They would arrive each morning, stay for while and then leave. This is of particular interest as similar incidents occurred at the birth of the First, Seventh, Eighth and Twelfth Dalai Lamas. After their births, a pair of crows came and remained. In my own case, in the beginning, nobody paid attention to this. Recently, however, perhaps three years ago, I was talking with my mother, and she recalled it. She had noticed them come in the morning; depart after a time, and then the next morning, come again. Now, the evening the after the birth of the First Dalai Lama, bandits broke into the family's house. The parents ran away and left the child. The next day when they returned and wondered what had happened to their son, they found the baby in a corner of the house. A crow stood before him, protecting him. Later on, when the First Dalai Lama grew up and developed in his spiritual practice, he made direct contact during meditation with the protective deity, Mahakala. At this time, Mahakala said to him, Somebody like you who is upholding the Buddhist teaching needs a protector like me. Right on the day of your birth, I helped you. So we can see, there is definitely a connection between Mahakala, the crows, and the Dalai Lamas.[6]

Clearly an aspect of Nick, Crow heralds death and birth, and apparently spiritual preeminence. Nick's dream is significant, indeed. As the Divine feminine releases Crow, only to land dazed and confused on a wall in India, so too, did an injured Nick travel to India (for the first of five times) a few years after his hang gliding accident. What a profound synchronicity that he actually "found" a picture of Crow and Nun the very next day. Perhaps it should be no surprise that Nick's dream saga continues with the Crow and Nun motif.

The Crow Dies
Standing in a field I hold a number of bulky items: a large cardboard box and perhaps a coat. By my shoulder I feel something twitch a couple of times. Now I just hold a knit cap with something inside. A black feather then a Crow wing appears. And

there is more twitching. A Crow is in the cap, very nearly dead. The Nun is witnessing this. I see a lot of blood on my clothing from my shoulder down the front of me and down my leg. The Crow is on the ground, *on* the cardboard box. I ask the Nun, "What should we do?" She answers, "We should help it die." I think that we should use a shovel to chop off its head, and say, "I don't have a shovel." The Nun answers, "Well, I just happen to have a shovel." She is going to chop off its head but as we look down on the cardboard box we see only a bit of black tarry residue, perhaps a bone and part of a feather. But nothing more—no Crow. There is nothing to be done—no Crow to kill.

Nick's dream augurs the end of his treatment. Again, a box. Perhaps a brain structure, or nerves under repair, as in his tent dream. Crow emerges from a cap (typically worn on one's head), very nearly dead. Crow *on top of* the cardboard box indicates a top-down connection between death, spiritual transformation *and* brain structure. Top-down is when executive function changes behavior and, ultimately, brain structure, according to neuropsychology. In Nick's case, *the software has altered the hardware of his brain.*

Now Crow can be killed. Disappeared. *Nothing more to be done.* The dream signals the end of our dream treatment for Nick's head injury. Completion. Recognizing this, Nick informs me that he *no longer identifies with being "head injured."* That work is done. Nick now has other identities to fulfill. Fully conscious, Nick. Cognizant of details *and* overall organization, Nick. Planner of his life, Nick. Spiritual adept through the transformation of traumatic brain injury, Nick.

Nick's final dream:

I Dream of 20 Owls

I look out my window and see many great white snowy Owls sitting on a clothesline in the yard. They fill the clothesline, there are so many of them. I know I have to tell somebody about these Owls and so I start counting. It is a little difficult because occasionally they fly to the ground and back up to the clothesline. They are constantly in motion, looking each direction. One very small Owl perches on the shoulder of its mother . But I am finally able to count 20 Owls. This is a remarkable dream. A dream introduction to Owl spirits.

Counting **20** indicates executive function, for sure. Owls galore, looking in each direction.

"Thank you, Janet, for witnessing these important dreams. I'm looking forward to reading the chapter when it's finished." Little does Nick know, but Owl is often an archetypal screen memory for alien contact—the calling card of otherworldly denizens. I look forward to *that* chapter.

CHAPTER 14

CONCLUSION:
THE INNER AND THE OUTER

Jesus said to them:
When you make the two one, and
when you make the inner as the outer
and the outer as the inner and the above
as the below....
then shall you enter [the Kingdom].

The Gnostic Sayings of Jesus

The dark face of heaven. Trauma *and* transcendence. The *inner* and the *outer*. Inner transcendence is required to balance outer trauma. At first we soar through darkness and confusion. At length we find our balance. We ascend and ultimately seek to reach the stars. Through our exploration of transformation *through* trauma, we arrive at the final door. The cosmos beckons even as I bear witness to each step on the threshold ... until we reach the final passage:

"It is the *nirvana* of Buddhism, the *samadhi* of yoga, the *satori* of Zen, the *fana* of Sufism, the *shema* of the Kabbalah, and the Kingdom of Heaven of Christianity."[1] *Enlightenment*. The ultimate healing. *Non-duality*. No one in these pages has fully attained enlightenment, much less stabilized this stateless state of consciousness—though it may ultimately be as natural an evolution as achieving puberty. Congratulations are scarcely due for such a developmental achievement.

But journeying *through* trauma is also a decisive achievement evolutionarily. It has been said that shamanism is an exploration of humanity's collective subconscious. Not for nothing have I highlighted Abbey's shamanic powers, or Judith's Kundalini snakes. Power, self-affirmation and egoic healing are highlights of their transcendence through trauma. These are necessary developments or precursors to conscious immersion in a reality that supercedes ego. One cannot submerge one's ego until it has seen the light of day, that is, the full light of consciousness.

The Gnostic saying of Jesus steadfastly points the way to that transformational door, as surely as we in our current collective have lost it. What do the signposts say of our collective disorientation? What diagnosis can be given for our collective state of *un*consciousness? With so much trauma and darkness within its individual members, surely we suffer from collective dissociation. We are frozen in shock and horror. Held senseless, pinned like a butterfly to a table, or an impala in the jaws of a tiger, we are hypnotized by commercial television and hand-held technologies. So manipulated and brainwashed are we that we cannot tell the difference between black and white and color. Balance is lost. Little wonder. The *inner* has been blocked, systematically and seemingly blocked by vested interests. The *outer* has a hold over us, even as our senses are barraged and overwhelmed. We have overridden our innermost awareness. Through disuse, we have lost the ability to discern and trust our own insides.

Materialism holds sway. As succinctly expressed by John Locke (1823), "Nihil est in intellectu guod non antea fuerit in sensu." ("There is nothing in the intellect that had not first been processed through the senses.")[2] Materialism is the theory that physical matter is the only essential reality; that the brain produces consciousness in much the same way as the kidneys produce urine. However, the truth is far from it. Human experience teaches us the limitation of materialism. A full human experience allows for the sacred and the numinous—signposts of dimensions beyond matter. Such as *synchronicity, the progeny of the marriage between matter and the psyche.*

As for our materialist world, thus writes one who sojourns in the subtle realm, who emerged through traumatic "close encounters of the third kind," compelled by body terror to take his place as a citizen of the cosmos:

> The current paradigm on our planet is one of polarization and isolation. A deep, fear-based, mass *un*consciousness has seized control and will not stop until everything it touches is destroyed. I have felt this very strongly most of my life, and the sense that there is something out of balance in the world at large has guided many others and myself to the realm of spirit.... What we have been programmed to accept is that this is the state of the world—as it is. Despite this darkness, I now know for absolute certain that the world as I have always been told to accept *does not exist.*[3]

Just as the Wizard of Oz and the Emperor's clothes do not exist. Oh, there is substance there but it is *virtual* substance. Mental constructs. Like a value added tax, our conditioned consciousness takes over and adds (or subtracts) value and meaning to our every sensory occurrence.

Now, I am not saying that the subtle realm has nothing whatsoever to do with our physical senses. Not for nothing did Judith and I test Eagle's grasp of physical reality. But no, Eagle did not know that her missing glasses were in her jacket pocket; nor do we know for certain that Eagle steered animals out of the path of her car. Of course I would like solid evidence (in the form of brain scans) that Nick's neurophysiology has been altered by his lucid dreaming. And I do look forward to further validation by Abbey's *subtle realm* soul mate some-day. But sometimes synchronicity is the best shot the subtle realm has of impacting material reality. Like Nick's find of an uncanny artistic rendering of the nun and crow of his dreams.

Naturally, some sensory validation is ... well, validating. However, too stringent a requirement I liken to what mathematicians and logi-cians call a *type error*, that is, when the rules and conditions of one state or level are applied inappropriately to another level. It is impor-tant not to mix up levels. The subtle realm is not the material, nor do they necessarily completely correspond. Separate but equal is our rule of thumb.

Nor do I hold that the subtle realm belongs part and parcel to an individual psyche, confined to its vagaries. External trauma beckons us to go within—to utilize our facility with psychological absorption, that is, our predilection for altered states engendered by dissociation. And in so doing, we encounter the subtle realms: the astral and the shamanic, the karmic and akashic. Near-death experience. If not ma-terially real, then so be it. They exist nonetheless, and objectively so. Separate but equal.

But for ordinary consciousness to be transcended, a perfect blend or balance is highly recommended. So perfect that the polar oppo-sites—inner and outer—melt away. Like Oz's Dorothy, perhaps we need not look for balance any further than our own front yard.

Our truest self resides at the core of who we are always. But the more we seek to improve and expand on that *externally*, the more we shrink away from reality. The veil of darkness thickens. *Truth is within* despite our current life circumstances. Go within, and be present for your own life, no matter what it looks like. I offer these words only because I have experienced this repeatedly in my life. It is as though I have always been two halves: one of the "world," and one of "spirit." I am only just now beginning to discover the path of making the two halves into one.[4]

If anything, my stories detail the manifold ways trauma disrupts, freezes and "sets" our nervous system to apprehend altered state re-alities. According to renowned trauma researcher, Judith Herman: "The capacity for induced trance or dissociative states, normally high in school-age children, is developed to a fine art in severely punished

211

or abused children. They may learn to ignore severe pain, to hide their memories in complex amnesias, to alter their sense of time, place or person."[5] Freud himself held the Medieval theory of possession to correspond with his early theory of the splitting of consciousness.

First made manifest through dissociation, altered states become *de rigueur* for spiritual seekers. Other past eras employed the use of now illegal "entheogens," an anthropological term meaning "spirit-facilitating," a term that has since come into prominence for a class of substances such as psilocybin, peyote and LSD. But beyond using such substances as access, it is largely trauma that initiates one to the spiritual subtle realm, from whence healing comes.

It is our fail-safe position for the expansion of human consciousness.

Even within transpersonal or transformational psychology such a view is revolutionary.

Transpersonal psychology has been described as a discipline that bridges science and the spiritual traditions.[6] Yet transpersonal findings remain largely un-integrated within psychology and psychiatry. Such findings include the effect of the perinatal (birth) trauma upon development[7]; as well as the intrinsic and healing nature of non-ordinary experience. Such findings are not reflected in psychiatry's pharmacological trend towards suppressive medication, nor found within in its classification scheme of mental pathologies, the Diagnostic and Statistical Manual of Mental Disorders (DSM).

Given the task of integrating transpersonal psychology, the bridge analogy is apt. To begin with, the materials of the bridge have long been at hand. Consider the unique role trauma plays in the psyche's functioning. It can be said that we form our egoic structure through successive shocks and traumas beginning in the womb, and that conversely, we liberate ourselves from the encasings of the skin-encapsulated ego through the healing of trauma. However, clinical psychology does not deal with transcendence, and the role of trauma in transcendent experience is largely overlooked by transpersonal psychology:

> Years ago as a SEN [Spiritual Emergency Network] helper I was taught that true spiritual emergencies ... *generally happen to mentally healthy people*, probably as a developmental step (see Appendix A). In contrast, real mental illness was categorized as somehow not spiritual, as it was more devastating, permanent, the realm of therapists and drugs, and by implication hopeless.... I've come to reject that SEN model. [8]

These pages attempt to redress this issue, to re-balance these two fields.

That the transpersonal is anchored in trauma is evident in Stanislav Grof's findings: "The *perinatal level* of the unconscious, therefore, represents an important interface between the individual and the collective unconscious, or between traditional psychology and mysticism."[9] Although Grof's cartography did not imply a strict linear process, nonetheless, in LSD psychotherapy a person would generally gain access to post-natal and perinatal trauma *prior to* accessing transpersonal material. And birth was the most traumatic imprint of all experience.

Other transpersonal phenomena engendered by trauma include near-death life reviews and veridical perception during NDEs.[10] These latter involve accurate accounts of remote objects or events that are outside the field of vision or otherwise impossible to perceive through the sense organs. Veridical OBEs have occurred under laboratory conditions: Charles Tart conducted experiment s where a subject correctly identified a 5-digit number placed on top of a shelf—invisible to the subject—after an OBE. In the laboratory of life, Michael Sabom reported 32 cases of cardiac arrest patients who were able to describe their resuscitation in great detail. Near-death researchers Pim van Lommel and Kenneth Ring published studies with numerous cases of veridical OBEs that imply that consciousness is *non-local* to the brain. The dissociation that trauma engenders may find its ultimate validation in veridical OBEs. The inner has indeed met the outer.

Stanislav Grof and others have given evidence of objectively authenticated perinatal memories, as well as memories of being in the womb.[11] Yet the attitude of psychiatry toward that is best summed up by Bessel van der Kolk in his lecture, "The Psychological and Biological Processing of Traumatic Memories." "Basically, before age three, unless you live on the West coast, nobody has memories for what happens to them. A few people in California remember being in the fallopian tube, but that never happens in Massachusetts." General laughter ensued. There was tacit agreement to put such notions on hold in order to focus on the more pressing issue of childhood traumatic memory. "Does this mean you can mess with kids, starve them, put them in closets—does that mean the kid won't hold it against you?... It's not that there is *no* memory, things do get stored. But they don't get stored in verbal memory—[they are] stored in *sensory-motor memories.*"[12] That last point was the fulcrum for the revolution that took place in psychology that began in the late seventies regarding delayed recall of traumatic memories. Unfortunately, such ridicule as van der Kolk's supports a view of transpersonal psychology as west coast whacky. Transpersonal psychology remains relegated to a minor role, despite the major finding of the role trauma plays in initiating transformation.

Ultimately, the task of bridge building falls to those who can comprehend both realms. Trauma *is* the structural underpinning of both transpersonal and clinical psychology. A solid footing in mainstream trauma work is needed to help people process the oft life-shattering events that usher in spiritually transformative experiences.

Moreover, the chasm between transpersonal and clinical psychology may run counter to the experience of the practicing clinician, who may range freely between the two. I help people process and integrate the numinous signals of life, whether physical symptoms resulting from a traumatized nervous system; disturbing relationships occupied by projections; or experience such as Kundalini awakening, past life recall or close encounters. When we follow Nature's signs, whether dreams, accidents, or symptoms, we are living in the fullness of Creation. The jewel truly *is* in the lotus, if "lotus" signifies the entire world of human experience, both outer *and* inner.

It is through the mechanism of dissociation that consciousness unfolds, and through healing dissociation that consciousness expands. Ordinary people now perceive what used to be deemed *non*-ordinary, and regardless of the widespread cultural denial, the extraordinary threatens to become ordinary—with trauma as the initiatory event. The veil between realities—material and subtle—is thinning. Reassurance that these are natural human domains is needed now more than ever.

That radical a position bears repeating. The transformative healing from trauma allows such expansion that our human evolution is virtually guaranteed. It is essentially vouchsafed. Sexual abuse, traumatic brain injury, near-starvation, cancer, ridicule and physical and emotional neglect, physical assault, suicide and its aftermath—what trauma have these pages *not* recorded? What external trauma have my clients *not* faced internally and transformed?

Psycho-spiritual transformation is realizable with help from the subtle realm.

Without a doubt, the growth of the human personality is facilitated through trauma and its recovery. Spiritual emergence naturally unfolds. Those who have experienced trauma, deep disturbance, or *dark night of the soul*, often develop special awareness or perceptual abilities. Extraordinary experience appears to be the portal to a biologically-based transformation of the human personality.

Yet such growth or transformation is a natural evolutionary process that everyone can access. Disturbances such as depression, anxiety or physical illness, can be vehicles of growth. Consciousness transforms when our egos are threatened and our hearts are challenged to open. Thus does the emergence of the Self and the collective planetary awakening unfold.

What trauma have these pages recorded? What disturbances of the psyche have been utterly transformed?

My own childhood story of near-starvation outlines the seeds of conflict that would replay in my bout with cancer. But thwarted instincts make for more than mere revenge. Above all, my story embodies the Jungian principle of regeneration. Instincts that are thwarted—by redoubling back to the source of life—lead ultimately to renewal. When I was seriously ill with cancer, I dreamt of dolphins. My dream announced that I would be facilitating encounters between cancer patients and dolphins. My faith in that dream enabled me to make the long-dreaded decision to initiate medical treatment, as well as initiate psychospiritual transformation.

Monica is consecrated to witnessing her internal state of near-debilitating panic. That alone brings about profound change. Not to mention, *desensitization*. Instead of continuing to suppress her panic with medication, with support Monica uses her awareness to simply *be with* her panic. The relaxation response is naturally induced, and a greater awareness is born. Popping pills is a thing of the past. The witness within dares to *feel* and thereby heals Monica.

Spirit guide Eagle teaches cancer patient Judith to balance her fears, her own dark images of victimization—with empowering choice. "I have control over what goes on in my head! That's what Eagle is teaching me." In the aftermath of surgery, Eagle teaches Judith to compartmentalize pain as well. Thus began our practice of delving into Judith's inner space to consciously transform her own violent scenarios, a lifelong destructive process. Dangerous threats transpose into simple worries, and finally, peace comes.

Together, we discover a dissociated part living in a cave. Dark Judith ("DJ") lived in darkness for forty-five years. This vital part speaks of the traumatic splitting when fifteen year old Judith witnessed her father's brutal assault. DJ was expelled into darkness—until we rescued her, along with her five snakes. DJ's helper snakes authenticate the Eastern spiritual view of Kundalini: our vital, life-force energy that when *un*awakened is symbolized by a coiled or unfurled snake. Judith's has awakened.

Judith is eager to "integrate" DJ, who wisely resists. DJ remains autonomous yet freely communicates with Judith as her deepest, wisest part. Her soul. Judith embodies *functional dissociation*. Having learned how to alter her perspective early in life through trauma, she can now easily tune into other realities. Judith can now communicate with her own (and others') body parts, such as Skin and Scar Tissue.

Three hundred pound Abbey has an eating disorder. Born with a life-threatening condition, Abbey survived multiple medical procedures. Physical trauma set the stage for a profound initiation into dissociation. Abbey is a profound teacher not only about the issue of weight and its correlation with childhood abuse, but about the power of the fractured psyche to heal itself, precisely through the growth and integration of its fractured parts. Abbey has become a subtle realm adept.

We "time travel" with EMDR to childhood when Abbey first began to overeat. Admitting abuse happened in her home when her father drank is a big step: "I don't ever remember feeling this unburdened." Abbey excels at active imagination. A dissociated part emerges: three year old *Little Abbey*. Thus began our work with Abbey's parts—fractured aspects formed during her greatest traumas, such as Abbey-Apple, who weighs 600 pounds. *Abbey-Apple took on Abbey's unfelt pain.* She eats and eats.... Abbey places her in a house by the ocean with animal helpers. At long last, all Abbeys merge into one.

We target invasive medical procedures during Abbey's infancy and early childhood with EMDR. Abbey has *non-local* access—to virtually any time or space. The hospital room becomes bright as Blue-eyed Angel appears above Little Abbey. "It's okay, everything's going to be fine. You're going to have a beautiful life." A radical shift occurs. Abbey begins to feel safe in her physical body.

Abbey has a special relationship with a well-known musician, with whom she mainly consorts in the astral realm. What seems to be a past life with Jay spontaneously unfolds during EMDR, and its impact on her eating disorder is revealed. Overeating facilitates an altered state in which she self-soothes. Habitual *neural networks* of addictive overeat-

216

ing are seemingly re-routed as she learns other means of managing her distress. Abbey's physical body undergoes a major makeover—from the *inside* out. Finally, Abbey loses weight.

Two stories of traumatic near-drowning illustrate the ongoing therapeutic value of NDEs. Mary's near-drowning in a swimming pool floods her with overwhelming love and support. Victimized by sexual abuse, her sense of self-worth has been virtually annihilated. But after her NDE, she remembers *love*. Seven year old Mary is henceforth emboldened to stand up to her adult abusers and stop the abuse. Clinical psychology understands that trauma can arrest the course of normal development. Yet with transcendent experience, that arrested development can be dramatically healed.

Lori is saved by a disembodied voice that directs her to "go with the current." Lori's initial NDE had happened much earlier in life, in the aftermath of childhood abuse. But the therapeutic value of her NDE, specifically, the availability of, and her susceptibility to otherworldly guidance, continues to this day.

Nick flies and dies multiple times throughout his life, illustrating how key traumatic events are relived throughout one's life span. Five year old Nick is thrown against a wall by his mother. "I'm flying!" he believes. That is, until impact. Nick relives this defining incident most notably when he crashes in a hang-gliding accident. A near-death experience in the hospital and other experiences of traumatic dissociation affect Nick profoundly. Namely, trauma has facilitated a higher-order consciousness.

Nick's life unfolds with startling parallels to central themes of early childhood trauma. Infant Nick almost dies when born with the umbilical cord wrapped around his neck. This dynamic pattern is relived during Nick's intubation during his hospitalization. During EMDR, Nick spontaneously relives and more fully processes his birth trauma. Suffering from symptoms of traumatic brain-injury (TBI), Nick is prompted to manifest a lucid dream recovery. Only the long-lasting effects of trauma and his recovery enable this extraordinary intervention.

All seven stories document the journey from outer trauma to the inner, subtle realms, and its integrative healing function. Such that the inner *healed* the outer, and greatly expanded its reach and compass. In short, the polar opposites melted away. Peter Levine wrote the following, having studied our innate capacity to transform overwhelming experiences by virtue of our physiological and instinctual nature: "It is universally true that the renegotiation of trauma is an inherently mythic-poetic-heroic journey."[13] *More than that, a profound evolution of human consciousness is in the offing.*

Countless times I have been amazed by what is born—by the new growth of consciousness. "The most important requirement for the therapist employing non-ordinary states of consciousness is not to master specific techniques and steer the client in the desired direction, but to accept and trust the spontaneous unfolding of the process."[14] Faithfully I follow the unfolding of the process through uncharted territory. We fly together—me and my clients. Flying blind at times but guided ultimately by otherworldly sources. I know of no greater active practice of trust. May it lead us one and all to enlightenment. May we all enter the Kingdom....

I finish with a prayer and Sanskrit word so often used to complete a mantra or prayer, a word translated as "I bow." *Namah* means the act of bowing. Obeisance. Adoration, homage, respect.

That the light of consciousness, both within us and without us, may merge. Namah.

Notes

Introduction

1. Just Betzer, Bo Christensen, & Benni Korzen (Producers), Gabriel Axel (Director). *Babette's Feast* [Film], (Available from Janus Films, 1987). The first Danish film to win the Academy Award for Best Foreign Language Film.
2. C. G. Jung, *Memories, Dreams, Reflections.* (New York: Vintage Books Edition, 1989), p. 107.
3. Ibid., p. 107.
4. Ibid., p. 107.
5. Kenneth Ring, *The Omega project: Near-death experiences, UFO encounters, and mind at large* (New York: William Morrow,1992).
6. Judith Herman, *Trauma and Recovery* (New York: Basic Books, 1992), pp. 96-7.
7. Melvin Morse and Paul Perry, *Transformed by the light: The powerful effect of near-death experiences on people's lives* (New York: Villard, 1992).
8. Ring, op. cit., p. 221.
9. Jung, op. cit., p. 189.

Chapter 1

1. Jeanne Achterberg, *Imagery In Healing: Shamanism and Modern Medicine* (Massachusetts: Shambhala Press, 1985), p. 71, italics added. The discussion of Western medicine is also based in part on this source.
2. Arnold Mindell, *Working with the Dreaming Body* (Portland, OR, Lao Tse Press, 2001), and other books by this author, who is known for his innovative synthesis of dreams, bodywork, Jungian therapy and shamanism.
3. Bessell van der Kolk, *22nd Annual Trauma Conference: Psychological Trauma: Neuroscience, Attachment and Therapeutic Interventions* (Premier Education Solutions, Day 3, Disc 1, May 21, 2011).
4. C. J. Jung, *Memories, Dreams, Reflections* (New York: Vintage Books Edition, 1989), p. 135.
5. Margaret Wilkinson, *Coming into Mind: The Mind-Brain Relationship: A Jungian Clinical Perspective* (New York: Routledge, 2006), pp. 9, 74.
6. Jack Kerouac, *On the Road* (New York: Viking Penguin, 1997 ed.), pp. 5-6.
7. Gerald Nicosia, *Memory Babe: A Critical Biography of Jack Kerouac* (Berkeley and Los Angeles, CA: University of California Press, 1994), p. 697.
8. C. G. Jung's letter to Bill Wilson, Jan. 30, 1961. http://www.barefootsworld.net/jungletter.html
9. Hugh Burnett (Producer), *Face to Face: Carl Gustav Jung with John Freeman* (Lime Grove Studios/BBC, Oct. 22, 1959).
10. Jenny Wade, *Changes of Mind: A Holonomic Theory of the Evolution of Consciousness* (Albany, NY: State University of New York Press, 1996), p. 203.

11. Bill Wilson's letter to C. G. Jung, 1961, Jan. 23. http://www.barefootsworld.net/wilsonletter.html

12. Swami Satyananda Saraswati, *Shree Maa: The Life of a Saint* (Napa, CA: Devi Mandir Publications, 1997), pp. 143, 188.

13. Walter C. Langer, *The Mind of Adolf Hitler: The Secret Wartime Report* (New York: Basic Books, Inc., 1972), p. 103. Langer, a psychiatrist, was commissioned by the Allies in 1943 to prepare a thorough psychological study of Hitler. His report, kept under wraps for 29 years, was published in book form in 1972.

14. Countee Cullen, "Any Human to Another," *This Quarter*, Vol. 2 (1929, New York: Kraus Reprint Corporation), p. 249.

Chapter 2

1. Amy Stechler (Editor), *The Life and Times of Frida Kahlo, A film by Amy Stechler* (Washington D.C.: Daylight Films/WETA, 2005).

2. Hayden Herrera, *Frida: A Biography of Frida Kahlo* (New York: Harper & Row, Publishers, Inc., 1983), p. 144.

3. Ibid., p. 49, bolded italics added.

4. Ibid., p. 52.

5. Ibid., p. 15.

6. Ibid., italics added, p. 15.

7. Susan Lacy and Stephanie Bennett (Producers), *American Masters: Joni Mitchell: Woman of Heart and Mind* (New York: Eagle Rock Entertainment and Thirteen/WNET, 2003).

8. Brian Hinton, *Both Sides Now: The Biography* (London: Sanctuary, 2nd ed., 2000), p. 134.

9. Ibid., p. 98.

10. Ibid., p. 134-35.

11. Lacy and Bennett, op. cit.

12. Hinton, op. cit., p. 135.

13. Ibid., p. 26.

14. Lacy and Bennett, op. cit.

15. Lacy and Bennett, op. cit.

16. Hinton, op. cit., p. 106.

17. Lacy and Bennett, op. cit.

18. Lacy and Bennett, op. cit.

19. Hinton, op. cit., p. 264.

20. Kenneth Ring, *The Omega project: Near-death experiences, UFO encounters, and mind at large* (New York: William Morrow, 1992), p. 146.

21. Ibid., pp. 155-156.

22. Ibid., p. 169.

23. Ibid., p. 168.

24. Karen Armstrong, *Through the Narrow Gate: A Memoir of Spiritual Dis-*

covery (New York: St. Martin's Press, 1995), p. 252.
25. Ibid., p. 242.
26. Judith Herman, *Trauma and Recovery* (New York: Basic Books, 1992), p. 87.
27. Margaret Cho, *I'm The One That I Want* (New York: Ballantine Books, 2001), pp. 12-13.
28. Stephen Davis, *Jim Morrison: Life, Death, Legend* (New York: Gotham Books, 2004), pp. 22-24.
29. Cho, op. cit., p. 171.
30. Cho, op. cit., p. 196.
31. Cho, op. cit., p. 199.
32. Cho, op. cit., p. 168.
33. Cho, op. cit., pp. 44-45.
34. Cho, op. cit., p. 30.
35. Cho, op. cit., p. 146.
36. Herman, op. cit., p. 208.
37. Cho, op. cit., p. 85.
38. Herman, op. cit., p. 43, italics added.
39. Davis, op. cit., p. ix.
40. Ibid., p. xii, italics added.
41. Ibid., p. 125.
42. Ibid., p. 131.
43. Ibid., p. 269, italics added.
44. Ibid., p. 291.
45. Ibid., p. 298.
46. Ibid., pp. xi-xii.
47. Ibid., p. 235.
48. Ibid., p. 51.
49. Ibid., p. 5.
50. Ibid. p. 15.
51. Ibid., p. 24.
52. Armstrong, Op. cit., p. 253.
53. Cho, Opt. cit., p. 152.
54. Joseph Conrad, *The Heart of Darkness* (New York: Random House, 1993), pp. 75, 79.

Chapter 3
1. Stanislav Grof, *When the Impossible Happens: Adventures in Non-ordinary Realities* (Boulder, Colorado: Sounds True, 2006), p. 228.
2. S. A. Swanson, S. J. Crow, D. LeGrange, J. Swendsen, K. R. Merikangas. Prevalence and correlates of eating disorders in adolescents: results from the National Comorbidity Survey Replication Adolescent Supplement. Archives of General Psychiatry. Online ahead of print March 7, 2011. http://www.

nimh.nih.gov/science-news/2011/most-teens-with-eating-disorders-go-without-treatment.shtml

3. Osho, *Autobiography of a Spiritually Incorrect Mystic* (New York: St. Martin's Press, 2000), pp. 63-64.

Chapter 4

1. Richard Moss, *The Black Butterfly* (Berkeley, CA: Celestial Arts, 1986), p. 25.

2. Ibid, p. 2.

3. William McGarey, *Edgar Cayce and the Palma Christi* (Edgar Cayce Foundation, 1981), p. 51.

4. Ibid, p. 19.

5. Ibid, p. 18.

6. Ibid, pp. 32, 44.

7. Kathleen Herber, R.N., was my compassionate counselor, without whose support I likely would not have survived cancer.

Chapter 5

1. "Cry Baby Cry" is a song by The Beatles, written by John Lennon, from their 1968 album *The Beatles.*

2. For a description of four perinatal matrices, see Stanislav Grof, with Hal Zina Bennett, *The Holotropic Mind: The Three Levels of Human Consciousness and How They Shape Our Lives* (New York: HarperCollins, 1993).

3. See Panic Disorder, Statistics and Related Conditions, http://www.pani-chub.com/panic-disorder.html

4. Richard Moss, *The Black Butterfly* (Berkeley, CA: Celestial Arts, 1986), p. 43 (italics added), Introduction, Chapters 4 and 5; also see *The Second Miracle* (Berkeley, CA: Celestial Arts, 1995), p. 62, and Chapters 12 and 13.

5. Stanislov Grof, *Beyond the Brain: Birth, Death, and Transcendence in Psychotherapy* (Albany: State University of New York Press, 1985), p. 360. This language ("inner healer") and strategy derive, in part, from the Holotropic Breathwork module, *The Power of Holotropic Breathwork*, taught by Tav Sparks (5/11/2007); and *Psychopathology,* taught by Stanislav Grof (2/10/2008). It is also the strategy of Process-oriented Psychology, taught by Arnold Mindell, Ph.D.

Chapter 6

1. *The Gospel According to Thomas: The Gnostic Sayings of Jesus,* trans. A. Guillaumont, H. C. Puech, G. Quispel, W. Till, and Yassah Abd al Masih (San Francisco: Harper & Row, Publishers, 1959), Log. 22, lines 22-34.

2. David Cherniack, *The Oracle: Reflections on Self,* 2006, (Producer, Director, Scriptwriter), Television Documentary, David Cherniack Productions, Ltd., Toronto, Ontario, DVD Release Date: December 7, 2010.

Chapter 8

1. Thomas Dale Cowan, *Fire in the Head: Shamanism and the Celtic Spirit* (New York: HarperCollins Publishers, 1990).
2. Jeanne Achterberg, *Imagery In Healing: Shamanism and Modern Medicine* (Massachusetts: Shambhala Press, 1985), p. 21, italics added.
3. Ibid., p. 45.
4. Courtney Brown, *Cosmic Voyage* (New York: Dutton, 1996), Chapter 1: A Brief History of the U.S. Military Psychic Warfare Program, pp. 11-15. Also see R. Targ and H. Puthoff, *Mind Reach: Scientists Look at Psychic Ability* (New York: Delacorte Press/Eleanor Friede, 1977); H. E. Puthoff, "CIA Initiated Remote Viewing Program at Stanford Research Institute," *Journal of Scientific Exploration* 10 (1996), pp. 63–76; and Dean Radin, *The Conscious Universe* (HarperSanFrancisco, 1997).

Chapter 9

1. Lynda Barry, *Big Ideas* (Seattle, WA: The Real Comet Press, 1983). p. 16.
2. Alan Schore, *Affect Regulation and Disorders of the Self* (New York: Norton, 2003). As cited in Margaret Wilkinson, *Changing Minds in Therapy: Emotion, Attachment, Trauma & Neurobiology* (New York: Norton, 2010), p. 23.
3. Ray Bradbury, *The October Country* (New York: HarperCollins Publishers Inc., 2003) pp. ix-x.
4. Stanislav Grof, *Beyond the Brain: Birth, Death and Transcendence in Psychotherapy* (Albany: State University of New YorkPress, 1985), p. 39.
5. See, for example, Stanislav Grof, *LSD Psychotherapy: Exploring the Frontiers of the Hidden Mind* (Ben Lomond, CA: Multidisciplinary Association for Psychedelic Studies, 4th ed., 2008); Stanislav Grof, with Hal Zina Bennett, *The Holotropic Mind: The Three Levels of Human Consciousness and How They Shape Our Lives* (New York: HarperCollins, 1993); *When the Impossible Happens: Adventures in Non Ordinary Realities* (Boulder, CO: Sounds True, Inc., 2006). See C. M. Bache, *Lifecycles: Reincarnation and the Cycle of Life* (New York: Paragon House, 1990). See also D. B. Chamberlain, *Babies Remember Birth: And Other Extraordinary Scientific Discoveries About the Mind and Personality of Your Newborn* (Los Angeles: Tarcher, 1988); and "The Expanding Boundaries of Memory," *Pre- and Peri-Natal Psychology Journal 4* (3) (1990), pp. 171-189. See also D. B. Cheek, "Prenatal and Perinatal Imprints: Apparent Prenatal Consciousness as Revealed by Hypnosis," *Pre- and Per-Natal Psychology Journal 1*(2) (1986), pp. 97-110; and "Are Telepathy, Clairvoyance and "Hearing" Possible in Utero? Suggestive Evidence as Revealed During Hypnotic Age-Regression Studies of Prenatal memory," *Pre- and Peri-Natal Psychology Journal 7*(2) (1992), pp. 125-137.
6. Stanislav Grof, *Realms of the Human Unconscious* (New York: The Viking

Press, 1975) pp. 111-13.

7. Bessel van der Kolk (Speaker) *The Psychological and Biological Processing of Traumatic Memories* (Cassette Recording). (Seattle, WA: XYZ Audio, Sept. 29, 1995).

8. Wilkinson, op. cit., p. 22.

Chapter 10

1. Notes from Grof Transpersonal Training (GTT) *Spiritual Emergency: Understanding and Treatment of the Crises of Transformation*, with Stanislav Grof (Joshua Tree, CA, 2/11/2007).

2. Leslie D. Weatherhead, *The Christian Agnostic* (Abingdon Classics, 1990). See also http://en.wikipedia.org/wiki/Asian_Century

3. Wade, op. cit., p. 111. See also D. Christie-Murray, *Reincarnation: Ancient Beliefs and Modern Evidence* (Garden City Park, NY: Avery, 1988); I. Wilson, *All in the Mind: Reincarnation, Hypnotic Regression Stigmata, Multiple Personality, and other Little Understood Powers of the Mind* (Garden City, NY: Doubleday, 1982); D. Scott Rogo, *The Search for Yesterday: A Critical Examination of the Evidence for Reincarnation* (Englewood Cliffs, NJ: Prentice Hall, 1985).

4. Ian Stevenson, *Cases of the Reincarnation Type* (Vols. 1-3) (Charlottesville: University Press of Virginia, 1975-1980); and *Children Who Remember Previous Lives: A Question of Reincarnation* (Charlottesville: University Press of Virginia, 1987).

5. Mary Craig, *Kundun: A Biography of the Family of the Dalai Lama* (Washington, D.C.: Counterpoint, 1997), pp. 114, 117.

6. John Lennon, "I Am the Walrus" on *Magical Mystery Tour* (Los Angeles, CA: Capitol Records, 1967).

Chapter 11

1. For statistics and criteria, see The International Association for Near-Death Studies (IANDS) website, particularly http://iands.org/about-ndes/key-nde-facts.html

2. The subjective perception of a life-threat can itself initiate a NDE, irrespective of the event's objective nature. For example, the NDE of one research subject resulted from an imminent car accident, though she did not actually sustain any physical injury.

3. Our physical body may allow non-local communication via the *zero point field* (ZPF). See Thomas E. Beck and Janet E. Colli, "A Quantum Bio-Mechanical Basis for Near-Death Life Reviews," *Journal of Near-Death Studies* 21(3) (Spring 2003), pp. 169-189.

4. This chapter contains only one of three cases. The other two may be heard on the audio recording, available as Tape T-10: "Victims No Longer: Healing Chronic Abuse in the Context of NDEs," (Jamestown, CO: Perpetual Mo-

tion Unlimited: (303) 444-3158).

5. Jenny Wade, *Changes of Mind: A Holonomic Theory of the Evolution of Consciousness* (Albany, NY: State University of New York Press, 1996), pp. 175-176.

6. Judith Herman, M.D., *Trauma and Recovery* (NY: Basic Books, 1992 & 1997).

7. Wade, op. cit., pp. 225-227.

8. Bruce Greyson, M.D., "Dissociation in People Who Have Near-death Experiences," *The Lancet,* 355 (2000), pp. 460-463.

9. Wade, op. cit., pp. 234-235.

10. This case was highlighted in *The NDE's Healing Effect on Abuse* (Vital Signs, Vol. 22, No. 3, 2003) pp. 7-9.

11. Wade, op. cit., pp. 238-239.

12. See C. R. Lundahl, "Near-Death Visions of Unborn Children: Indications of a Pre-earth Life," *Journal of Near-Death Studies 11*(2) (1992), pp. 123-128.

13. See discussion in Wade, op. cit., pp. 237-239.

14. Wade, op. cit., p. 238.

15. Kenneth Ring, *The Omega Project: Near-Death Experiences, UFO Encounters, and Mind at Large* (New York: William Morrow, 1992), p. 146.

16. See Janet E. Colli and Thomas E. Beck, "Recovery of Bulimia Nervosa through Near-Death Experience: A Case Study," *Journal of Near-Death Studies,* 22(1) (Fall 2003), pp. 33-55.

Chapter 12

1. Arny Mindell, *The Dreammaker's Apprentice: Using Heightened States of Consciousness to Interpret Dreams* (Charlottesville, VA: Hampton Roads, 2001), pp. 169-70. Mindell has long emphasized the connection of childhood dreams and life patterns, chronic symptoms and illness.

Chapter 13

1. Theodore Esser IV, *Lucid Dreaming, Kundalini, the Divine, and Nonduality: A Transpersonal Narrative Study* (California Institute of Integral Studies, 2013), 545 pages, 3560741.

2. Janet Elizabeth Colli, *Sacred Encounters: Spiritual Awakenings During Close Encounters* (Xlibris Corp., 2004), p. 34.

3. Randolph E. Schmid, Associated Press Oct. 5, 2007 Crows Bend Twigs Into Tools. http://dsc.discovery.com/news/2007/10/05/crows_ani.html?category=animals&guid=20071005130000&dcitc=w19-502-ak-0000

4. http://en.wikipedia.org/wiki/Crow

5. Ibid.

6. http://www.dalailama.com/biography/questions--answers

Chapter 14

1. Jenny Wade, *Changes of Mind: A Holonomic Theory of the Evolution of Consciousness* (Albany, NY: State University of New York Press, 1996), p. 203.

2. John Locke, 1823. *Essay Concerning Human Understanding.* In *The Works of John Locke.* As cited in Stanislav Grof, *Beyond the Brain: Birth, Death and Transcendence in Psychotherapy* (Albany: State University of New YorkPress, 1985), p. 22.

3. Jesse Paquin (2013). *Beyond Body Terror.* Unpublished manuscript.

4. Ibid.

5. Judith Herman, *Trauma and Recovery* (New York: Basic Books, 1992), p. 102.

6. Christina Grof and Stanislav Grof, *Spiritual Emergency: When Personal Transformation Becomes a Crisis* (Los Angeles: J. P. Tarcher, 1989), p. xii.

7. Stanislav Grof, with Hal Zina Bennett, *The Holotropic Mind: The Three Levels of Human Consciousness and How They Shape Our Lives* (New York: HarperCollins, 1993), p. 210.

8. Grant McFetridge, "Spiritual Emergency and the Triune Brain," *Revision,* 1.0 (Nov. 19, 1997).

9. Stanislav Grof, *LSD Psychotherapy: Exploring the Frontiers of the Hidden Mind* (Ben Lomond, CA: Multidisciplinary Association for Psychedelic Studies, 4th ed., 2008), p. 10.

10. Janice Miner Holden (Ed), Bruce Greyson (Ed), and Debbie James (Ed), "Veridical Perception in Near-Death Experiences," *The Handbook of Near-death Experiences: Thirty Years of Investigation* (Santa Barbara, CA: Praeger/ ABC-CLIO, 2009), pp. 185-211. For a scientific view of non-local, ND life reviews, see Thomas E. Beck and Janet E. Colli, "A Quantum Bio-Mechanical Basis for Near-Death Life Reviews," *Journal of Near-Death Studies,* 21(3), (Spring 2003), pp. 169-189.

11. Stanislav Grof, *When the Impossible Happens: Adventures in Non-ordinary Realities* (Boulder, Colorado: Sounds True, 2006), Part 2.

12. Bessel van der Kolk (Speaker) *The Psychological and Biological Processing of Traumatic Memories* (Cassette Recording). (Seattle, WA: XYZ Audio, Sept. 29, 1995).

13. Peter A. Levine, *Waking the Tiger—Healing Trauma: The Innate Capacity to Transform Overwhelming Experiences* (Berkeley, CA: North Atlantic Books, 1997), p. 119.

14. Grof, with Bennett, op. cit., p. 210.

Acknowledgments

While it is appropriate to thank nearly everybody I have ever known for helping me write this book, those mostly deserving acknowledgment are within its pages. Their remarkable courage and healing light have served as my inspiration. For their special guidance and support, as well as practical help and advice, I especially want to thank the following.

Pamela Stockton helped birth this book and has been a stalwart friend throughout the process. Without her wisdom and midwifery, I would not have survived the birth. Pammy's faith in the birth process helped sustain me. Pam functioned additionally as a discerning reader whose keen editorial skills were a vital contribution.

Several teachers within the disciplines of psychology and psychiatry deserve recognition as I regard my own work to be within their lineage. I stand very firmly upon their broad shoulders. Arny Mindell, modern-day shaman and founder of process-oriented psychology, grounded me through working therapeutically with practically everything—from extreme states to body symptoms.

Stanislav Grof, one of the founders of transpersonal psychology, taught me about the healing power and saving grace of non-ordinary states, in short, the heritage and birth right of humanity.

Tav Sparks, director of Grof Transpersonal Training, taught by sharing the wide open door to his heart. He inspired me to strive to keep my own heart open while traveling through hell.

Kenneth Ring's near-death research provides an overarching *overview effect* to everything I research.

Will Bueche, of the John Mack Institute, is an exceptional designer. Dark Face's striking book cover, I owe to him. Fortunate I am to have his assistance.

Brian Short and Scott Aaron Gaul provided practical help with formatting and photography.

Thomas Beck, my partner (and his unseen spirit guide, Henry), cheered me on and blessed me with their company.

With the help of all those acknowledged, what Edna St. Vicent Millay wrote in *Renascence* happened through the vehicle of this book:

> I know not how such things can be! —
> I breathed my soul back into me.

Bibliography

Achterberg, Jeanne. *Imagery In Healing: Shamanism and Modern Medicine*. Massachusetts: Shambhala Press, 1985.

Armstrong, Karen. *Through the Narrow Gate: A Memoir of Spiritual Discovery*. New York: St. Martin's Press, 1995.

Barry, Lynda. *Big Ideas*. Seattle, WA: The Real Comet Press, 1983.

Beck, Thomas E., and Colli, Janet E. "A Quantum Bio-Mechanical Basis for Near-Death Life Reviews," *Journal of Near-Death Studies* 21(3) (Spring 2003): 169-189.

Bradbury, Ray. The October Country. New York: HarperCollins Publishers Inc., 2003.

Brown, Courtney. *Cosmic Voyage*. New York: Dutton, 1996.

Cho, Margaret. *I'm The One That I Want*. New York: Ballantine Books, 2001.

Christie-Murray, D. *Reincarnation: Ancient Beliefs and Modern Evidence*. Garden City Park, NY: Avery, 1988.

Colli, Janet Elizabeth. *Sacred Encounters: Spiritual Awakenings During Close Encounters*. Xlibris Corp., 2004.

Colli, Janet E., and Beck, Thomas E. "Recovery of Bulimia Nervosa through Near-Death Experience: A Case Study," *Journal of Near-Death Studies,* 22(1) (Fall 2003): 33-55.

Conrad, Joseph. *The Heart of Darkness*. New York: Random House, 1993.

Cowan, Thomas Dale. *Fire in the Head: Shamanism and the Celtic Spirit*. New York: HarperCollins Publishers, 1990.

Craig, Mary. *Kundun. A Biography of the Family of the Dalai Lama*. Washington, D.C.: Counterpoint, 1997.

Cullen, Countee. "Any Human to Another," *This Quarter*, Vol. 2. (1929). New York: Kraus Reprint Corporation.

Davis, Stephen. *Jim Morrison: Life, Death, Legend*. New York: Gotham Books, 2004.

The Gospel According to Thomas: The Gnostic Sayings of Jesus. Translated by A. Esser, Theodore, IV.

Lucid Dreaming, Kundalini, the Divine, and Nonduality: A Transpersonal Narrative Study. California Institute of Integral Studies, 2013, 545 pages; 3560741.

Guillaumont, H. C. Puech, G. Quispel, W. Till, and Yassah Abd al Masih. San Francisco: Harper & Row, 1959.

Greyson, Bruce. "Dissociation in People Who Have Near-death Experiences," *The Lancet,* 355 (2000): 460-463.

Grof, Christina, and Grof, Stanislav. *Spiritual Emergency: When Personal Transformation Becomes a Crisis.* Los Angeles: J. P. Tarcher, 1989.

Grof, Stanislav. *LSD Psychotherapy: Exploring the Frontiers of the Hidden Mind.* Ben Lomond, CA: Multidisciplinary Association for Psychedelic Studies, 4th ed., 2008.

_____. *When the Impossible Happens: Adventures in Non-ordinary Realities.* Boulder, Colorado: Sounds True, 2006.

_____. *Beyond the Brain: Birth, Death, and Transcendence in Psychotherapy.* Albany: State University of New York Press, 1985.

_____. *Realms of the Human Unconscious.* New York: The Viking Press, 1975.

Grof, Stanislav, with Bennett, Hal Zina. *The Holotropic Mind: The Three Levels of Human Consciousness and How They Shape Our Lives.* New York: HarperCollins, 1993.

Herman, Judith. *Trauma and Recovery.* New York: Basic Books, 1992.

Herrera, Hayden. *Frida: A Biography of Frida Kahlo.* New York: Harper & Row, Publishers, Inc., 1983.

Hinton, Brian. *Both Sides Now: The Biography.* London: Sanctuary, 2nd ed., 2000.

Holden, Janice Miner (Ed), Bruce Greyson (Ed), and Debbie James (Ed), "Veridical Perception in Near-Death Experiences," *The Handbook of Near-death Experiences: Thirty Years of Investigation.* Santa Barbara, CA: Praeger/ABC-CLIO, 2009: 185-211.

Jung, C. G. *Memories, Dreams, Reflections.* New York: Vintage Books Edition, 1989.

Kerouac, Jack. *On the Road.* New York: Viking Penguin, 1997.

Kierkegaard, Soren. *The Concept of Anxiety: A Simple Psychologically Orienting Deliberation on the Dogmatic Issue of Hereditary Sin*. Kierkegaard's Writings, Vol. VIII, Princeton University Press, 1980.

Langer, Walter C. *The Mind of Adolf Hitler: The Secret Wartime Report*. New York: Basic Books, Inc., 1972.

Locke, John. 1823. *Essay Concerning Human Understanding*. In *The Works of John Locke*. As cited in Stanislav Grof, *Beyond the Brain: Birth, Death and Transcendence in Psychotherapy*. Albany: State University of New York Press, 1985.

Lundahl, C. R. "Near-Death Visions of Unborn Children: Indications of a Pre-earth Life," *Journal of Near-Death Studies 11*(2) (1992): 23-128.

Levine, Peter, A. *Waking the Tiger—Healing Trauma: The Innate Capacity to Transform Overwhelming Experiences*. Berkeley, CA: North Atlantic Books, 1997.

McFetridge, Grant. "Spiritual Emergency and the Triune Brain," *Revision*, 1.0 (Nov. 19, 1997).

McGarey, William. *Edgar Cayce and the Palma Christi*. Edgar Cayce Foundation, 1981.

Mindell, Arnold. *The Dreammaker's Apprentice: Using Heightened States of Consciousness to Interpret Dreams*. Charlottesville, VA: Hampton Roads, 2001.

_____. *Working with the Dreaming Body*. Portland, OR: Lao Tse Press, 2001.

Morse, Melvin, and Perry, Paul. *Transformed by the Light: The Powerful Effect of Near-Death Experiences on People's Lives*. New York: Villard, 1992.

Moss, Richard. *The Second Miracle*. Berkeley, CA: Celestial Arts, 1995.

_____. *The Black Butterfly*. Berkeley, CA: Celestial Arts, 1986.

Nicosia, Gerald. *Memory Babe: A Critical Biography of Jack Kerouac*. Berkeley and Los Angeles, CA: University of California Press, 1994.

Osho. *Autobiography of a Spiritually Incorrect Mystic*. New York: St. Martin's Press, 2000.

Paquin, Jesse. "Beyond Body Terror." Unpublished manuscript.

Puthoff, Harold E. "CIA Initiated Remote Viewing Program at Stanford Research Institute," *Journal of Scientific Exploration* 10 (1996): 63–76.

Dean Radin, *The Conscious Universe*. HarperSanFrancisco, 1997.

Ring, Kenneth. *The Omega project: Near-death experiences, UFO encounters, and mind at large*. New York: William Morrow, 1992.

Rogo, D. S. *The Search for Yesterday: A Critical Examination of the Evidence for Reincarnation*. Englewood Cliffs, NJ: Prentice Hall, 1985.

Schore, Alan. *Affect Regulation and Disorders of the Self.* New York: Norton, 2003.

Stevenson, Ian. *Cases of the Reincarnation Type*,Vols. 1-3. Charlottesville: University Press of Virginia, 1975-1980; and *Children Who Remember Previous Lives: A Question of Reincarnation*. Charlottesville: University Press of Virginia, 1987.

Satyananda Saraswati, Swami. *Shree Maa: The Life of a Saint*. Napa, CA: Devi Mandir Publications, 1997.

Targ, Russell and Puthoff, Harold E. *Mind Reach: Scientists Look at Psychic Ability*. New York: Delacorte Press/Eleanor Friede, 1977.

Wade, Jenny. *Changes of Mind: A Holonomic Theory of the Evolution of Consciousness*. Albany, NY: State University of New York Press, 1996.

Wilkinson, Margaret. *Coming into Mind: The Mind-Brain Relationship: A Jungian Clinical Perspective*. New York: Routledge, 2006.

Wilson, I. *All in the Mind: Reincarnation, Hypnotic Regression Stigmata, Multiple Personality, and other Little Understood Powers of the Mind*. Garden City, NY: Doubleday, 1982.

Made in the USA
Charleston, SC
26 September 2014